DUNE

THE DAVID LYNCH FILES: VOLUME 2

Six months behind the scenes on one of the biggest science fiction movies ever made.

By Kenneth George Godwin

DUNE, THE DAVID LYNCH FILES: VOLUME 2
By Kenneth George Godwin
Copyright © 2020 Kenneth George Godwin
   No part of this book may be reproduced in any form or by any means, electronic, mechanical, digital, photocopying, or recording, except for inclusion of a review, without permission in writing from the publisher or Author.

Published in the USA by:

BearManor Media
4700 Millenia Blvd.
Suite 175 PMB 90497
Orlando, FL 32839
www.bearmanormedia.com

Paperback ISBN 978-1-62933-541-4
Case ISBN 978-1-62933-542-1
BearManor Media, Orlando, Florida
Printed in the United States of America
Book design by Robbie Adkins, www.adkinsconsult.com

To Stephen R. George,
who always goes above and beyond

Table of Contents

Introduction vii
Dune Diary 1
Week 1: March 21-27, 1983 3
Week 2: March 28-April 3, 1983 13
Week 3: April 4-10, 1983 15
Week Three Documents 27
Week 4: April 11-17, 1983 28
Week Four Documents 36
Week 5: April 18-24, 1983 38
Week Five Documents .... .51
Week 6: April 25-May 1, 1983 64
Week Six Documents 73
Week 7: May 2-8, 1983 78
Week Seven Documents 85
Week 8: May 9-15, 1983 .... .91
Week Eight Documents 99
Week 9: May 16-22, 1983 107
Week Nine Documents 115
Week 10: May 23-29, 1983 121
Week Ten Documents 126
Week 11: May 30-June 5, 1983 129
Week 12: June 6-12, 1983 133
Week Twelve Documents 138
Week 13: June 13-19, 1983 139
Week Thirteen Documents 142
Week 14: June 20-26, 1983 143
Week Fourteen Documents 148
Weeks 15 & 16: June 27-July 10, 1983 150
Weeks Fifteen and Sixteen Documents 153
Weeks 17 & 18: July 11-24, 1983 155
Weeks Seventeen and Eighteen Documents 162

Weeks 19 & 20: July 25-August 7, 1983 167
Weeks Nineteen and Twenty Documents 172
Week 21: August 8-14, 1983 173
Week 22: August 15-21, 1983 178
Weeks 23 & 24: August 22-30, 1983 183
Weeks Twenty-Three and Twenty-Four Documents 187
Epilogue...191

DUNE GALLERIES.. 193
Riding the Worm: Estudios Churubusco Backlot....................... 196
Arrival at Arrakeen: Azteca Stadium 200
The Attack on Arrakeen: Aguilas Rojas....................................204
Rabban at the Arrakeen bridge: Aguilas Rojas 208
After the Final Battle: Estudios Churubusco Backlot..................212

INTERVIEWS 216
David Lynch 217
Jack Nance (Nefud) 232

ACTORS 244
Max von Sydow (Doctor Kynes) 244
Jurgen Prochnow (Duke Leto)... 249
Patrick Stewart (Gurney Halleck)... 256
Sting (Feyd Rautha) and Sean Young (Chani) 260

CREW 270
Aldo Puccini, Construction Manager..................................... 270
Bob Bealmear, Apogee, Inc. Supervisor 273
John Dykstra, special effects director, Apogee, Inc. 275

Appendix: My adventure with Jack Nance on the fringes of Hollywood .. 282

Introduction

Atreides House Brand

I first met David Lynch as a fan. In the summer of 1980, I became obsessed with his first feature, *Eraserhead*, which I saw repeatedly over a period of three months. I felt compelled to come to terms with the film's unique world, to understand just how it exerted its power over me. And so I wrote an essay, essentially just for myself, in order to clarify my thoughts and feelings about the film.

Through a series of fortuitous events, that essay found its way to David Lynch himself ... and he agreed to cooperate in the writing of a history of the production, which I had been commissioned to write for the magazine *Cinefantastique*. This was the first time Lynch had been willing to go into any detail about his work; and with his permission, many of the people involved with *Eraserhead* also spoke to me during my trip to Los Angeles in December 1981. I then spent the winter of 1982 writing the article.

I sent the draft to David Lynch that spring because I had agreed to let him vet it for any revelations he would prefer not to see in print. His response was very favourable, and I began to lobby for some kind of job – any job! – on his upcoming *Dune* project. At that time, he was still working on the script, no dates had been set for production ... and it was still up in the air where the film would be made. Possibly at studios in England, with location work in North Africa.

I didn't hold out much hope of getting involved – after all, I had virtually no filmmaking experience, and the still-unpublished article was my first piece of professional writing. And yet twice during the rest of that year possibilities arose – only to evaporate quickly. But then in early 1983, Lynch contacted me about something much more promising. By that time, the production was set

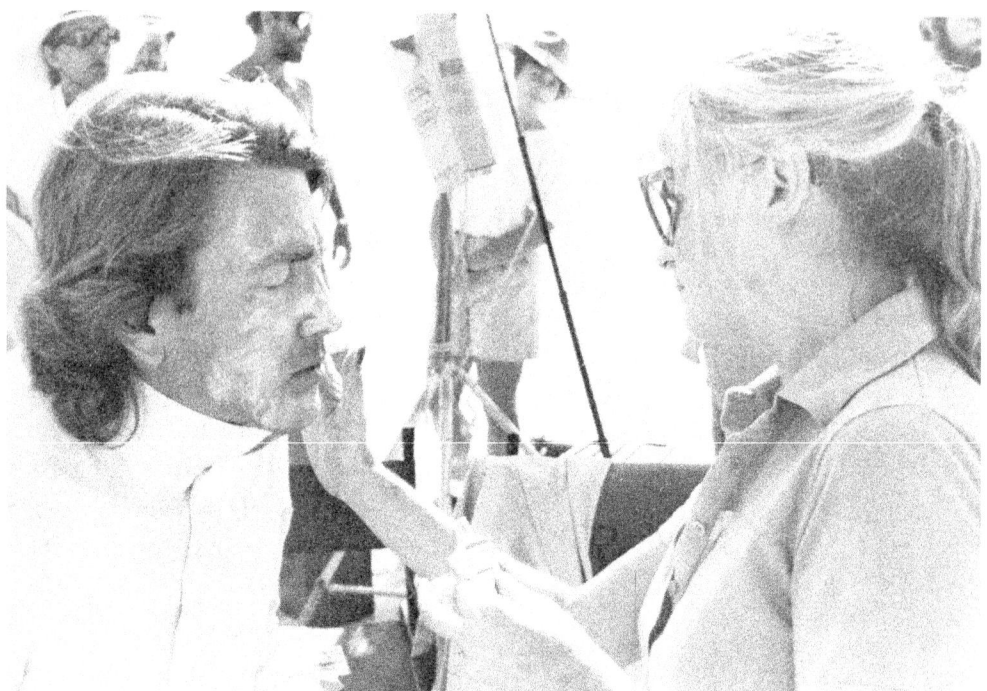

That's me peering around the woman's hat just above David Lynch's head: on location in the desert outside Ciudad Juarez. Photograph by George Whitear, copyright Universal/De Laurentiis.

for a Spring start and would be located at Estudios Churubusco in Mexico City, with locations on the outskirts of the city and a week of shooting scheduled in the desert outside of Ciudad Juarez (a less threatening place then than it became just a few years later).

Apparently an ambitious Vice President of Publicity, Promotions and Advertising at Universal had floated the idea of using *Dune* as a test case for creating more extensive behind-the-scenes material than was usually the case. It was normal at the time to have a crew drop in on a major production two or three times during principal photography to get a few interviews, shoot some B-roll, and generate what was known as an EPK (Electronic Press Kit). But this executive, Gordon Armstrong, wanted to place a documentary crew with the production for the full duration of principal photography, shooting interviews and behind-the-scenes material – documenting the day-to-day process of making what was, at that time, one of the most expensive movies ever produced. Faced with this prospect, Lynch responded by telling Universal that he would only consent if the omnipresent video crew consisted of people he approved of. Specifically, he told them that they would have to hire Anatol Pacanowsky, a cameraman from San Francisco who had been with Lynch at the AFI, and a writer from Canada – me.

And so, quite remarkably, I found myself hired by Universal Studios for a six-month job in Mexico for which I was unqualified. There was no interview, no negotiations; I was sent a ticket and told to report to the studio in Los Angeles on March 21.

Over the next six months, Anatol and I shot about 75 hours of videotape, only to find ourselves dismissed at the end of principal photography (we never did get a written contract from Universal). The tapes, in a format new at the time – a high-speed Panasonic VHS system – were shipped back to Los Angeles and disappeared into the "black tower". Apparently there was a "making of *Dune*" shown on TV in 1984 which I assume used some of the material (there's a very spartan listing on IMDb), and it seems likely that our tapes were used extensively by Ed Naha in preparing his *Making of* Dune book to give the impression (false) that he had been around for much of the shoot.

But what happened subsequently to all that footage was a mystery to me for almost three decades. I made numerous unsuccessful attempts over the intervening years to find out whether it still existed, possessed by a doomed-to-be-frustrated dream that one day maybe it would resurface, making it possible to put together a *Hearts of Darkness*-type documentary about the production. Then, in 2010, in response to the *Dune* material on my website, French filmmaker Jerome Wybon contacted me with the news that, while working on extras for a French DVD release of the film, he had learned from writer Paul Sammon that all our tapes had been quickly destroyed when it became apparent that Lynch's epic was not going to be the box office hit Universal was hoping for.

I would like to think that someone at the studio feels some guilt about this in light of Lynch's subsequent rise to the status of cultural icon … but somehow I doubt it.

What follows is an edited version of the journal I kept during the six months I worked on David Lynch's *Dune* in Mexico, not so much a record of the production itself as my account of being adrift and alone on location in a big foreign city. It's difficult for me now to identify with the person who wrote this: an inexperienced, insecure 28-year-old who knew very well that he was out of his depth, and was fully aware that he had been handed an amazing opportunity – if only he could figure out how to make the most of it! That insecurity comes through in the sometimes stridently defensive tone. Still, it may be of some interest as the perceptions of a naive observer involved in a monumental, troubled production …

Photographs were taken by the author, except for a handful of publicity stills taken by the production's stills photographer George Whitear and images taken directly from the *Dune* Blu-ray.

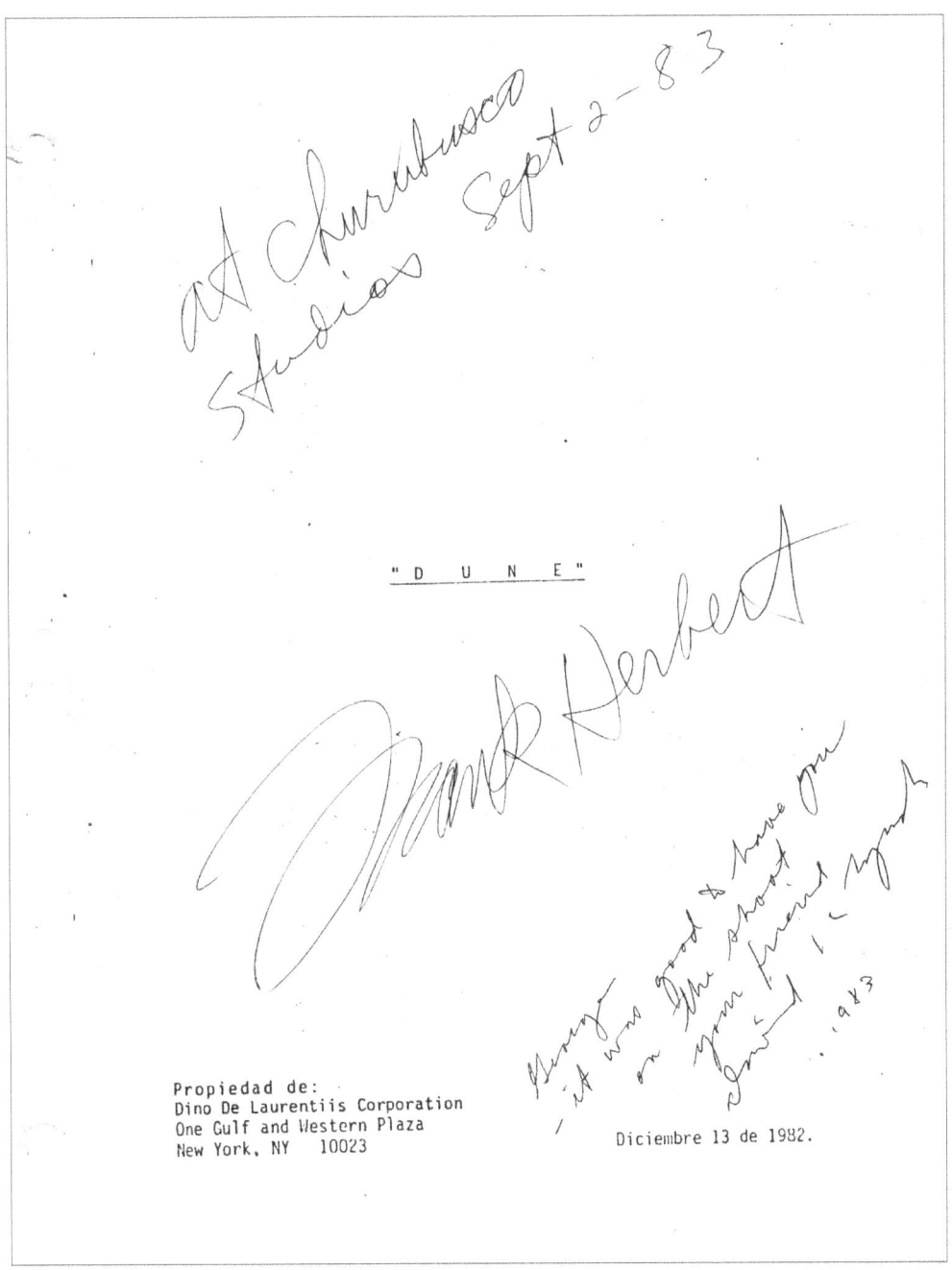

Title page of my copy of the Dune *script, signed by David Lynch and Frank Herbert.*

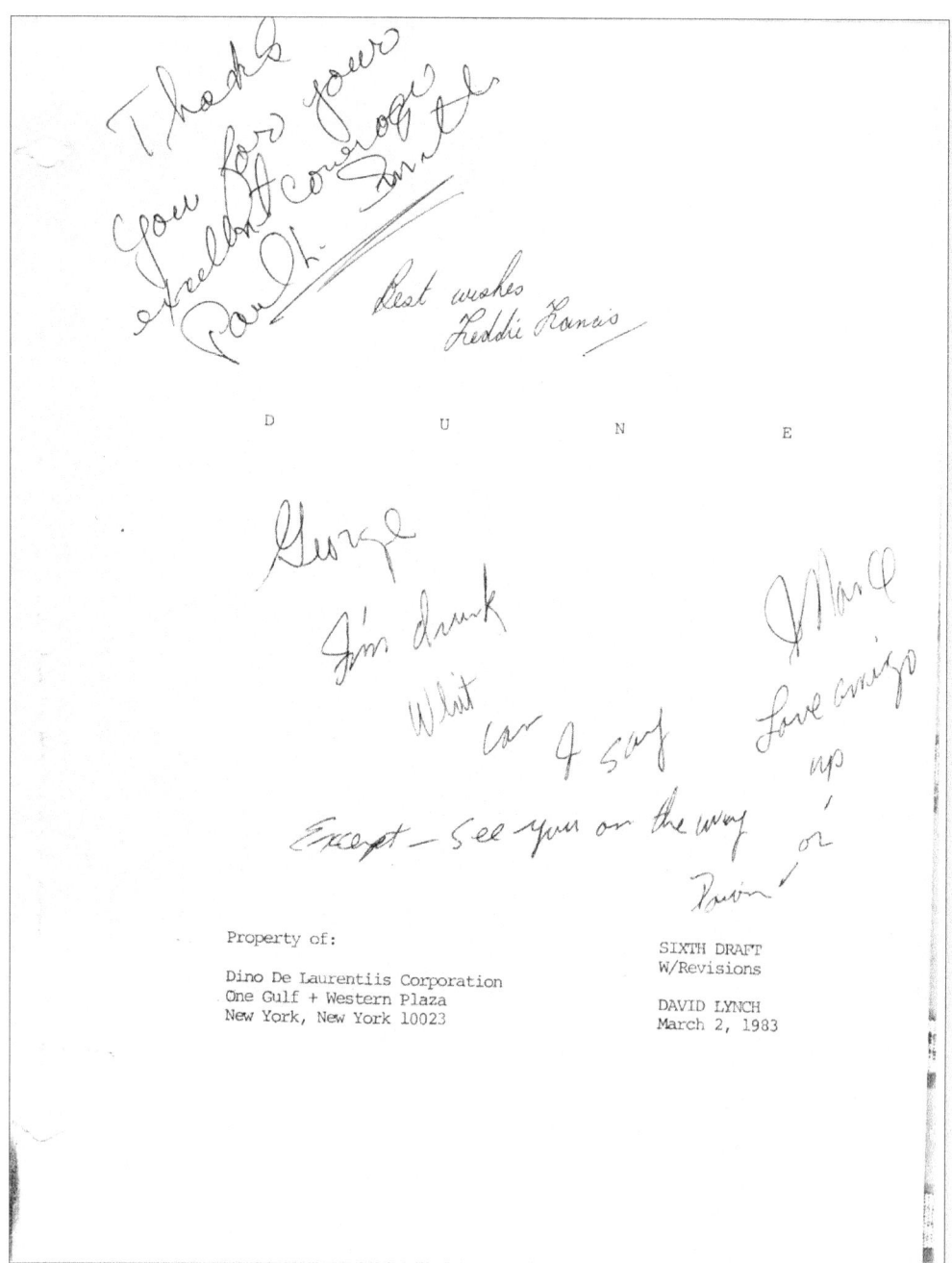

Duplicate title page of my copy of the Dune *script, signed by Jack Nance, Freddie Francis and Paul L. Smith.*

Dune Diary

Week 1: March 21-27, 1983

Los Angeles, March 1983.

Monday, March 21: DAY ONE

Not a good day, I have to confess. So, I can deal with the would-be producer on the bus from the airport, a man getting old fumbling around for a last chance to make something of himself. But I was simply not ready for my first foray into corporate-land. Down the rabbit hole and through the looking glass into the world of a third-rate Kafka.

I got back from breakfast this morning to find the little red light flashing on my phone. A message. Anatol had arrived. He's a friendly guy in his late thirties – grey-streaked beard and hair. He drove all night from north of San Francisco in the jeep we'll use to get down to Mexico.

We called Armstrong's office and went over there about ten-thirty. Met Ruth. Briefly saw Armstrong. Were shown a bunch of electronic press kits – a gruelling experience. Shit, in a word. Bland, unimaginative. This is what we're supposed to do?

We were sent to lunch after twelve – still no meeting. Burgers in the Universal cafeteria. Anatol wanted to go to the bank to make a payment due on his jeep. Only to find there were no funds – six-hundred dollars gone since he checked in at six-fifteen. Funny business. We're brought down here to do a job and they take money from us. So we get fired up, ready to fume when we meet with Armstrong at two-thirty.

So we arrive, and who's there? Paul Sammon, a writer (did *Cinefantastique*'s *Conan* issues, among others). He's in on the meeting. Now, I can't recreate that meeting. It was a strange affair, an amorphous thing which left us with less of an idea than when we went in. What exactly did Armstrong have in mind? This press kit stuff? A documentary? Sammon talks of a TV thing using material from old epics (*The Ten Commandments*?!?) culminating in *Dune*. And – get this: *Charlton Heston* narrating (or at least introducing) it – "the voice of God," he said. I didn't know whether to laugh or barf. On the whole, I kept quiet, letting it flow over me. What to say when he asks, "You haven't done anything like this before, have you?" I said no. Okay, I was put on the defensive as soon as I met Sammon: is he getting control? He's sucking up to Armstrong, throwing out these stupid PR ideas. Because he was there I couldn't bring up my salary, so I still don't know how much I'm to be paid. It didn't seem all that important considering we were being told they want shit.

We managed to straighten out the hotel situation, though. And, although we spent the rest of the afternoon kicking all this idiocy back and forth, getting angry, venting our frustration, we went for drinks and supper (it all goes on the bill now) and began to relax. And then Anatol hit on a possibility which may explain why Armstrong was so vague, so annoying. Tomorrow we're to go over to the *Dune* people here; we're to be attached to them for the duration, says Armstrong, until Universal buys it back. But maybe the truth is, we've simply been taken out of his hands and he's struggling to maintain the appearance of control.

After a couple of margaritas and a bottle of wine, we felt much better. If we're going to be dealing with the *Dune* people rather than the Universal PR unit, we'll be freer – because we'll be closer to David, who understands what we want and appreciates that we want to do right by him. So maybe, once we're away from this place it'll go smoothly (more smoothly). Because, frankly, this guy Armstrong seems to be an insecure idiot, wanting to keep us down so that we won't present a threat. Tomorrow may tell...

One thing I *don't* like: we've been instructed to enter Mexico as tourists. Visas, Armstrong says, will be fixed up by the company in Mexico City. I really don't want any unnecessary complications.

Frankly, getting down here hasn't allayed any of my fears. It's heightened them.

Tuesday, March 22: DAY TWO

More corporate bullshitting this morning. But at least I know how much I'm being paid – twenty-five thousand. Tomorrow, we'll bring up the matter of points again; today Armstrong just waved his hands about and said, "We'll take care of you, don't worry." Already, Anatol and I know that we have to take care of ourselves.

I spent some time in the office of Armstrong's boss. He was suddenly invited to lunch with Ed Schreyer [Govenor General of Canada], who's apparently in town. Since I'm Canadian and I was there, he just wanted to brush up on what he knew about the country. I didn't get to say much, but I got a view of executive behaviour – the abrupt mood shifts, friendly calls, hostile calls, jokes, threats, all flowing fast and furious.

High point of the morning: we got copies of David's *Dune* script. Looks very good.

A business lunch with Armstrong and two guys from Panasonic. More surrealistic behaviour; the gossip, the jollity, the plastic camaraderie. Anatol would bring up matters; the Panasonic guys would respond – but obviously Armstrong doesn't know the technical end and he would redirect the conversation, most pointedly when Anatol again brought up the idea of us having a basic editing capability down there.

But after this long tedious business, Armstrong left us and we followed these two back to their office to meet the camera and to talk. The machine turns out to be very good – Anatol found himself instantly comfortable with it. After a short test, we retired and drew up a list of basic requirements – including the editing capability (which, it seems, will in the long run save Armstrong money because it'll cut down on the amount of time his people will have to fuck around up here; we'll be shooting a lot of tape, a vast amount of material which it would take someone unfamiliar with it ages to wade through; they're talking three hundred hours). The package would be about twenty-five thousand to buy outright – they're working out a rental figure. Tomorrow we have to sell it to Armstrong, persuade him it's all necessary (which it is).

Then on Thursday, we'll drive out.

We still haven't met the *Dune* people here yet, though.

This evening we again went for drinks in the bar, had a leisurely supper. Anatol talked of some of his experiences – born in Russia with a Polish father, years of statelessness in France and elsewhere, time spent at the AFI (not very happy), disappointing experiences trying to get going in film, people who messed him around (like Roman Polanski), marriage to a White Russian countess in Paris, the bizarre circles of the exiled aristocracy there.

Los Angeles, March 1983.

After that we got on to future plans: our first feature. We have to start thinking about it now, come up with some property, so that we can attack it fresh from this project.

It seems crazy, but I suddenly seem to be plugged into this business – all because I was fascinated by *Eraserhead* three years ago.

Wednesday, March 23: DAY THREE

Much waiting around today. This morning, a brief meeting with Armstrong, in which he is informed as to the cost of the support package we worked out yesterday. He looks a little queasy, so we work to assure him it's all necessary.

Today he seemed a bit better – more positive, less slippery, to the point where he made remarks about what lies beyond. Could Anatol and I be in line for another six months or so, working on post-production here in L.A.? And what's this about visiting Frank Herbert's ecologically balanced ranch in Washington state? and – gulp! – effects people in London?

This afternoon, we were each given a fifteen hundred dollar cheque for travelling expenses (here I get for pocket money more than I'll be paid for my article in *CFQ*...). And we visited the *Dune* office on the lot – another breath of fresh air. Hester, a friendly dark-haired young woman, was very straightforward and businesslike. She took down the details – was going to contact Mexico City to clear everything, and their agent in El Paso who will take care of customs, insurance, etc. (we'll hear back on that tomorrow)(so we won't be taking the coast route south after all).

But then this evening it all got sour again. We had a meeting with the people at Westgate who put together the electronic press kits which Armstrong is so enamoured of. Theirs will be the project editing facility; they obviously have a deal with Armstrong that covers these matters. Too bad. Not only is their material technically poor (the shooting is sloppy, the sound a mess); their attitude – like Armstrong's – is that of TV ad-men. It's all product; everything becomes bland and homogenized. They like lots of zooms in and out; they love talking heads (as Anatol terms static on-camera interviews). And they sat there instructing us on how to shoot things while showing us this awful shit. Interviews were done badly – they'd interrupt because the camera wasn't properly set; they'd record where ambient noise was loud enough to drown voices; they destroyed spontaneity with their clumsiness. If I worked like that, I'd become too embarrassed to deal with anyone.

But what's worse is that subject matter means nothing to them. The guy thought David might be a problem because he'd heard he was "very low key" – now Hal Needham is great because he's very active and loud ... Lynch and *Dune* mean nothing to them – all they want are their zooms and pans (fill the vacuum with an illusion of action) and their pat interviews.

So – we'll go and shoot the way we want to shoot. They'll get the material and make their PR stuff. We hope that we'll be able to put together *our* film too. Anatol is already talking of keeping back the material we really like, the special stuff. Certainly I intend to keep my audio cassettes (we can re-record bits of them, but I'll keep the originals). And very early we'll sit down with David to talk out this situation. Because Armstrong today said he'll be showing our "rushes" to virtually every tom, dick and harry – home movies for the office staff and friends. Obviously David won't want the stuff tossed around that carelessly. At least Anatol managed to convey that the original tape shouldn't be screened – it looked as if Armstrong really didn't know the difference.

This may be a battle all the way. But perhaps it'll smooth out once we get to Mexico. We certainly got the impression that these guys envy our position. We're in a privileged position, being close to David, and we're using technology they've never even seen. Maybe they want to hold us down – we're just a means to their end, a tool they have to use to placate David as they seek their bland video package. We want as little to do with them as possible.

Anatol and I are getting along together very well. We have similar views of David and this project, we have similar responses to the shit around here. David had a great idea, Anatol says, bringing us together. Anatol needs someone who writes to accompany his visual work; and I need someone to help shape what I write. Talking about things, I've come to feel much better, more confident about all this because of Anatol's openly expressed confidence in

Anatol with his new shades.

me. I feel very comfortable with him (I was able to explode in disgust this evening when we left Westgate and explain exactly what was wrong with what we were shown and how I felt about the apparent position we hold in relation to those guys – at least in their minds). Whatever else might go wrong, I think at least Anatol and I will develop a good relationship.

Halfway through the script. A bit too heavy on explanatory dialogue perhaps (inevitably) – but the action is relentless and the imagery incredible. If he can get it on the screen, it'll be – well, a uniquely Lynchian epic – unlike anything else.

Thursday, March 24: DAY FOUR

(Hastily scribbled the next morning.)

Another sour day, a feeling of wasted time. We didn't get out of L.A.

I had some problems cashing the fifteen-hundred dollar cheque – they're very touchy about ID here. Finally got it sorted out and bought fifteen-hundred dollars worth of travellers' cheques.

We went over to Shoreline, the Panasonic people, late in the morning to cover a couple of details. They'd spoken to Armstrong, but things were still vague (of course). A few more items were added to the package and the head of purchasing for Universal was coming down to see what he was supposed to be getting. First of all: he didn't know who Anatol and I were – this was the first he knew of the project(!). Second: just before he arrived something went wrong with Shoreline's playback system, so the equipment he was to see wasn't even working when he got there. That did little for our confidence – and as for the guy from Panasonic, Paul Carey, he was almost in tears.

Maybe we'll have to end up with a 16mm system after all (Anatol hopes).

We had a big lunch with some friends of Anatol's – charging it to the studio of course.

In the afternoon we went shopping. I bought a flight jacket, but couldn't find desert boots. A couple of pairs of jeans. In the evening we cruised Hollywood in search of something to play my tapes on. Finally, down in Westwood, Anatol found the Porsche Carrera sunglasses he was looking for – but the store would take only its own credit card. So I paid the hundred-and-thirty for them. Then we found a big warehouse store, Federated, which was loaded with junky equipment. We almost gave up. Until we found an incredible little JVC stereo with mini-components – complete with short-wave radio, equalizer, and a noise reduction system going beyond Dolby. And it was only two-hundred-fifty dollars! So we each bought one.

But when Anatol went to pay with his credit cards, he discovered he was being fucked from all sides. His MasterCard hadn't been cleared of the six-hundred dollar hold put on it by the hotel on Monday. And his Visa hadn't been cleared by the bank, even though he paid all his bills yesterday with the expense cheque – apparently it's legal here for the bank to "float" a cheque, that is, not to put the transaction through for several days so that it holds onto the money a while longer and collects more interest. Apparently it's like that all over the States. So Anatol's credit was fucked – and I paid for his stereo.

When we finally got back here – having driven through downtown L.A. (unbelievable), he complained at the desk and was told it usually takes seven work days to clear the hold on a card – but they'd try to fix it Friday morning.

On the bright side, the little JVC system gives excellent sound. Only hope we don't lose them getting into Mexico (or during the stay).

As it is, it looks as if we may not get our equipment down there for another week or two. No wonder movie-making is so expensive – the inefficiency is like a drain that they pour money into.

Friday, March 25: DAY FIVE

As Eric Burdon sang: We gotta get out of this place, if it's the last thing we ever do...

We didn't get out of the city. Hester didn't call back from the *Dune* office, so it hasn't been clarified as to how we are supposed to travel down. Both Anatol and I have developed a serious aversion to being "reverse wetbacks", going down as tourists and working illegally for six months. Anatol has quickly lost faith in the equipment. Paul Carey at Shoreline turned out to be like everyone else we've met here: before, it was all friendly and confident, call him anytime if

Los Angeles, March 1983.

there was a problem ... since Thursday morning he's changed his tune; since we witnessed the equipment failure, he's "just a salesman" and we'll have to find a technician at Universal to have on standby. It was all bullshit – he doesn't really know anything about the system he's selling us.

On top of this, we still don't know *where* our money is or how we're to get access to it.

So we're stuck here for the weekend. We'll descend on Armstrong on Monday and demand clarification of the situation – and that we sign some kind of agreement right away instead of continuing this "don't worry, we'll take care of you" garbage. We want some kind of commitment that *shows* that we're being taken care of.

We even tried to call David, though we really don't want to trouble him – but of course he's not just sitting around in the office down there.

Anatol hopes we'll be able to get a 16mm system after all since the video equipment may be unreliable. But maybe this whole thing isn't going to work out at all.

We fled the hotel and drove to the beach, to see what's left of the storm-ravaged Santa Monica pier. Anatol lived there when he first came here; talked about those days of hippies and cockroaches and the AFI.

We ate later at a place called La Figaro, a former bohemian hangout. Pleasant atmosphere, quite good food. We met a pleasant, friendly actress-waiter named Jill (Anatol strikes up conversations with any and every woman he meets, asking them to come down to Mexico – this one took it with very good humour).

We wandered around Westwood, near UCLA, and went to see Bill Forsyth's *Local Hero* – a truly magical film made in Scotland (now I *really* regret not having seen his *Gregory's Girl* last week). So full of inventive detail, warm humour, and love for the people in it, that watching it was like being cleansed of the noxious atmosphere we're caught in here. Film as true poetry, achingly beautiful.

Afterwards we returned to La Figaro and were joined for a while by Jill, chatting about what we've all done and are doing or planning to do. She seemed charming and natural – and since we'll probably never meet again I can hold that pleasant image and think that perhaps not everyone here is as phony as Armstrong or Carey or those guys at Westgate.

Bought some tapes: the new Pink Floyd (a rehash of the styles and tricks of *The Wall*), Roxy Music's live EP, and Marianne Faithful's *A Child's Adventure*.

Saturday, March 26: DAY SIX

Some potentially good news at last. Anatol spoke to Fred Elmes' girlfriend this morning. Fred came into L.A. yesterday, is going back to Mexico this afternoon. So Anatol gave her the whole story – from the shaky equipment situation to the lack of any written agreement to this "tourist" business ... and she'll tell it all to Fred when she drives him to the airport – and he'll convey it to the people down there (David himself possibly). So perhaps by Monday somebody will start pushing from that end.

Fred called here while we were at lunch – left his number in Mexico City, so Anatol will call him tomorrow just to make sure he knows exactly what's going on. We might get this cleared up yet.

Sunday, March 27: DAY SEVEN

Mexico, it seems, is a filmmaker's hell. Reality may sour the dream terribly.

Anatol spoke to Fred for an hour this morning. The studio is primitive; all the equipment must be imported. The city is bathed not just in gaseous pollution, but in particulate pollution too. There's no air conditioning – tending the video equipment will be a major job.

The start keeps getting delayed. The cameras are out-dated Todd-AO, because De Laurentiis owns the company. This stuff was the hot new thing in the mid-Fifties, but it's long since been by-passed. The lenses are slow, so they have to have masses of light... Worst of all, they've started cutting effects out of the script – "too expensive". With De Laurentiis' cheap-jack mentality, David's going to be fighting against the *Battlestar Galactica* style all the way. If only they could have got Trumbull (but I guess his quality comes at a higher price). They pump forty million or more into crap like *Flash Gordon* and *Star Trek*, but when someone like David comes along they try to tie him down...

On the more positive side (?) Fred says we're not missing anything yet – that we should stay here to get the deal worked out properly, get the editing equipment, before we leave. Communications are so bad that we'd never get it done once we were down there.

Los Angeles, March 1983.

He'll tell David what's going on – so hopefully some pressure will be applied to protect us (and the film) from Armstrong's more excessive stupidities.

I suppose it's valuable to be getting this first-hand view of the way these people work – in such a way that Anatol and myself aren't going to be seriously harmed personally (think how much worse if we were trying to do a feature!) – but my heart aches for David. He should never have to put up with this ridiculous shit.

Two films today. Both French, both good. Tavernier's bizarre, twisted morality tale *Coup de Torchon*, with a superlative performance by Philippe Noiret. And Jean-Jacques Beineix' *Diva*, a thriller so slick, so polished, so stylish, that it's almost too much of a good thing – the technique is so awesome that you wonder if Beineix might not have exhausted all his potential on this, his first film; but it's a glorious entertainment.

Bought Stephen King's new novel – a big one called *Christine*.

Week 2: March 28–April 3, 1983

Tuesday, March 29: DAY NINE

Yesterday, we had a brief chat with Armstrong – he came in, red of face (wind burn from skiing) saying, as we'd anticipated, "I thought you guys were in Mexico!" So we explained the equipment question, the lack of information from Mexico City, our unease. He put a call through to Raffaella – she wasn't available. And scheduled lunch in the Universal commissary with Paul Carey (of Shoreline) and the owner of a company called Bexel, who's renting us the rest of the equipment.

Luckily, Armstrong was delayed and we managed to talk to the two of them and clarify things a bit.

Although it got down to gossip and such when Armstrong arrived (and ideas like live satellite links to transmit what's happening on the set to distributors all over the world for promotional value), some other things became a bit clearer. Such as: we have no connection whatever with Westgate. That was just an informational meeting. The material will be stored at Universal. And we're not getting the tape for free – Armstrong is paying for it. So we might not get the ten gross (four-hundred-eighty hours worth) after all – which means the demand for two-hours per day might be eased.

Afterwards Anatol and I went over to Bexel to check the list again. The package will be ready tomorrow (supposedly) and we're to go over and look at it. Our departure is delayed until Thursday now – so we should arrive in Mexico City on Easter Monday, exactly one week late. It's a pity; shooting is supposed to start tomorrow – but, according to Fred, it's small stuff – and it'll only be for three days – there's the long Easter weekend.

I'll be taking a small recorder so we can at least get a little background material before the camera arrives.

We are going as tourists – they're supposed to arrange work permits after we get there. As for pay – we have to speak to the production manager and the accountant when we get there. We may be getting an apartment(s) – neither of us wants to stay in a hotel. The per diem is twenty-four-thousand pesos (just under two-hundred dollars) a week.

In the evening we went to see *Missing*. It hit Anatol quite hard (he hadn't seen it before); he's from Poland, so the situation was close to home. And when we came out he was in a strange mood – depressed, a bit aggressive. He said he wondered why he'd ever taken out U.S. citizenship – the country could slip into fascism at any time.

We're talking about a movie set in Europe – a *cinema verite* black comedy about chaotic terrorism and political decay. With David as an artist on the brink of success in Paris and Sissy Spacek as a naive, middle-class American who becomes involved in complexities she doesn't understand. Anatol said he'd like her – but she's so big … so I said, she's married to David's brother-in-law, why not just ask. It was like a revelation to him…

Today was virtually wasted. New tires for the jeep, some spare parts. Desert shoes for me; a jacket for Anatol. A lot of driving around, getting almost nowhere.

We came back here, found the locks on our doors had been changed ("on-going security measures") – and went for drinks and a big supper (the best we've had here so far – Anatol had lobster tails, I had duck). Wine, brandy…

Wednesday, March 30: DAY TEN

We, my friend, are going to be some kind of celebrities. We went over to Bexel, the rental facility, this afternoon. And took a look at most of the equipment. We've got the optimal package – almost too much – what a crew would ideally want, but generally couldn't afford. We don't have to settle for second best. It's a fucking bonanza, Christmas in March – worth about a hundred-thousand. Everyone down there will want to take a look. Of course, there may be a few jealousies too.

Tomorrow I pick up the audio recorder, a Sony – the smallest professional stereo recorder (complete with two VU meters and Dolby) – and a modular Sennheiser microphone set – almost fifteen-hundred bucks worth all together and absolutely gorgeous.

Also, I'm going to buy an auto-winder for my Nikon – I bought a pile of film today (ten rolls of Tri-X, five of Plus-X, ten of a brand new format – 1000 ASA colour print stock).

Armstrong called Anatol this morning – rambling. Has these ideas about a series of video "texts" on film-making – four hour-long programs… Seems that perhaps he now thinks we're capable, not just friends of the director who wangled a cushy job. Maybe we'll get another six months or a year out of it – amazing job prospects for this business. But I really don't want to live here (the smog's been rolling in lately) – particularly after six months of Mexico City's pollution.

Week 3: April 4-10, 1983

Monday, April 4: DAY FIFTEEN

So much to write – but I'm exhausted. I'll have to try to catch up tomorrow.

But we were at the studio today, saw the sets, met David – a brief, friendly greeting in the midst of an amazingly busy schedule.

What we saw was a knockout. The sets are incredible – dense, intricate mazes; large, brooding halls... A strange amalgam of vastly different periods and styles – Aztec, Mayan, Egyptian, Medieval, with a dash of 20th Century military, and a dominant aura of Victorian/ Edwardian design right out of Wells and Verne. Totally unlike any other science fiction epic ever made – but, of course. It's David. The man is brilliant and unique. It's not a hodge-podge mixture, a grab bag – it all blends together into an overwhelming unity. The sets in themselves are works of art, densely atmospheric. Added to that is the visual design of the life-forms and action set-pieces ... and it's awesome.

I won't spoil it now with all the petty problems that greeted us...

A rumour over supper with Fred Elmes: the equipment might be arriving tomorrow.

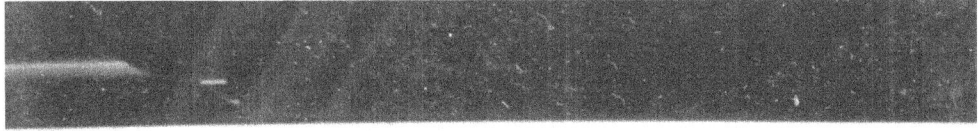

On the road: Mexico, April 1983.

Further: we may actually shoot some material for use in *Dune* – an x-ray display of an autopsy performed by Dr. Yueh, to be filmed from a monitor later and rear-projected into the scene...

Tuesday, April 5: DAY SIXTEEN

The drive down was deadly. We only got away at about two, Thursday afternoon. Anatol packed that morning. I bought an auto-winder for the Nikon. When the jeep was finally loaded – an awful task – we didn't have room for the second spare. So we drove back to the tire dealer where Anatol had already bought three new radials (using the spare for a fourth, and keeping the two best old ones for spares) and bought a fourth new one, putting the old spare back where it came from, and trading in the two used ones. All of which took time, though the people were very quick and helpful.

We drove south and east through a smog which stretched as far as Palm Springs and beyond. The California desert and Arizona were pretty damn boring – we kept asking ourselves how anyone could actually live in those towns; no answer offered itself. TV sets must sell very well.

In Phoenix we stopped for something to eat – just after ten. Nothing was open along the highway, so we finally stopped at a MacDonald's – yechh. Then drove on to Tucson, where we got a couple of not too hot motel rooms for what was left of the night.

Next morning – Friday – we headed south to Nogales, on the border. More delays there; getting a hood lock installed. Having a last, very bad, American hamburger. Then across the border. They just waved us through, so we made the rest of the journey without any official papers.

Immediately, on the Mexican side, things seemed better. The atmosphere was different – "more organic", as Anatol put it. We drove south through quiet agricultural land – on roads which left much to be desired, and on gas which – though lead-free – immediately affected the Jeep's performance: engine knocking, poor acceleration.

We drove on into more barren land, through small towns where the roads often got even worse – sometimes vanished in a mess of dust, gravel, potholes. But worst of all were the Mexican drivers – absolutely crazy, taking appalling risks. By the end of the journey, we'd seen about half a dozen burned and rusted bus carcasses in ditches and ravines – not surprising, since the bus drivers were the most maniacal. As it got dark there seemed to be more and more buses, roaring at us down the centre of the road at horrifying speeds. The trucks were just about as bad; we saw quite a few rolled semis, often tankers.

Anatol at the wheel: Mexico, April 1983.

As the evening drew on, we stopped for a while – I had coffee, Anatol had beer. He tried his Spanish out on the very attractive, part-Greek cashier – he can more or less get by, by ransacking his Italian and French. Deciding we didn't like most of the towns we passed through, as regards motels, we made a decision to head on to Mazatlan, figuring it would take another four hours or so.

We rolled in finally sometime around seven. Surprised we made it. We had both become weird, Anatol was all over the road. It was far more dangerous, I believe, than either of us thought at the time. And then it looked as if we might have to drive on; it was Easter weekend and the place was packed. We had a hell of a time finding a motel, but at last lucked into a decent one by accident. We crashed for the day, then went out in the evening. Anatol luckily asked a woman for the best restaurant in town and she recommended a little place called La Herradura (the horseshoe) which specialized in seafood. We had some very good shrimp and then wandered around for a while. Neither of us liked the place – a dirty, ugly, crowded town with thick oily air, too much humidity, and an unpleasant smell of decay from the sea. It killed all the interest we might have had in Mexican vacation spots. Interesting point: Anatol commented that it was like a bad movie depiction of Mexico.

Anatol was still hungry – or thought he was – so we went into a Mexican place and ordered some Mexican food. They dumped some sludge on us which wasn't even warm. We couldn't eat it. It sort of spoiled the earlier meal, and sealed our dislike of tourist places. So we went back to the motel and slept.

(To be continued.)

Kyle MacLachlan (Paul Atreides) & Linda Hunt (Shadout Mapes) outside the Dune *restaurant at Estudios Churubusco.*

We were given a fuller tour of the studio today. It just gets more and more incredible – the sets are massive and complex and awesomely beautiful. The design is amazing, thought out so carefully. And the craftsmanship so detailed and skillful. The sets themselves are genuine works of art. And David's genius shines through them all.

We were introduced to many people – too many to absorb. Some of them biggies. Finally met a couple of the actors – one being Richard Jordan, the other – much to my pleasure – being Linda Hunt, who played Billy Kwan in *The Year of Living Dangerously*.

But the topper was a ride in a VW microbus into a less savoury part of the city, along narrow unpaved lanes, through waste grounds and dereliction, to a place called Aguilas Rojas but known (we were told) as "dead dog dump" – for reasons which became clear. And there we found a huge construction crew which had spent the last seven months digging out the volcanic rock and building some small mountains and a big castle wall. Everything seems to be bigger, more staggering than whatever came before.

Wednesday, April 6: DAY SEVENTEEN

A certain amount of aggravation developed during the journey of course. Anatol would get worked up and barrel ahead without taking time to work things out. When something looked wrong, he wouldn't stop to reason it out and find our way back – he'd roar ahead saying "this looks like a good road..."

But we only lost our way a couple of times – in Culiacan late at night, and in Mazatlan in the morning as we were leaving. He pulled up at a seedy street stall in Culiacan and a drunk set upon him, wanting to buy him a Pepsi. The place was filthy and stank – and Anatol, having unwillingly shaken hands with the drunk (who was also filthy and stank), was worried about picking up some unpleasant disease.

Arriving in Mazatlan in a state of utter exhaustion, we had an argument. He insisted on having someone unload all our stuff for a small tip – and attacked me for pitching in. That's what those people are there for ... mustn't over-exert ourselves... But I didn't like acting like a tourist.

(Since then we've had a few more run-ins; he has an annoying habit of ceasing to understand what I say – and then when I get tired of pointlessly repeating and trying to clarify, he looks at me as if I'm stupid and gives up as if I'm a hopeless case. And yesterday it seemed that as far as he was concerned we were to take care of our own areas and he wasn't going to remind me of anything – and, I suppose, I don't have to remind him. If either of us forgets anything, too tough – we have to suffer from our own mistakes. I got pissed off because if anything comes into my mind, I tend to mention it. At least yesterday, he didn't return the favour – and made me feel stupid for having forgotten something [which turned out to be unimportant later].)

We left Mazatlan Sunday morning and went up into the mountains. From the map, we'd figured on hitting Mexico City ten or eleven in the evening. But the roads were bad, winding, often clogged with heavy Easter traffic. At one point we ran low of gas in an area where there wasn't much in the way of habitation. Luckily, we found a gas station in time. We made a decision not to let the needle fall much below half. Later on, having struggled through mountain roads and Mexican holiday weekend traffic, Anatol didn't like to stop and lose our position (we were constantly fighting to get by loud, filthy buses and trucks). We would gas up and eat at Guadalajara. But when we got there, all the stations we stopped at were sold out. We kept getting told there was a place twenty, thirty kilometres down the road. Whenever we reached the place, though, it was either sold out or had never even had unleaded. We were literally running on empty. It was dark. The country was empty. We got bloody nervous – it wasn't the sort of region we would want to get stranded in for the night; we were apparently wealthy *norte americanos* – and country people have big knives and machetes...

A miracle occurred. We rolled into a small town, swearing to stay there the night. Found a gas station. Asked desultorily if they had any no-lead. Sure, the guy said. We filled up. And across the street was a restaurant at which we had a fine Mexican meal. After the tensions of the last few hours, it was like a rebirth.

So we rolled on and ultimately found ourselves on a genuine highway which carried us right on to Mexico City. We got here between three and four in the morning – and what greeted us was just like *Blade Runner*'s Hades landscape made real – a vast, glittering expanse of lights and flame and smoke.

We found ourselves on the Periferico – the perimeter highway – a huge futuristic road complex passing through vast deserted concrete landscapes. As it turned out we passed half way round the city, turning into it from the south. Eventually we found the Zona Rosa, the hotel-cluttered tourist centre where most of the crew are living. We had breakfast at four, exhausted. A group of youngish people, five male, two female, were eyeing the Jeep unpleasantly. Anatol had gone to wash his hands; the food had just arrived; I rushed outside – afraid someone would grab me for not paying – and had to stand guard for a while. I wouldn't have done it if I'd had any real idea of what things are like around here. I was shaken up – more so because I was so tired. But when I came back a while later from washing my hands, I found Anatol heading out the door; a fight had started across the street and some people had a guy down on the ground and were kicking the shit out of him. That made me feel even worse. We were both shaken, disliking the city already.

Eventually we found our way to Churubusco Studios and sat there from six-fifteen until Fred Elmes arrived to take us in hand.

Since then we've been looking around, meeting far too many people, seeing far too many things – and feeling lousy because we have no equipment and we look useless amongst the bustle of production. (The equipment, by the way, is still in L.A.)

We toured the backlot this morning – a marvellous place full of a bizarre mixture of architectural styles. The exterior of the Atreides castle on Caladan is there. And they're building a huge Arrakis exterior – dunes and a mountain wall. Fred was there, setting up a shot of a miniature in which thousands of tiny Fremen are pouring out of caves into open sand.

We saw some of the model construction and the furniture shop (they're whipping up a case for my Sony portable recorder).

The craftsmanship here – from the largest sets to the smallest details – is absolutely incredible.

Thursday, April 7: DAY EIGHTEEN

Today was both good and bad. We actually seem to be slowly getting into the feel of things at the studio. We visited Stage 2 this morning where they're building the world's largest blue screen; unless something goes horribly wrong, we'll be able to get some film of them making and raising the actual screen in about six weeks.

We also spent quite a bit of time on Stage 8 where Fred's crew were setting up to film some "filmbook" inserts of a sandworm's innards. Just after noon a whole frozen bull calf was delivered, which was to be sliced and filmed. But there were a lot of problems – particularly the apparent impossibility of making the Mexican vet and butcher understand the simple cross-section cuts that were necessary. When we finally left at about three they'd made quite a mess of it, hacking their way through. It was badly thought out, I'm afraid, with no one having really considered what equipment would be required. It would have been much better, as one of the effects people pointed out, to buy a mess of guts, arrange them as desired, freeze them, and slice them. Which is probably what they'll end up doing.

```
                            Sc: 78B pt.
REQUIREMENTS:
CAMERA: As per Fred Elmes' instructions.
            *Según instrucciones de Fred Elmes.
ELECT: Window light to get lighter - Shutters for arc light.
            *La luz de la ventana se aclara más y más - Dimmers para arco.

            NOTE: PROPS DEPT: Freeze cow's guts to be shot SATURDAY APRIL
                                23 (Sc: 113B) - Director must SUPERVISE the
                                position of guts inside wooden box before
                                shooting.
                                *Congelar vísceras de vaca para filmar el SABADO
                                ABRIL 23 (Sc: 113B)- El Director debe SUPER-
                                VISAR la posición de las vísceras en caja de
                                madera.

            NOTE: ART DEPT: -11.00am: RECEE to Lake location (CALADAN)
                                        *VISITA a Locación de lago
                                        Del Lago Restaurant
                                        Revised Scene: 52C
                        ATTENTION:
                        ATENCION:   Tony Masters
                                    Kit West
                                    Pierluigi Basille
                                    Alejandro Ferrer
                                    Fernando Ramírez
                                    Benigno Ramírez (LABORER)
                                            *(TRABAJADOR)
```

Unusual instructions for the B-camera crew.

Meanwhile, the stench of the carcass is making the stage intolerable. Poor Fred...

Also meanwhile: Armstrong's rep down here – Anne Strick – is revealing herself by the moment to be a flake of inconceivable proportions – ignorant, helpless, pretentious. And she's latched on to us, trying to appropriate us to her PR department. We hope, once the equipment arrives, to lose her.

Other people:

Bob Bealmear is John Dykstra's man down here – an almost too friendly and helpful type, the kind who makes you a bit distrustful. But he seems to be quite genuine, willing to help get stuff from the States if we need it. Gray haired, tall, in his forties, he's lived all over – Europe, South America... – has been an actor, is a writer. This is his first real effects work (he's supervising the blue screens). Yesterday he introduced us to some Mexican film types who've done

Production Designer Tony Masters at Estudios Churubusco.

documentaries. Three women (Mara, Alexandra, and Alexandra) and two men (David, a young guy who's even worked a bit with Jack Nance, and an older man whose name I forget). We didn't know quite why he introduced us and we were a little wary because there's a lot of local resentment against the production and the secrecy surrounding it. We were invited to the women's place for the evening – a poker game – and Anatol figured we should go, strictly as a matter of business; the women (production managers) could get us access to some one-inch video equipment which we might use for the hospital sequence if our own is delayed much longer. As it turned out, it was a decent evening; we went over after a good meal at a decent local restaurant (El Refugio), taking a couple of bottles of wine with us (a decent bottle costs about three-hundred pesos – two dollars). The people were friendly, Bob showed up; and one of the effects people (he did the big boulder in the cave in *Raiders of the Lost Ark*). We stayed until almost eleven (too long) and drank a fair bit of wine (a mistake for me). And walked back here, not far.

Raffaella seems tough – a hard businesswoman. Apparently she has powerful feelings about people of different nationalities: Italians are best; Spanish and Mexican next; then the British; with Americans at the very bottom – and worse, she seems to lump David in with the rest of the Americans (he's a director Daddy hired to make his big film). I have a feeling very few people on the production side realize what they've got in David.

Golda Offenheim is an old, eccentric lady, very English, who's production coordinator; Aldo Puccini is an old Italian who's worked with all the great Italian filmmakers – he's in charge of all the construction and doing an amazing job; Tony Masters is a tall, very English man, who has interpreted David's ideas into the physical design of the film...

We still haven't met Freddie Francis and I've forgotten the names of so many others we have met.

A young guy from the States introduced himself to us this morning on Stage 8; an admirer of "Mr. Lynch", he'd been looking around for a project to get in on (film school is too expensive). He tried *Dune*. They turned him down flat. So he saved some money, flew from New York to Mexico City and walked into the office here. Unpaid, he's been a production assistant for the past two weeks – he's to speak with Raffaella at the end of this week to see if he's actually got a job. I respect his nerve, and if he's actually worked on all the facets of film he claims to have done, we might be able to get his help on our project.

Yesterday, we finally saw Kyle MacLachlan, the young Seattle stage actor who's playing Paul Atreides. He looked impressive in the hallway dressed in full Atreides regalia. But I couldn't remember his name. So I said, "Are you Paul Atreides?" He said, "Some of the time," and hurried away before proper introductions could be made.

The cow incident will keep coming back to haunt us. Because it was surreal, pure Bunuel; and also the essence of David Lynch – the bizarre mind of *Eraserhead* made flesh – gruesome, horrifying and weirdly funny. And also because we had no equipment and so lost one of the strangest, most fascinating things we're likely to encounter in these six months.

Friday, April 8: DAY NINETEEN

On the equipment: we got a list this morning – nine crates, supposed to fly in today. So we might get it by the middle of next week. However, there's no tape listed in the manifest. So we might not be able to shoot, even if we get it all set up. (Tape is one of many items on which there is an import ban because of the virtual collapse of the country's economy; the fact that we're not actually importing may not make it easier to bring it in.)

Fred's crew has a night shoot this evening – we may go along (we haven't spoken to him about it yet).

And we started using company transportation today, after four days of tense city driving in the Jeep. The studio has a plentiful supply of vehicles (seventy) and drivers, and we arrived at the studio much more relaxed than usual.

It's going to be very difficult filming the first unit a lot of the time. So many of the sets are so tight that they can barely get the necessary personnel into them – let alone extraneous observers. I hope David doesn't live to regret the way things have been designed.

We still haven't seen a full cast list, but neither Anatol nor I think Francesca Annis is right for Jessica – a rather cool British actress cast as the passionate concubine of a Duke and the mother of a messiah; and Kyle MacLachlan looks much too big for Paul (who becomes known as Muad'Dib, the tiny, quick desert mouse). But Linda Hunt as the Shadout Mapes is perfect.

How much say has David had in casting the film?

The first *art nouveau* science fiction film, with Spanish detailing added.

I just called Fred – he's about to leave for the studio (the call is for five – they'll set up then wait for dark). It's okay for us to drop by and watch. Now I hope Anatol hasn't changed his mind – he gets upset about seeing things he's unable to shoot (for myself, I want to see as much as possible).

Saturday, April 9: DAY TWENTY

Yesterday developed into a long session – a good one.

I got back to Churubusco at about four-thirty, checked in at the office and discovered that a separate shipment of tape was supposed to have been sent (all ten gross, for some stupid reason). But we don't know if the special permit which is required had first been obtained – if not, the whole shipment might be lost. Also, we don't know whether Armstrong, having discovered that he has to buy the tape, has bought the cheapest he could find. It's highly likely.

I walked over to the backlot where the crew had erected a couple of towers at the Caladan castle set during the afternoon – one for lights, one for camera. Ran into Doug, the young guy from New York. He'd been assigned to second unit, which pleased him because he could be closer to the action there than he had been on the crowded first unit (and further from departmental politicking). He was needed only occasionally, so we chatted. Quite enterprising. He's virtually the only person around here with a work visa because he faked a letter from Universal, flashed it at the Mexican consulate in NY and said he needed papers immediately – and they gave them to him.

I got to play the expert on *Eraserhead*, telling the tale of my acquaintance with David, which puffed me up pleasantly.

Later in the evening, after the first unit wrapped sometime after eight, David paid a visit to look at the set-up – and he greeted both Anatol and myself warmly – much more relaxed than before; shaking hands, stopping to chat (impressed with our flight jackets, asking where we got them, how much they were...). When he came back down off the camera tower, Anatol started snapping some shots with his new fully automatic little Pentax; as soon as David saw who it was, he didn't mind. So if they come out, there'll be a few shots of me with David... All of this produced a massive ego boost for Anatol and myself; from being two vague, scruffy guys lurking about the set for unspecified reasons, we were suddenly stars, seen by the crowd to be closely connected to the director.

And then coming back from supper, we rode with Fred in his limo. And drove away with him at the end of the shoot at about one-fifteen. Our stock must have risen considerably, which could be a great help when we start poking around with the camera.

Just before supper, Doug showed up looking despondent. He'd been transferred again – this time to the office. He asked me to keep him mind if we need to expand our crew (he's had some video as well as film experience; and his father is an NY documentary filmmaker). But even if we do expand, it would be to acquire backup – editing, technical – because we have to remain at a minimum on set; that's the primary consideration – to be as invisible as possible.

The shoot itself was wonderfully entertaining. There are some marvellous characters involved. Pepe Rodero, the film's associate producer, was serving as Fred's assistant because Jesus (Chu Chu) Marin was off sick. Pepe has a superb on-set manner – active, full of humour, and a sensitivity to what's being shot. He kept the atmosphere friendly and pleasant.

The two British effects men – Yves and Jeff – were also great; full of humour, yet totally professional, constantly aware of all the details.

The session illustrated the essential unreality of filmmaking. All that time and effort, all those people, all that money (how many thousands?) – it was all for just two shots, lasting a total of a few seconds. A rainy night on Caladan; a troop of Atreides soldiers stand to attention as the house's banner is lowered preparatory to leaving for Arrakis; two men step forward to fold it; another steps forward to watch with tears in his eyes. The first shot is a high angle slow

View from my living room at the Hotel Suites Amberes, Mexico City, 1983.

zoom looking down on the flagpole and following the banner down; the second, a close up of the crying guard. It involved rain and wind effects and a flag which didn't operate too smoothly (less so as it got wetter).

Pepe exhibited the essence of his manner by quietly stepping forward at the end to shake hands with and thank the extra whose eyes were repeatedly assaulted by the makeup woman to create the necessary tears.

So again we missed a lot of good material – visually interesting, with excellent dialogue.

Today we didn't get to the studio until about one-thirty. And only stayed an hour. Checked about our equipment – maybe within a week. And looked in on the first unit on Stage 4.

A piece of, for me, interesting news: Chani is being played by Sean Young – Rachael in *Blade Runner*. If she's anything in person like she is on screen, I'm going to fall in love.

Not yet seven, and I'm at a total loss. What to do with a Saturday evening in Mexico City?

Sunday, April 10: DAY TWENTY-ONE

Anatol moved into this building today. He'd had it with the Hotel Royal, checked out this morning, telling them what he thought of their power cuts, faulty fans, jamming elevators…

On the whole, he seems to be worse than I am for letting things get to him – generally, I just remove myself from a situation; he wants to explode and strike out. His moodiness could become a real drag over the next six months (year?).

Yet at other times… He, Fred, and I went in search of a supermarket this afternoon, taking the Jeep. We found a big one on Insurgentes Sur not far from here, did a bit of shopping. Then went further down Insurgentes in search of an appliance place where we might buy some humidifiers (it might be difficult; it's not the "season" since the rains are supposedly due – but they only fall a couple of hours a day, we've been told, so it'll still be uncomfortably dry). Anyway, we went too far and found ourselves in a more rundown area – where we were stopped by a cop car. The cop was aggressive and unpleasant, it didn't help that Anatol doesn't have the necessary vehicle permit (since we were just waved across the border). It turned out to be a good lesson though. The cop took ten thousand pesos (about seventy dollars) and let us go. Legally it could have cost a lot more and the Jeep could have been confiscated – so the graft system seems to work both ways. But it wasn't a particularly pleasant experience.

Week Three Document

```
                              CALL SHEET
        PRODUCTION TITLE: DUNE                      DAY OF SHOOTING: # 6
        PRODUCER: RAFFAELLA DE LAURENTIIS           DATE: SATURDAY APRIL 9, 1983.
        DIRECTOR: DAVID LYNCH                       CREW CALL: 8:00 AM AT STUDIOS
================================================================================

        SETS AND SCENES NUMBERS:            D/N             LOCATION STAGE

        TO COMPLETE:
        INT. JESSICA'S CHAMBER - CALADAN CASTLE    N         STAGE # 4
        SC. NO.: 35pt., 39pt., 41pt.,

        INT. JESSICA'S ROOM - ARRAKEEN PALACE      D         STAGE # 4
        SC. NO.: 88,90,92

        NOTE: NO LUNCH BREAK - CONTINUE HOURS TILL 3:00 P.M.
--------------------------------------------------------------------------------

          CAST          CHARACTERS      D/R      P/U       M/U      WARD    ON SET

        KYLE MACLACHLAN    PAUL      218    7:30 AM    8:00 AM            10:00 AM.
        SIAN PHILLIPS      R.M. MOHIAM 207  6:30 AM    7:00 AM            10:00 AM.
        FRANCESCA ANNIS    JESSICA   217    7:30 AM          AFTER REHEALSAL  8:00 AM
      * LINDA HUNT         SHADOUT MAPES 209 7:30 AM         AFTER REHEARSAL  8:00 AM.
      * SC. NO. 92 ONLY


        HUMBERTO ELIZONDO  HARKONNEN GUARD #1                            10:00 AM
        RAMON MENENDEZ     HARKONNEN GUARD #2                            10:00 AM
        * FIGHT TRAINING   W/R. HUMPREYS IN MOCK-UP OF HARKONNEN THOPTER
        * SC. NO. 130pt.


        STANDS INS:

        GONZALO IRIGOYEN       FOR PAUL                          7:45 AM   8:00 AM
        PATRICIA PALM L.       FOR REV. MOTHER MOHIAM            7:45 AM   8:00 AM
        JOSEPHINE LOVELL       FOR JESSICA                       7:45 AM   8:00 AM
        LOURDES . CUELLAR      FOR SHADOUT MAPES                 7:45 AM   8:00 AM

        REQUIREMENTS:  Keep Stage front clean for actors car.
                       *Mantener frente del Foro libre para coche de actores.
                       Security Guards in Stage #4 - Coffee sevice on Stage and Dress Rooms
                       *Guardias de seguridad en Foro 4 - Servicio de cafe en Foro y Camerinos
                       A.D.'S desk Rigged to Stage light, Bell & Telephone
                       *Mesa de Asist. Dir. conectada a luz de Foro, campana y teléfono.
                       Running Buffet from 11:00 AM for 50 People (shooting crew only)
                       *Buffet desde las 11:00 AM para 50 personas (solo personal de rodaje)

        PROPERTY:      4 Lamps for Jessica's Chamber - available - Jessica's Note
                       *4 Lámparas para aposento de Jessica - disponibles - Nota de Jessica

        SP/FX:         Gom Jabbar needle - 2 Small battery operated Glow Globes (arrakis)
                       2 Sets of Recharble spare batteries
                       *Aguja Gom Jabbar - 2 Glow Globes operado con baterias pequeños (arrakis)
                       *2 Juegos de baterias de repuesto recargables

        MAKE UP/HAIR:  R.M. MOHIAM GLEAMING METAL TEETH
                       Scratched line on Shadout Mapes right breast - blood.
                       *R.M. MOHIAM dientes de metal brillosos
                       *Linea de raspón en pecho derecho de Shadout Mapes - sangre

        WARDROBE:      SC. 92 Opening blause for Shadout Mapes
                       *SC. 92 Blusa abierta para Shadout Mapes

        CAMERA:        As per F. Francis instructions
                       * Según instrucciones de F. Francis

        ELECTRIC:      Stand by generator rigged to Stage #4
                       *Generador conectado a foro 4

        SOUND:         As per Nelson Stoll instructions
                       *Por instrucciones de Nelson Stoll

        ADVANCED SCHEDULE:  INT. JESSICA'S ROOM, ARRAKEEN PALACE SC.NO. 88,90,92 to complete

        TRANSPORTATION:  STAND BY ACTOR'S CAR & COMBIE IN FRONT OF DRESS/ROOMS * Coche de actores
                         y Combie frente a camerinos. Transp. movement ord. attached
```

Dune call sheet for April 9, 1983, the 6th day of shooting.

Week 4: April 11-17, 1983

Monday, April 11: DAY TWENTY-TWO

Finally made contact with the Customs people this afternoon. Through Belinda, one of the women at the office (very friendly and helpful), we had to go through the manifest virtually item by item over the phone. We were told they'd release it all Wednesday. It remains to be seen.

Saw a partial cast list. Jurgen Prochnow, the captain in *Das Boot*, is to play Duke Leto. That's good. Not so good is Kenneth MacMillan as the Baron – a good actor, but totally without a threatening presence. Believe it or not, Sting was also on the list…

Spent some time watching Kyle and a guy named Judd Omen training for the fight between Paul and Jamis, guided by Kiyoshi Yamazaki (he also trained the actors in *Conan*). Omen is a pushy know-it-all, far too aggressive. Kyle turns out to be a very pleasant guy – friendly, interested in what we're doing.

We ran into David in the hallway this morning. He stopped for a brief chat – wanted to know again where we got our flight jackets (he's going to order some, maybe – and get *Dune* patches for them?). With him was the DGA trainee (Ian something) from New York, who's rapidly pissing us off; his manners

John Dykstra at Estudios Churubusco, Mexico City, 1983.

are lousy. The first day we visited the set, instead of saying, "Hi, I'm ..., who are you?" he came up to Fred and blatantly whispered behind his hand "who are these guys?" Today, after our first encounter with David, he came back to try on my jacket. I put it back on. Then he said, take it off and leave it here so David can try it on. Now, I'm happy to let David try it on – but this guy made it like an order and as if David wouldn't have time to stop with us for a minute. Then when David returned, we showed him the release forms we're supposed to get signed (his response was good – he wouldn't sign anything unless it said he'd get approval of what we use; that's protection for us as well as him). But while he was reading it over, this asshole Ian just piped up, "Can we sign this later?" *We?* He obviously doesn't understand our position in relation to David. Indeed, he doesn't seem to understand *his* position in relation to David. This was an important point and one which David had to consider carefully. If the guy acts the officious little prick with us again, he'll definitely have to be put in his place.

Tuesday, April 12: DAY TWENTY-THREE

I feel good today. For some reason, on some level, I seem to be developing new kinds of assurance.

I was on my own most of the day; Anatol had to move again – he seems to have found a satisfactory place, at least for the moment.

So I went around with John Dykstra and his crew most of the morning. We met Dykstra yesterday – a big, beefy guy with a beard, a relaxed (yet oddly fast-paced) manner. He toured the studio with Marty Kline, his number one man here, and Janice, his assistant. Checking the sets where effects-related shooting is to be done. Again, a lot of good material lost. Marty has the action and camera moves locked in his head and he laid it out for Dykstra, who rapidly evaluated everything, checking the effects storyboards, and dictating to Janice how the shots were to be done. He's obviously an excellent technician, knows what he's doing – but he also has a practical filmmaking sense, concerned that Stage 8, with its dune set, is going to become too familiar from the number of shots that have to be done there, working out ways to vary camera angles to disguise the set...

At least one major problem cropped up: a shot in the first worm sequence, in which the worm attacks the cliff where Paul and Jessica are clinging to a crack in the rock. There's a breakaway rock. In order to get the matte, it has to be filmed in front of the blue screen. But the full breakaway section is in the outdoor set on the backlot...

Fred had to shoot some simple animation this afternoon – some 16mm stuff, moving patterns which are to be front projected into someone's eyes on stage. He had to do it in a small room – and eleven other people squeezed in ... this whole thing is ridiculously overmanned.

Among his many other credits, Bob Bealmear did a spell as a writer of soaps. Apparently, he may be doing some similar work down here in his spare time (a company is producing an English language soap for sale up north); he asked if I'd be interested. I wasn't. But he's got my name, the Manitoba address, and says he'll keep me in mind in the future if anything turns up; he seems the kind who'd do it, too.

Through him I met a young Apogee employee named Greg Gubi who used to be a sports reporter, turned to script writing (apparently has someone backing a project to the tune of a hundred-thousand right now). I'm meeting all kinds of people, making all kinds of contacts – and becoming known to them as a *writer* (everyone seems impressed with the story of how I got here).

I was just finishing lunch when Sean Young came into the commissary. Not at all like Rachael. She seems fairly tall, slim – and pale and dreamy. I felt an initial disappointment, which subsequently faded away. Neither Bob nor Greg knew who she was – but when I told them, their interest was suddenly piqued (both have seen *Blade Runner* and thought Rachael gorgeous).

So, coming out of Stage 2 this afternoon after our chat, we saw her sitting on a bench in the sun. I was emboldened by their presence; and I have a legitimate

Sean Young (Chani) at Estudios Churubusco, Mexico City, 1983.

position. And, as Greg said, "You'd better make your move fast, 'cause she's going to be snapped up." So I walked over to her and introduced myself, explaining who I am and what I'm doing here. She shook hands, said thanks for introducing myself, asked my name again to make sure she'd got it. I said, "You'll be seeing a lot of us; I hope we'll see a lot of you." And then was called to the van which was just leaving. So I don't know where she's staying.

Wednesday, April 13: DAY TWENTY-FOUR

The equipment is supposed to be delivered to Churubusco at seven this evening. If so – and if the tape arrives – and if nothing essential was left out – we should be going next week – maybe even Saturday – or Friday…

Introduced Anatol to Sean Young this morning. She seems friendly. When she came into the commissary at lunchtime, she smiled and waved. She sat with Everett McGill (Stilgar – previously star of *Quest For Fire*).

On our way out, I introduced myself to McGill and said a few words to her, too. A little later, as Anatol and I were standing around in the sun with the Apogee people, Sean appeared with a super-8 camera, shooting home movies for Mom and Dad – shooting everything, including a bunch of shots of us.

Finally introduced myself to Freddie Francis; he knew who we were already. He's a friendly, unassuming little man who walks around with a look of quiet amusement on his face. Unlike Tony Masters, who's tall and thin and strides around with sharp-eyed assurance.

Janice, Dykstra's assistant, was carrying around a script which Dykstra is considering taking on: *The Stars My Destination*, from Alfred Bester's novel – the best science fiction adventure ever written … *my* movie, dammit!

Thursday, April 14: DAY TWENTY-FIVE

I'm feeling really bad. The tension came close to breaking point this afternoon. The equipment didn't arrive yesterday. There was a power cut at the studio – so, with the darkness and the waiting, we joined a tequila party, finally coming back here with Kyle about eight-thirty.

Anatol and I walked around, looking for a place to eat. He asked a couple of women on the street – and we wound up eating with them. The older, manager of a nearby new-wave boutique, the younger, her assistant. A weird evening, with Anatol acting a little crazy. We walked back to the boutique afterwards to get their address and phone number. A strange place, full of peculiar clothes, with Laura Mars-type pictures of dead women on the walls – punky, decadent; a superb set for bizarre stories…

After we left them, we walked around for a while before turning in.

The revised estimate was that the equipment would come at three this afternoon. So we waited the day away again. Greg and I discussed the possibilities surrounding Sean Young. I haven't asked her out yet – no opportunity ever really presents itself, and you know me; I've never been able to create my own...

Anatol and I watched Fred shooting a second-unit scene. We visited the first unit. David looked a bit tired – not surprising; it must be a strain dealing with people who take at least twice the time necessary to do anything.

I visited the first unit again this afternoon; it was interesting, because I got to see Freddie Francis lighting a shot – a long, complicated business. Another ego boost: Freddie noticed me, said hello, asked how it was going with the equipment... These are really decent, friendly people (except for Raffaella, who looks right through me).

Sometime after five, we got the word: no equipment today. Now it's twelve noon tomorrow... We aren't even going to bother going in tomorrow morning. We've developed into a kind of joke there – not vicious, but it's becoming too much to take.

The tension hit me like a brick then – it made me feel almost physically sick.

The DGA trainee, Ian whatever, fucked up seriously; he didn't tell anyone on the second unit that they were supposed to view the dailies yesterday – including David's assistant, Leslie Werner, who's now doing continuity. Yesterday afternoon David started talking to her about the dailies and she didn't have a clue (which was rough on her); and the second unit work this morning had to match some stuff previously shot by the first unit. How can you do continuity if you don't know what you're continuing?

More bad news: the script for *The Stars My Destination* was written by Lorenzo Semple, Jr. – renowned for such classics as De Laurentiis' *Ping Pong*. A hack who's afraid to take fantasy seriously. Dykstra says it's a shallow, campy script. It's possible I'll get to read it sometime in the next couple of weeks...

My mood has developed into a profound depression. I walked over to Anatol's hotel a while ago, called his room – he was crashing with a glass of brandy. I saw Sean Young in the lobby of the Century across the street – white dress, bare feet. She hurried out, went to the Royal around the corner. I wound up sitting on a window ledge across from my hotel, watching the street. I saw Bob Bealmear heading off, probably to dinner, with some woman. I saw the two soundmen, Nelson [Stoll] and John [Haptas], apparently heading back from dinner. Raffaella arrived at the hotel. I saw a few more faces I recognized from the studio. About an hour after I saw her go into the Royal, I saw Sean and a tall bearded man going up the street, presumably in search of a restaurant. She was still in white, with bare feet. It appears that she's down here with someone.

And all the time I couldn't stop thinking how Anatol and I were turning into a joke, couldn't shake the feeling that this is all turning sour on me – that it's all gone badly wrong and I don't know where or why. And worst of all: there's really no one here I can talk to, call when I need someone. I've met a lot of people, but it's the same old thing – there are really no friends here (or, rather, there's one – but I can't talk to him because he's too deeply entangled with his own problems: David).

Friday, April 15: DAY TWENTY-SIX

I got up late today, about ten. The phone had rung earlier, but I didn't answer it. I had a shower, then went over to Anatol's hotel and called his room. He'd tried to reach me, got no response – looked in here at the Amberes, saw my key wasn't at the desk (indicating I was in). He said he was worried I'd gone and killed myself. He also said the studio had called and our stuff had arrived. It turned out that the *tape* had arrived (minus a few cassettes).

So – another day of waiting around. By five o'clock, I'd given up on it. But Belinda called the shipper again; it'd be there in twenty-five minutes. By six, I was suggesting we leave the studio – it wouldn't be arriving until next week. Well – it finally arrived about six-thirty. In an old, beaten up, open truck (thank god it didn't rain). It was being treated like vegetables, this hundred-thousand dollar electronics package. Everything had been opened and (in some cases) resealed. It turned out that someone had poked into everything (in the camera case, a small circuit board had been removed from its plastic, transparent envelope and left loose – with god knows what finger marks all over it).

Tomorrow we really unpack it, check what's there, and start setting up. And if the camera hasn't been thrown off completely by the rough handling, perhaps we'll be able to shoot some tentative footage Monday.

I watched them setting up a shot on a Harkonnen 'thopter this afternoon. The machine is beautiful – the Harkonnen soldiers amazing; dressed in thick oily-looking space suits, they have bright red hair with a shaved patch on top in which there are scars (from brain surgery, I assume). They look like big, hulking, mindless brutes.

Saturday, April 16: DAY TWENTY-SEVEN

A day of tension, mistakes, unpleasant clashes.

It started badly. I was standing on the corner at seven-forty-five this morning, waiting for Anatol and the eight o'clock bus. Suddenly the transport captain came over and said, "Do you want to ride with the director?" I looked up and saw David's car sitting in the middle of the intersection. He was alone. I said,

"I'd better wait for Anatol." So I blew it. A chance for half-an-hour alone with David. I just wasn't thinking.

As if I didn't feel bad enough about it, Anatol kept harping on it during the bus ride – I've got to be thinking all the time, can't afford these stupid mistakes… So I got really depressed about it. Then he said, "I don't want to hear any more about it." Just don't fuck up again. But later, when things were getting tense, he laid into me about not making any more mistakes, like this morning with David…

I now see very clearly that it's not going to be fun working with Anatol. He gets all worked up – pushing things, pulling things, taking very little care (he kept forcing the tripod head because he wouldn't pause to see how all the locks work) – I'm surprised he hasn't broken anything yet.

We finally got the camera-recorder-player-monitor links set up, but we weren't getting sound. Bob was there watching, so I jokingly said, "Do you know anything about video?" And Anatol snapped, "I've got the video. It's the sound that's not working and that's your department." By that time, I'd had enough. If he wants to play the prima donna, fine. I'd helped him rig the camera – now it's suddenly my fault alone there's no sound (actually there was – on the tape; it just doesn't run direct from camera through to monitor). So I walked out and got myself some tea, taking a break to calm down.

When I went back, "We've got to talk," he said. "Yes, we've got to talk," I said. And he went into a long spiel about how you don't "walk off set," no director would stand for it. And once again, everything that doesn't go smoothly is my fault – and I'm supposed to sit still for his attacks. The thing is, I can't argue back because when he gets worked up, it's as if he switches off a circuit and he simply no longer understands English…

Eventually things smoothed out. We took the camera out and shot a test cassette (twenty minutes). It needs some minor adjustment, but the image is sharp. I must admit I felt a little gratified that he quickly found the camera uncomfortably heavy.

But I don't know if I'm going to be able to take six months of his bullshit (we work together until we hit a snag, then the problem is my fault). As for working with him beyond this job … frankly, I don't see it.

Fred was off sick this morning. I ran into him about five. I'd gone over to David's hotel, El Presidente, hoping to catch him (partly because I wanted to apologize for this morning, partly because he and Anatol and I must get together soon to talk about this project) and was standing around outside. Fred looks beat – and he's got a heavy shooting schedule. I don't know how he holds up.

He said David would be back in an hour or so – he'd gone back to the studio from the garbage dump set (where Fred will be shooting Monday) to see the dailies. So I'll try to call in a little while.

On top of it all, I feel as if I'm coming down with something myself...

Anatol called; all smooth and decent again.

I just talked to David on the phone. No problem about this morning – I mean, he wasn't insulted or anything. It doesn't look as if we'll ever really be able to get together for a chat, but he says he thinks we should just get out and shoot what we want to and it should be good.

Once again he said it's great that "you guys" are down here. I really think he likes us around for moral support.

More on the cast: we were wrong about Francesca Annis – she's gorgeous.

Jose Ferrer as the Emperor; Freddie Jones as Thufir; Aldo Ray as Gurney; Dean Stockwell as Dr Yueh; Sting as Feyd; Jack Nance as Nefud; Max von Sydow as Dr Kynes; Silvana Mangano as the Reverend Mother Ramallo. There's one hell of a cast coming together for this film...

Sunday, April 17: DAY TWENTY-EIGHT

I slept in today, until some time after noon. Took a shower, wrote a letter. Then went out – partly to buy postcards, partly just to walk. I walked around a couple of blocks, and spotted Dykstra crossing Amberes with what I thought was his crew. Actually, it was Marty, Anatol and Raffaella – on their way up to the rooftop pool at the Royal. I tagged along. A relaxing afternoon, part of the clique. Bob, Janis, Greg were there; Nelson and John, the sound crew, arrived later. Raffaella was talkative and outgoing (in English!). Work only poked its way into the conversation occasionally (Dykstra seems to be having a few problems with the way the film is being shot, from the effects point of view).

The group gradually thinned out, planning to gather again later for supper. Sean Young showed up – a wave and a smile. Not long after that, Ian Woolf, the DGA trainee, also appeared. I left soon after.

A pleasant evening. I had supper with John Dykstra, Marty Kline, Janis, Ed George (Freddie F.'s assistant), and Nelson and John, the sound crew. A decent seafood restaurant. Lots of wine and easy conversation. I could very easily become addicted to this social atmosphere (and at the same time do my best to develop these people as contacts – if I'm to have any kind of career...).

It's funny – after just two weeks, I can run into far more people I know and who know me in this area of Mexico City than I ever could in Winnipeg.

By the way – Ron Miller, the production illustrator, mentioned yesterday that there's a small east coast publisher who's interested in putting out an *Eraserhead* book. He said he'd get the address for me...

Week Four Documents

```
                        CALL SHEET.              Production N° 12

PRODUCTION TITTLE :  DUNE                        DATE : Saturday April 16th,1983
PRODUCER : RAFFAELLA DE LAURENTIIS .
DIRECTOR : DAVID LYNCH                           CREW CALL:  8.00am at Studios
```

SETS & SCENES NUMBERS : TO COMPLETE :		D/N			LOCATION/STAGE	
INT.HARKONNEN ORNITHOPTER - Sc.: 130pt, 13/A,135		(N)			STAGE #2	

ARTIST	CHARACTERS	D/R	P/U	M/U	WARD	ON SET
FRANCESCA ANNIS	JESSICA	217	TIME TO BE CONFIRMED			
KYLE MacLACHLAN	PAUL	218	TIME TO BE CONFIRMED			
HUMBERTO ELIZONDO	HARK. GUARD #1	212		7.00		8.30am
RAMON MENENDEZ	HARK. GUARD #2	214		7.00		8.30am
SEAN YOUNG	CHANI	208	TO MEET WITH MAGGIE ANDERSON			
EVERETT McGILL	STILGAR	207	TO MEET WITH MAGGIE ANDERSON			
JUDD OMEN	JAMIS	216	FIGHT TRAINING AT			9.00am
RICHARD HUMPHREYS	STUNT CO-ORDINATOR				at Studios	8.00am

STAND-INS :
JOSEPHINE LOVELL	FOR JESSICA				7.45	8.00am
GONZALO IRIGOYEN	FOR PAUL				7.45	8.00am
A.N. OTHER					7.45	8.00am
A.N. OTHER					7.45	8.00am

REQUIREMENTS :
PRODUCTION : Security guards on Stage #2-coffee service on Stage & Dress.Rooms-A.D's desk rigged to Stage light,bell & telephone.
* Vigilancia en Foro #2-cafe en Foro & Camerinos-mesa de Asst.Dir. conectada a luz Foro,campana y telefono.

PROPERTY : Paul & Jessica bonds -telescopic knife for Hark.-sharp knife to cut stripes-Yueh's satchel (fremkit)-Leto's signet ring-Hark.rifle & dummy rifle- /* ataduras para Paul & Jessica-cuchillo telescópico para Hark.-cuchillo afilado para cortar ataduras- cartera de Yueh (fremkit)-anillo de Leto -fusil para Hark. y fusil de truco.

ART: Yueh's triangular tattoo in cabin roof */Tatuaje triangular de Yueh en techo de cabina.

SP/FX : Rocker - /* columpio-

MAKE-UP/HAIR : Head symbol on Harkonnen heads/*Símbolos en cabezas de Harkonnen.

CAMERA : EICI 16mm projector with 2 lenses-animated 16mm film-art card-
* EICI 16mm proyector con 2 lentes- pelicula 16mm animada-

ELECTRIC : Stand by generator rigged to Stage #2 /* generador conectado a Foro #2 preparado .

GRIP : Zeus Chapman crane /* grua Zeus Chapman.

CATERING : Running buffet ready from 11.30am ./*running buffet desde las 11.30

ADVANCE SCHEDULE : Monday April 18th,1983.
1) TO COMPLETE: INT.HARKONNEN ORNITHOPTER, Sc.:130pt,135,137A (N) STAGE #2
2) IF TIME PERMITS : MOVE TO LOCATION "AGUILAS ROJAS"("TRASH DUMP") EXT.FREMEN PLACE-DEEP DESERT . Sc.:164,165,166,167,168,210
On Saturday it will be decided if the call is at 8.00am or 5.00pm

RUNNING BUFFET : ONLY FOR SHOOTING CREW .
RUNNING BUFFET : SOLO PARA PERSONAL DE RODAJE.

J.Lopez Rodero
Assistant Director.

First unit call sheet, April 16, 1983.

```
TRANSPORTATION:

OWN INSTRUCTIONS :   R.DE LAURENTIIS,D.LYNCH.P.LOPEZ,G.ANGOSSE,L.BARNARD,M.B.FARRELLY,
                     V.ESCRIVA,J.CLEMENTE,A.BADIN,A.CAMACHO,K.LOPEZ,T.MASTERS,G.MASTERS,
                     P.L.BASILE,B.FERNANDEZ,J.VELAZQUEZ,A.PUCCINI,K.WEST,G.SUMNER,G.GALLO,
                     E.RUIZ,J.SORIA,A.ARRIOLA,G.DESIDERI,Y.DE BONO,T.WOODS,J.STIRBER,
                     T.GIBBS,P.SHAW.

PRODUCTION CAR #2    8.00am         G.OFFENHEIM,A.STRICK,ALISON .                   8.30am
(LUIS RAMIREZ)
PRODUCTION CAR #3    8.00am         F.FRANCIS,Y.AXWORTHY,G,HAYMAN.                  8.30am
(J.L.CONTRERAS)
CAMERA COMBI         8.00am         T.ROSS,E.GEORGE.                                8.30am
(C.VELEZ)
WARDROBE COMBI       (own inst.)    B.RINGWOOD,T.CASTERLINE,M.JONES,
(J.RODRIGUEZ)                       A.INFANTE,N,VITALI.
WARDROBE COMBI                      E.PERCIVAL,B.HIGGINS,K.ORR,C.STREETER,D.HARKNESS,
(C.CHAVEZ)                          R.WARD.M.LANG (as per B.Ringwood inst.)
MAKE UP COMBI        6.00am         G.DE ROSSI, M.DE ROSSI,                         6.30am
(J.CRUZ)                            M.TAMAGNINI,L.ROCCHETTI,M.SCUTTI.
YELLOW COMBI         8.00am         R.DIAZ.                                         8.30am
(S.AGUIRRE)
SOUND COMBI          8.00am         N.STOLL,J.HAPTAS.                               8.30am
(SELF DRIVEN)
SP/FX COMBI          (as per K.West) D.GALLIANO,A.KELLY,J.HATT,J.CLIFFORD,
(D.RIOS)                             A.PARRA,A.BALANDIN.
SP/FX COMBI          (as per K.West) J.BAKER,T.COX.
(O.CRUZ)
PROPS DPT. COMBI                    M.BENSTED,L.ROMERO (as per G.Sumner)
(J.ERAIS)                           R.DOWNING


PRODUCTION CAR       (own inst.)    A.PACANOWSKI, G.GODWIN.
(UNIVERSAL)
PRODUCTION CAR       8.00am         R.LARNER,M.SCHIAVONE,I.MACCARONE,G.WHITTEAR.    8.30am
(A.ROMERO)
SCARLET PICK UP      7.30am         J.MATTHEWS                                      8.00am
(VILLAREAL)
BEIGE COMBI          8.00am         K.PHIPPS , A.PATON.                             8.30am
(V.ROMERO)


PRODUCTION COMBI                    U.VENTURA,S.CATARINELLI,T.SERINI,M.MARTA.A.MARTA,
H.ROYAL  : 6.30am                   J.BOLAÑOS,A.DEL TORO.
S.NIZA   : 6.35am
```

ARTIST CAR #1	6.00am	FRANCESCA ANNIS	Hidalgo 161-2	6.30am	Studio
ARTIST CAR #2	8.00am	KYLE MacLACHLAN	Vallarta #47-	8.30am	Studio
ARTIST CAR #3	12.30 noon	SYLVANA MANGANO	Fuego 990	1.00pm	Studio
ARTIST CAR #4	12.30 noon	EVERETT McGILL	Camelias #18	1.00pm	Studio
ARTIST CAR #5	12.30 noon	SEAN YOUNG	Cda.Gomez Farias N°21	1.00pm	Studio
ARTIST CAR #6	12.30 noon	MOLLY WRYN	H.Presidente	1.00pm	Studio
ARTIST CAR #7	12.30 noon	D.CORKILL & D.GONZALEZ	H.Century	1.00pm	Studio

Typical daily unit transportation schedule.

Week 5: April 18-24, 1983

Tuesday, April 19: DAY THIRTY

Yesterday was a *long* day. Fourteen hours at the studio (Anatol got there ninety minutes before me). But it went quite well. We shot off eight-and-a-half cassettes. Anatol has a very unstructured approach; he finds a vantage point (difficult on the tight set they were filming yesterday – the Harkonnen 'thopter in which Paul and Jessica escape to the desert); and then just fires the camera more or less continuously. Occasionally it throws up a good shot (we got a couple of excellent ones), but on the whole it's a rather generalized mess without much informational value. It was only the first day, of course, and he's just getting used to the camera, but if it goes on like this, everything will have to be covered by a lot of narration. He doesn't seem to think in terms of: if we see this, then we should go over there and see this other related thing which makes sense of the first thing. They were using the air gun rack which fires clusters of darts on yesterday's setup – we have it firing on tape – but we don't have Kit West operating the controls.

But there's a bigger problem. He has no interest in behind-the-scenes stuff; he doesn't want to tour the shops or talk to the technicians and artisans to find

Western Costume, Estudios Churubusco.

out how they make things, how things work... Yet, whether he likes it or not, that is definitely a part of our job.

After the wrap yesterday evening, the second assistant director, a Mexican named Arturo who's been a news cameraman all over the place (Central America, Europe, the Middle East...) came up to our room to check the camera out; the image was quite good, but the tubes weren't fully aligned – he spent almost two hours fiddling with it. He's a very nice guy with a wife and new baby, who's working for peanuts on *Dune* ($200 a *month*) so he can watch David work. Anatol wants to get him paid extra so he can regularly tweak the camera for us. And then Anatol started talking to me about testing Arturo's shooting style, so that if he's any good, we can get *him* to shoot all that "boring" stuff.

It looks as if I'm going to have to try to guide him into covering all the angles, not just David and Fred on set. I'm going to have to start thinking as the writer of the thing...

The atmosphere was very good yesterday. Anatol himself was in excellent spirits. We had a lot of contact with David around the set – he seemed very pleased to have us there. Kuki Rodero (Pepe's brother), the assistant director, didn't seem to like us at first – telling us to get out of the way, pushing my mike out of the way. But he warmed in the afternoon (maybe David spoke to him; maybe he just realized what our position is).

Anatol got in the way of the camera at one point – spoke to the operator and established a good rapport (all he has to do now is tell Gordon what he wants, and they'll be able to work it out).

During a break, I told David the 'thopter looked great – he seemed very pleased. Later, I mentioned that I'd read the script and said, "For someone who says he can't write, you're a very good writer. It reads better than any other script

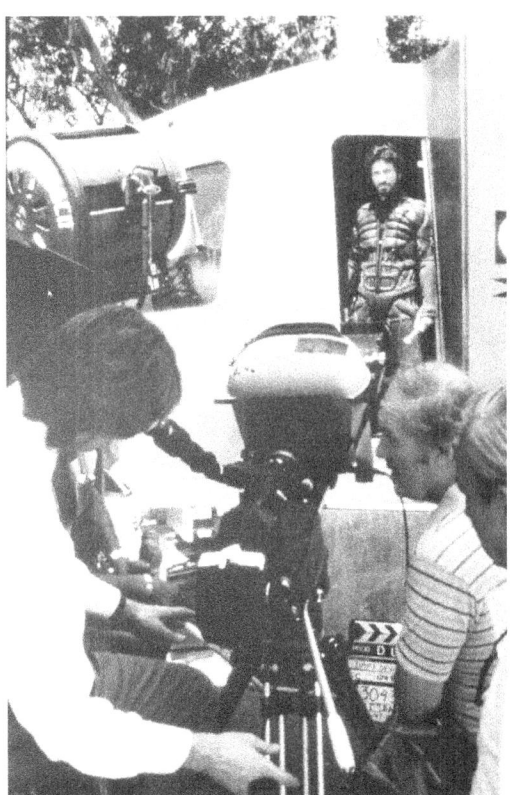

David Lynch and 2nd unit director Jimmy Devis line up a shot of Duke Leto (Jurgen Prochnow) exiting an Atreides 'thopter. Photograph by George Whitear, copyright Universal/De Laurentiis.

I've read." And I was gratified to see that he took it as the opinion of someone whose opinions count in that area.

Freddie Francis is also a pleasure to watch. Completely professional, with a sense of humour – he never loses his temper with people, speaks calmly but firmly until things are set the way he wants them.

On top of everything else, Raffaella actually said good morning to me yesterday – before I said anything to her.

A group of people from Universal are visiting. Among them Paul Sammon. He brought some news. We're to produce a series of little promo pieces – the first, about five minutes, to be ready in four to six weeks. He brought the script with him. We'll be working together a lot, he says.

We say, we contracted to produce a sixty-minute documentary. This stuff falls into the category of extra work. That means it must be paid for separately.

He said Armstrong told him we'd be getting extra for this. But he didn't tell us that until he came back later – as if to let the job sink in, then to appear generous about it.

And this is where I begin to sound like Anatol, I'm afraid; because I'll be only too happy to let Sammon take care of some of the interviews – at least initially. Today we have to do something with Ron Miller, the illustrator. I don't expect to get much out of it...

Dykstra at supper Sunday evening: there are concepts in the script which they haven't yet worked out the technical means of executing (like scenes which wrap around drops of water, fall away to be replaced by another...). Yet they had to put them in the budget somehow – kind of a seat-of-the-pants operation. But he said: whether they make any other films or not, this is the one they have to do right – no fudging... He does have respect for the project.

Today: there's a big night shoot at the dead-dog dump set (Arrakis). Far too much scheduled for one session: Paul and Jessica's first encounter with the Fremen – a lot of dialogue culminating in the fight between Paul and Jamis. The crew call is for five – cast to be on-set at ten. It'll be a *very* long night.

A surreal scene last night: we had to get a cab back from the studio, dropping Arturo off on the way. It was the most wrecked cab I've ever seen – doors hanging off their hinges, reluctant to latch, door handles missing off the outside. The trunk buckled and flapping. No suspension. A death trap. And the driver took a route completely different from any we've used before – it was like a strange French movie.

Then, just a minute or two after being dropped in front of Anatol's hotel we saw a spectacular crash at the corner of Amberes and Liverpool (around which we'd just come in the death-trap cab). A black Mercedes and a white American sedan, one coming down Amberes, the other along Liverpool, both at about thirty or forty miles per hour, met in the middle of the intersection with a roar, showers of sparks and steam, seemed to leap into the air, doing almost complete three-sixty degree turns before landing facing each other. All the people from the white car piled out; someone in the Merc was injured – people grabbed him and ran down the sidewalk with him (god knows what damage they did). The driver of the white car got back in and tried to start it, despite the completely crushed front end.

Two cops on motorcycles came down Liverpool, turned into Amberes and rode on past. The people involved seemed to vanish (apparently few people carry insurance). After a while an ambulance came to pick up the injured guy. A cop drove past. There was no one to direct the fairly heavy traffic which was squeezing past the wrecks. *Three* police tow trucks drove up, but went away without doing anything. There was no sense of order, no authority – this place is on the brink of chaos. It was a perfect nightmare scene.

Just after I left Anatol, I was stopped by a guy who asked if I'd seen what happened. We got talking. He's an American, from Tucson, who's been here about six months (teaching English at a nearby school), a writer, he said. He's interested in *Dune*, exchanged names and addresses. Someone he knew came by – an Englishman named Terry. A member of Kit West's effects crew (he built the dart gun). He says they're planning to send the foreign crew home once everything's been built and let the Mexicans run the machinery.

Wednesday, April 20: DAY THIRTY-ONE (16 hrs)

Christ knows what this'll do to my health.

We got to the studio at one yesterday afternoon, had lunch, did some stuff with Ron Miller, the production illustrator. Neither Anatol nor myself like interviewing, nor know how to do it. Mostly we pointed the camera and mike at the guy and hoped he'd talk. Luckily he did.

Spoke to Fred; they might want us for the hospital, x-ray stuff Saturday (maybe not). He also told me that David is planning an *Eraserhead* book (a visual one, not verbal).

Sammon stopped by to tell us he'll be hanging around with us as much as he can. Rah rah rah...

We left for the garbage dump location about five-twenty. It looks absolutely fantastic – something out of the Arabian Nights. I realized later what the turrets on the castle wall reminded me of subliminally (they look like faces) – the Easter Island statues.

We gradually got into the feel of it, moving in closer as we went. The preparation of the thirty-five Fremen (who look truly tribal), covering them with dust

The desert planet Arakis – aka "dead dog dump."

– in an atmosphere which was constantly thick with a fine, irritating volcanic dust (we'll probably get silicosis). The setting up of each shot (they got three before the wrap at three-thirty), the rehearsals, the takes – David coaching the actors...

Whatever actually comes out of this, it really is a remarkable, valuable experience for us personally. Already our presence seems to be generally accepted – people will turn to the light if they see us shooting what they're doing, they ask about our equipment, what we're doing here... Though the occasional person doesn't seem to like us (a wardrobe man pushed my mike away from Francesca Annis and told me to "get that thing away from here").

It was a bizarre scene – the dump (Aguilas Rojas – Red Eagle; the rock formation was used in the *Man Called Horse* movies) looked like a stadium, massive light banks on cranes, a tower behind the castle wall holding two brutes; and when we got there, there was a huge crowd lined along the wire fence watching the spectacle. They were still there at eight-thirty when we all broke for supper – we had an audience at the catering tent on the embankment just outside the fence, held back by cops and security people. This all in a poor area of the city. It was the kind of scene Dickens would write if he was still around.

There's a very good atmosphere on set – friendly, controlled. David looks completely self-assured, occasionally moving away by himself, contemplative. Occasionally looking lonely. On our way to supper I said, "How does it feel to

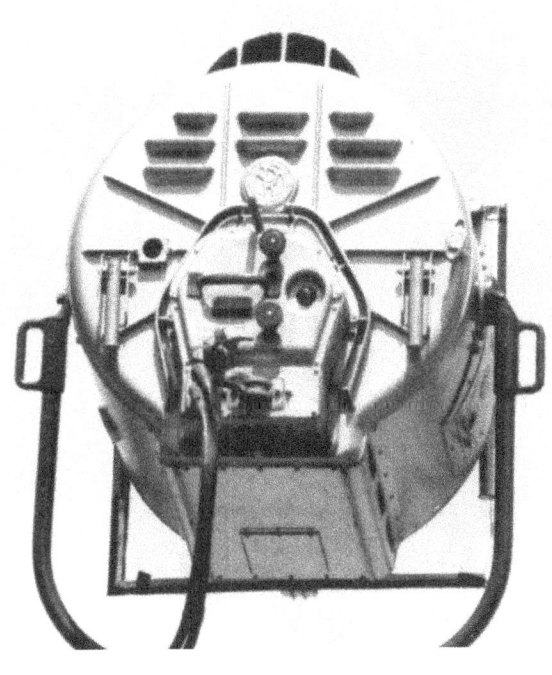

Brute.

have all this being done for you?" and he said, "It isn't being done for me." He still doesn't feel that this is *his* movie.

After taking the equipment back to the studio, we skimmed through the last cassette (some of it looked good, though Anatol has a tendency not to follow the conversations when we're filming, and there's a problem with framing – he holds the frame a bit too low, perhaps because of the read-out panel above the screen in the viewfinder). And had to get a taxi back because everyone else had already left. Finally got to bed just after five-thirty, stiff, dirty and aching.

Up again at noon. We're supposed to shoot something of Miller's wife, Judy, and the seamstresses this afternoon before heading back to the dump. We may be thoroughly wrecked by the end of the week.

Thursday, April 21: DAY THIRTY-TWO (15 hrs)

Yesterday didn't feel nearly so good. Tired. And rethinking. It has begun to seem that what looked so great about this project is actually the worst thing about it. Filmmaking is a tedious, repetitious business – you do the same things over and over again, only the places change and what the actors say and do. So being an outside observer becomes tedious. We've been shooting a lot, but it all starts to look alike. And we've only been doing it for three days! If we go on like this, we'll end up with a huge formless mass, hours and hours of mush. If we were doing this as a traditional documentary, it would be different; we'd come in for a short period, shoot specific things with a firm idea in mind, and put it together. But this shotgun effect diffuses our attention – and we wind up being Gordon Armstrong's electronic vacuum cleaner. Dispiriting.

There is no question in our minds that we have to expand our crew. We need Arturo Garciarubio as our video technician and technical advisor; and Doug Hersh for the logging and weeding out of the material we shoot. Because Anatol

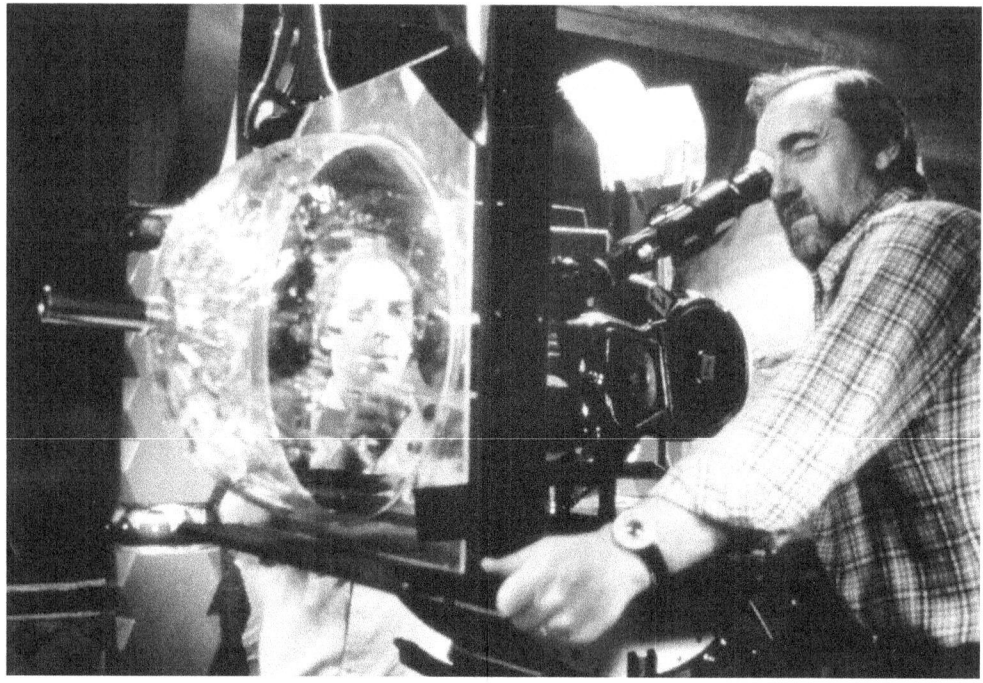

Camera operator Gordon Hayman [r] and clapper-loader Ed George working on a hunter-seeker POV shot. Photograph by George Whitear, copyright Universal/De Laurentiis.

and I simply don't have the time to look at all that we're shooting, let alone keep it in order and assemble it into any useful shape. But how to convince David and Raffaella of that?

I've just drafted a memo to them putting forward the situation. If Anatol agrees, I'll present it to them. Then we can only hope...

Friday, April 22: DAY THIRTY-THREE (12 hrs)

Yesterday was the busiest day on set yet. But we shot less than on previous days. Partly because we're getting used to it – we're becoming more selective about what we shoot, repeating ourselves less.

Partly because we were preoccupied with other things. Anne Strick brought a bunch of people to the location (a group of toy manufacturers and Universal people). Paul Sammon was with them. I can't help it: the guy makes me tense. He's a professional writer – I feel threatened by him.

Anatol and I were standing on the edge of the ravine, watching the crew set up a shot below. Sammon found us. I stepped away, back turned, and watched the action below with intensified interest as he talked to Anatol about his little script for a convention promo film he wants us to shoot (the one he says Armstrong says we'll get extra money for). He also spoke of his own film company which just finished some spectacular SF comedy. Anatol says my pointed snub was read clearly, that I made Sammon feel awkward. After a while I did join the conversation (at first, back still turned). And read the silly little script. Said he'd have to discuss it with David because he's very careful and has definite ideas himself...

A little later Strick spoke to us: what did Sammon say? what's this script? Raffaella hasn't approved it ... we don't take instructions from Sammon, we take our instructions from her(!?!). It was a regular little power struggle – for the control of us. We weren't particularly pleased. Strick told us we must meet with her on Monday so she can start telling us what to do; she seems displeased that we're spending so much time with the first unit, instead of shooting all the behind-the-scenes stuff (it was only our fourth day, for Christ's sake). In particular, she was annoyed that we hadn't got around to shooting the women who are embroidering Jessica's robe for the water ceremony – which she more or less ordered us to do Tuesday. We didn't have time Wednesday afternoon – so we're now doing it with Judy Miller on Monday.

But this little confusion about people who think they're in a position to tell us how to do our job wasn't the only thing.

I showed the memo to Anatol. He said okay. When we got to the studio, I gave it to Doug to type out. I thought he might not like it – and I was right. He came back a little flushed. "This just makes me an assistant ... Arturo told me that if you needed someone I could have the job ... he'd show me how to do it..." Ignoring the fact that this is not a thing to be arranged between Doug and Arturo, I had to point out that this was a complicated bit of office politics; first, at the moment Doug is not a qualified technician – we'd only be too happy to have Arturo teach him, but we need someone right now to tweak the camera – and second, they're more likely to assign Doug to us in an assistant capacity, and he can work up from there. Obviously, he was looking for an instant appointment to the top. He played his hand badly, pushing too much, demanding too much – also, when he typed the memo, he altered the wording slightly in the paragraph pertaining to himself. I didn't say anything, but the fact that he didn't speak to me about it first put me off; does he think I'm too stupid to notice?

His big complaint was that if they're willing to give us one person, going by the memo it would have to be Arturo. Sorry, but if it could only be one, *we'd* want it to be Arturo. I'm afraid this in an important matter of business, not a matter of favours.

It didn't stop there.

I had to wait for an opportunity to hand the memo to David. Supper is usually a good time, but he was sitting with Raffaella. Finally, quite late, there was a bit of a break as a new shot was being set up. I went over. "David, do you have a moment? I've got something we'd like you to read – and if you think it's reasonable, maybe pass it on to Raffaella." I thought he'd stick it in his pocket and look at it later. But he quickly read it, called Ian Woolf over and told him to take it to Raffaella. It seemed too fast. So Anatol and I sat there, all nervous tension – maybe it wasn't such a good idea; maybe it sounded as if we just weren't up to handling the job, maybe…

Then Raffaella appeared, had a brief word with David, and headed toward us. We arose, waiting. And she spoke to Anatol in French. They had a fairly long conversation – and I could only stand there silently. I couldn't judge it even from the tone because Raffaella tends to keep her voice quite flat.

Thus it transpired: she hadn't approved Sammon's thing – indeed, referred to Sammon as an asshole. So Strick had run to her with a report. This worries us (although, at the same time it relieves us of having to deal with Sammon for the moment) because Strick could be using Raffaella to appropriate us to her little publicity department. Raffaella's parting comment was that we'll have to "get organized like the stills" – ominous? we'll become just house photographers, told to shoot this, shoot that?

We're to have a meeting with Raffaella Monday afternoon to discuss everything. We hope Strick won't be present, but even if she is we're going to have to speak out and get the whole situation straight. The worst that can happen is that we get fired. And if their intention is to have us crank out garbage, maybe that's not so bad. In preparation, I'll get the earlier memo (our "statement of principles") typed out so that we can hand it to her if things start to get sticky. And we're going to have to spend the weekend putting together a little rough assembly of some of our best shots to date – a wide variety of them, to show that we're covering many areas, not just spending all our time on David.

We came to the conclusion that this whole thing is actually quite well timed – we've begun to work, have something to show, but haven't got too deeply in for things to be changed a little. One good point: Raffaella used the "*tu*" form with Anatol – we're all a family here, and so on. If we're accepted as part of the production, this working out of details might not be so terribly difficult.

Dino showed up on set yesterday, looking things over. Giving rise to yet another guy trying to make brownie points; he hurried over to us saying "that's the executive producer!" as if we were supposed to leap up and start shooting (even though it was too dark), as if we were so ignorant as to be unable to recognize the man.

The fact that we didn't leap up might be turned to our favour on Monday; we can tell Raffaella that out of respect we didn't want to bother her father, and would only shoot him if we'd cleared it through her first.

Judd Omen as Jamis challenges Paul to a knife fight. Photograph copyright Universal/De Laurentiis.

Saturday, April 23: DAY THIRTY-FOUR (15 hrs)

Yesterday was the most grueling yet – but despite the exhaustion, it was better than the previous day.

We arrived at the studio at three, found that we'd left our stuff in a real mess when we got back in the morning. Had to tidy up, then go over to shoot Fred on Stage 2. Unfortunately, they'd just struck a set-up, so we'll have to go back again later (we *were* going to go in again today, but decided this morning not to – like the first unit, we'll take Saturday off this week; but tomorrow we'll go to the studio and try to set up our editor – if it works, we'll try to put together a brief tape to show Raffaella, if she's interested).

Doug came in while we were packing for an early trip to the location (we wanted to get daylight shots of the crew setting up). We've turned cool towards him because of his pushiness, just told him it was all going through channels.

Having woken at nine-forty-five to a phone call from Paul Sammon (who knew I'd been working all night), who wanted to get a ride with us to Aguilas Rojas, I wasn't too thrilled to see him waiting in our car when we walked out with our equipment. It was generally more relaxed than before though; we all chatted idly on the trip. He stuck to us most of the evening. Said he'd spoken to Raffaella – we could shoot the stuff for his little promo piece (even had Anatol roll a shot of the twin rocks at the dump for a title background – "Your name will go over that," he said. No thanks, Anatol replied). He left sometime around midnight.

Much later, during a lull, Anatol went down into the ravine where Raffaella was sitting and chatted to her in French, hurried off to get her a mineral water when she expressed the need, made a good impression. He apologized about Sammon, saying we just couldn't shake him. She said she'd seen his script (piece of shit) and hadn't approved it. As for Monday's meeting, it sounds very informal – in fact, it's to be at *our* convenience!

Getting to the dump early didn't do us much good. No one showed up until almost six. So we stood in the wind and dust and talked to Sammon (who continually makes notes into a tape recorder). But we did get a few shots before sunset – though Anatol discovered he'd been shooting with 9 dBs enhancement (one-and-a-half stops), so the shots might be bad.

We started more slowly yesterday evening, our energies having run low. But we began shooting a lot more as time passed. David started with a big set up – leading into the fight between Paul and Jamis. It dragged on – we didn't break for supper until about ten – because Judd Omen (Jamis) turned out to be somewhat over his head. He talks very big – loud, pushy, cocky – but on set he's obviously terribly insecure; he builds himself up to such a pitch that he blocks himself. He comes on as if his brief moment is the whole of *Hamlet*, agonizing over it until he can't even deliver a couple of simple lines. He overplays horribly. It was a little embarrassing to watch.

At supper, I sat beside Josephine Lovell, Francesca Annis' stand-in. She's very friendly, an interesting character with the strangest accent I've ever heard. She was born in England, has lived in Australia, the States, England again, came to Mexico five years ago because of a Tarot card reading. Until now she hadn't done any film work for two years because of problems with a union man on *Caveman*; four weeks ago, she says, she just went to the studio to see what was going on – and found herself hired as Jessica's stand-in. She believes in fate – and who am I to argue? I'm here myself against all reason.

The day before (Thursday night) she'd turned up with an owl in a box – she'd just bought it as a pet (a big one, only two months old) and hadn't had time to take it home.

After all the preliminaries – establishing shot, close-ups, reverse angles, reaction shots – they finally got to the fight. Yamazaki, Richard Humphreys, and the other stuntmen moved in for some final coaching, Kyle and Omen ran through the moves a few times (very much refined from what we saw last week in the early days of training). Two cameras were set up. And the fight was shot as a continuous piece of action – twice. The choreography deteriorated somewhat on the takes, but it still looked quite good. It was after four when they prepared for the final set-up – a low angle of the fight's conclusion. After one take, they wrapped.

It was the longest, dustiest night of the week – and, thank god, the last. But we have to go back Monday night to finish the sequence. As Anatol says: David, why are you doing this to us?

The odd looks we were getting from David Thursday night apparently weren't because we were overstepping the bounds of our mandate. Must have been due to the pressure of Dino's visit, because last night he was friendly again, taking time out to ask how we and our equipment were doing in the cloud of dust he had Kit West's crew stirring up. That made us feel a lot better.

A surprising piece of information: Anne Strick, who seems to know almost nothing about almost everything, was once married to Joseph Strick, writer-director of *Ulysses*, *Portrait of the Artist*, *Tropic of Cancer*...

Had a leisurely supper with Fred at El Refugio, just the two of us. Talking about the film, his work on it – gradually going on to more general things. Very pleasant. He's a really nice guy. (He finally read my article, by the way; said he liked it very much – which, according to Anatol, is high praise from Fred.)

Coming back to the Amberes about ten, we ran into Raffaella – looking quite different, almost girlish, in a red-and-white knee-length dress with her hair down. She asked Fred how he was (he's been sick lately), smiling and friendly. When the elevator came, Golda, Maggie (dialect coach), Yvonne (continuity), and Tony Gibbs (the editor) got out. We stood around a few minutes as everyone chatted – and Raffaella seemed a totally different person; warm, playful, even likeable (she'd just got back from dinner with Dino, who was, she said, in a good mood). So a lot of her apparent coldness really is due to the pressures of her job (which must be considerable). If all goes well Monday, perhaps we can establish a completely different relationship with her – all we have to do is make her trust us and see that we have a clear and reasonable idea of what we're doing.

A moment of sheer unadulterated panic last night. We'd left our bags sitting by a rock down in the ravine (where we'd left them before). I went down there to collect them (we needed a fresh battery for the camera). Anatol's was sitting there, but mine – in which we keep the cassettes, both blank and used – was gone. *Theft!* rushed through my mind. I rushed back to Anatol, heart pounding – he said I was terribly white. We both set off in search. And luckily found the bag with a pile of other stuff which had been moved to one side. But it was a good object lesson: our material is really quite valuable. Some people might think it worthwhile (and profitable) to get hold of some tapes of set activity on *Dune*.

Sunday, April 24: DAY THIRTY-FIVE

Churubusco is apparently a union shop. Fred says it's been a source of problems because it's very tight; they tell the production who to hire – and the decision is based solely on seniority, not qualifications.

As far as Fred knows, the pictures for the *Cinefantastique* article are being taken care of right now. He wishes David hadn't waited so long before unloading the job onto him – he would have had much more time for it last year.

I've written a fairly concise one-and-a-half page outline for the Paris feature. I told Anatol about the basic plot idea at lunch – he likes it a lot. But going from outline to actual script is a pretty big step…

Didn't go to the studio today. Really needed the extra day off, just to bring the energy level back somewhere near normal.

Week Five Documents

```
                                                    Production #

              C A L L   S H E E T  (SECOND CAMERA)
PRODUCTION TITLE: "DUNE"              DATE: MONDAY 18th, APRIL, 1983.
PRODUCER: RAFFAELLA DE LAURENTIIS           *LUNES
DIRECTOR: FRED ELMES                  CREW CALL: 8.00am at Studios.


  SETS AND SCENE NUMBERS:              D/N         STAGE/LOCATION
  1) EXT. WALL-ARRAKEEN PALACE          D          RED EAGLES
     EXT. MURO PALACIO ARRAKEEN                    *AGUILAS ROJAS
     Sc: 64C
  2) EXT. WALL-ARRAKEEN PALACE          D          RED EAGLES
     Sc: 65B

  ARTISTS         CHARACTER    D/R   P/U   M/UP    WARD      ON SET


  ABEL WOOLRICH   CITY FREMEN                      8.00am    10.00am
                  *FREMEN CIUDAD


  CROWD
  -30 FREMEN MEN                                   8.00am    10.00am
      *HOMBRES
  - 5 FREMEN WOMEN                                 8.00am    10.00am
      *MUJERES


REQUIREMENTS:
PRODUCTION: Check details in all Departments-Coffee Service on Set-²Loud
            Hailers on Set - Walkie Talkies (CHECK CHARGING)-Drinking water
            for ALL PERSONNEl -Security on Set -Water Bowser for Set DUST.
            *Checar detalles en distintos Deptos-Servicio de Café en Set-
            2 Altavoces en Set- Walkie Talkis (CHECAR CARGA) - Aqua Potable
            para TODO PERSONAL- Seguridad en Set- Pipa de agua para POLVO
            en Set. (LOCATION DOCTOR ) [LABORERS PEONES on Set]
CAMERA: As per Fred Elmes' instructions -·40 KW GENERATOR (AC) for LIGHTFLEX-
PROPS: Oil lens Binoculars. *Binoculares de lente de aceite-Established acceso-
GRIPS: CRICKET Dolly with 15ft. TRACK *RIEL. (4 GRIPS)*(Accesorios establecidos
ELECT: 1,000 AMP/GENERATOR.
SOUND: As per José Carles' instructions. *Según instrucciones de José Carles.
TRANSPORT: BUS for TECHNICAL PERSONNEL -BUS for ARTISTIC PERSONNEL -
           TRANSPORT for: CAMERA - FOR DIRECTION PERSONNEL - FOR ACTOR/WARD/
           M/UP - PICKUP for staff's needs at Set.
           *AUTOBUS para personal TECNICO - AUTOBUS para personal ARTISTICO-
           TRANSPORTE FOR: Camera - Personal de Dirección - Actor/Ward/M-UP
           - Camioneta Pickup para necesidades de personal en Set.
     NOTE: TRANSPORT for SOUND CREW to leave STUDIOS at 8.30am for LOCATION.
           *TRANSPORTE para personal y equipo de Sonido para salir de Estudio
           a las 8.30am rumbo a LOCACION.
WARD: Arrange personnel as it has been established.
      *Arreglar personal de acuerdo con lo establecido.
HAIR/M-UP: Arrange personnel as it has been established.
           *Arreglar personal de acuerdo con lo establecido.
CATERING: Lunch ready from 12.30p.m. *Comida lista desde las 12.30pm'
S/FX: Standby for any necessities. *Pendiente para cualquier necesidad.
MEDICAL: Ambulance on set. *Ambulancia en Set.
CASTING:Check all personnel be ready at Set.*Checar que personal esté listo en
                                                                           Set.
       NOTE: ARTISTIC PERSONNEL WILL DRESS IN STUDIOS.
             *PERSONAL ARTISTICO SE VESTIRA EN ESTUDIOS.
ART/SET DRESS: Check any necessary detail for the shooting of these Scenes.
               *Checar cualquier detalle para el rodaje de estas Escenas.
NOTE/GRIPS:PLATFORM for Camera and Personnel. *Plataforma para Cámara y Perso-
                                                                          nal'
NOTE/ELECT: Complementary equipment as per Director's and Cinephotog. indic.
            *Equipo complementario según indic. de Dir. y Cinefotógrafo.
AVERAGE of Technic. and Artistic Personnel         Jesús Marín
ON LOCATION= 80 people.                            Assisstant Director
PROMEDIO de personal Técnico y Artístico EN LOC:=80pers
```

Second unit call sheet, April 18, 1983.

```
                SECOND CAMERA - TENTATIVE SCHEDULE
                *SEGUNDA CAMARA- PLAN TENTATIVO DE TRABAJO
```

TUESDAY, APRIL 19th   INT. PAUL'S ROOM-ARRAKEEN PALACE (D)   STAGE #4
*MARTES   HUNTER SEEKER Pickup shots
                       *Pickups de CAZADOR BUSCADOR
                       Sc: 80pt.

WEDNESDAY, APRIL 20   INT. PAUL'S ROOM-ARRAKEEN PALACE (D)   STAGE #4
*MIERCOLES   HUNTER SEEKER Pickup shots
                       (To complete)
                       *Pickups de CAZADOR BUSCADOR
                       (Para completar)
                       Sc: 80pt.

THURSDAY, APRIL 21   INT. PAUL'S ROOM-ARRAKEEN PALACE (D)   STAGE #4
*JUEVES   (Complete) *(Completar)
                       DYKSTRA SHOT (PART): Red droplets
                                          *Gotas rojas
                       This Scene will not be shot at Stage #4.
                       Window must be preserved as per John
                       Dykstra's indications.
                       *Esta Sc. no se filma en el Foro #4. La
                       ventana deberá conservarse según indi-
                       caciones de John Dykstra.

                       SECOND CAMERA SHOT(PART): Windows glow
                                                 white light.
                                                *Ventanas brillan
                                                 con luz blanca.

                       Sc: 78B pt.

REQUIREMENTS:

CAMERA: As per Fred Elmes' instructions.
        *Según instrucciones de Fred Elmes.

ELECT: Window light to get lighter - Shutters for arc light.
       *La luz de la ventana se aclara más y más - Dimmers para arco.

            NOTE: PROPS DEPT: Freeze cow's guts to be shot SATURDAY APRIL
                              23 (Sc: 113B) - Director must SUPERVISE the
                              position of guts inside wooden box before
                              shooting.
                              *Congelar vísceras de vaca para filmar el SABADO
                              ABRIL 23 (Sc: 113B)- El Director debe SUPER-
                              VISAR la posición de las vísceras en caja de
                              madera.

            NOTE: ART DEPT: -11.00am: RECEE to Lake location (CALADAN)
                                      *VISITA a Locación de lago
                                      Del Lago Restaurant
                                      Revised Scene: 52C
                            ATTENTION:
                            ATENCION: Tony Masters
                                       Kit West
                                       Pierluigi Basille
                                       Alejandro Ferrer
                                       Fernando Ramírez
                                       Benigno Ramírez (LABORER)
                                                    *(TRABAJADOR)

Projected B-camera schedule for the week of April 19, 1983.

```
                    CALL SHEET.              Production N° 14

PRODUCTION TITTLE :  DUNE                DATE :  Tuesday April 19th, 1983
PRODUCER  : RAFFAELLA DE LAURENTIIS
DIRECTOR  : DAVID LYNCH                  CREW CALL : 5.00pm at Studios/HOTEL
                                                     leave at Location
                                                     NIGHT SHOOTING .

SETS & SCENE NUMBERS :          D/N         LOCATION
EXT.FREMEN PLACE - DEEP DESERT .            TRASH DUMP / RED EAGLES
Sc.: 164,165,166,167,168,210    N           LAS AGUILAS ROJAS .

ARTIST            CHARACTERS          D/R    P/U      M/U      LINE UP   ON SET

FRANCESCA ANNIS   JESSICA             217    5.30   aft.line   6.00      10.00pm
KYLE MacLACHLAN   PAUL                218    5.30   aft.line   6.00      10.00pm
SEAN YOUNG        CHANI               208    5.30     up       6.00      10.00pm
EVERETT McGILL    STILGAR             207    5.30     "        6.00      10.00pm
JUDD OMEN         JAMIS               216    5.30     "        6.00      10.00pm
MARTIN LASALLE    FREMEN #1           212    7.30    8.00               10.00pm
HONORATO MAGALONE FREMEN #2           214    7.30    8.00               10.00pm
                                           (at Stud.)

RICHARD HUMPHREYS  STUNT CO-ORDINATOR       6.00pm on Loc
DAVID ELLIS        STUNT DOUBLE for PAUL    6.00pm on Loc
WILL HARPER        STUNT DOUBLE for JAMIS   6.00pm on Loc

STAND-INS :                                           M/U & WARD.
JOSEPHINE LOVELL   FOR JESSICA    at Studios at 4.30pm   5.15pm         5.30pm
GONZALO IRIGOYEN   FOR PAUL       at Studios at 4.30pm   5.15pm         5.30pm
A.N.OTHER          FOR CHANI      at Studios at 4.30pm   5.15pm         5.30pm
A.N.OTHER          FOR STILGAR    at Studios at 4.30pm   5.15pm         5.30pm
A.N.OTHER          FOR JAMIS      at Studios at 4.30pm   5.15pm         5.30pm

CROWD :                                              M/U at Loc.
30  FREMEN MEN (stillsuits)       at Studios at 6.00pm   7.00pm         8.00pm
 4  FREMEN WOMEN (stillsuits)     at Studios at 6.00pm   7.00pm         8.00pm

PRODUCTION REQUIREMENTS :
PRODUCTION :    Motorhomes for actors-honey wagon for shooting crew-tents for Ward.&
                Make-up- Production tent with radio communication to Production Office-
                coffee service on Dres.Rooms & Location-security guards on entrance &
                around location- 2 loud hailers-ambulance & Doctor on set-labourers
                on set - working lights-
             *  Caravanas para actores-honey wagon para equipo de rodaje-carpas para
                Vestuario y maquillage-carpa de Production con comunicacion radio con
                oficina Product.cafe en Camerinos y Locacion-vigilancia en entrada
                y alrededor de locacion-2 altavoces-ambulancia y Doctor en Loc.
                trabajadores en Loc.- luces funcionando.
CATERING :      Dinner for 200 people ready from 8.00pm./*Cena para 200 personas lista
                desde las 8.00pm.
PROPERTY :      Crysknives for Fremen-weapons-Jamis' knife-Chani's knife-dummy knife-
                telescopic knife-Leto's signet ring-fremkit for Paul-still tents to
                cover Jamis body-dipsticks-thumpers-ropes-hooks-
             *  Crysknives para Fremen-armas-cuchillo para Jamis & Chani-cuchillo de
                truco - cuchillo  telescopic-anillo de Leto-fremkit pata Paul-
                still tienda para cubrir a Jamis-varilla musical-golpeadores-cuerdas-
                ganchos-
SET DRESSING :  Small bushes-cacti-tiny clump odd leaves-cones for dew collecting-
             *  Pequeños matorales-pequeñas plantas de hojas  raras- conos para
                recoleccion de rocio
```

First unit call sheet, April 19, 1983, page 1.

Page #2

SP/FX :	Fremen SP/FX impacts on rocks- rig Jamis suit for water spill when killed by Paul- /* efectos de impactos de Fremen en rocas-preparar traje de Jamis para que agua se derrame cuando le mata Paul.
MAKE -UP : *	Jamis wound on chest- hand cut effect for Jamis-Make up take place on Loc. Herida en pecho para Jamis- efecto de mano cortada para Jamis-el maquillage tendrá lugar en Loc.
WARDROBE :	Cloaks or blankets to warm up artists-Artist dressing will take place on Loc Crowd dressing will take place on Loc. /* capas o mantas para calentar los actores- el vestuario de actores y extras se hará en Loc.
CAMERA :	As per F.Francis instructions /*Según instrucciones de F.Francis.
ELECTRIC :	5 D.C. generators on location ready from 2.00pm. 1 D.C. generator on location ready from 2.00pm.
TRANSPORTATION:	Equipment trucks,vans and combies as per each Dpt.request 2 crew buses 1 bus for crowd 1 Combi or car for Stand-ins 3 Actors cars 1 Direction Dpt. combi
NOTE :	TO ALL CREW AND ARTISTIC PERSONNEL WEAR WARM, WIND PROTECTION, CLOTHES.

ADVANCE SCHEDULE :

WEDNESDAY APRIL 20th, 1983.
TO COMPLETE :
EXT.FREMEN PLACE - DEEP DESERT .   LOCATION :
Sc.: 164,165,166.167,168,210   (N)   TRASH DUMP /AGUILAS ROJAS
         NIGHT SHOOTING .

                                    J.Lopez Rodero
                                    Assistant Director.

First unit call sheet, April 19, 1983, page 2.

```
.:SPORTATION :                                                    Tuesday April 19th, 1983.

OWN INSTRUCTIONS         R.DE LAURENTIIS, D.LYNCH, P.LOPEZ, G.ANGOSSE, L.BARNARD, M.B.FARRELLY,
                         V.ESCRIVA, J.CLEMENTE, A.BADIN, C.CAMACHO, K.LOPEZ, T.MASTERS, G.MASTERS,
                         P.L.BASILE, B.FERNANDEZ, J.VELAZQUEZ, A.PUCCINI, K.WEST, G, SUMNER, G, GALLO,
                         E.RUIZ, J.SORIA . G.DESIDERI

PRODUCTION CAR #2   (9.30am)      G.OFFENHEIM, A.STRICK, ALISON        10.00am at Studios
(LUIS RAMIREZ)
PRODUCTION CAR #3   (4.45pm)      F.FRANCIS,                           5.30pm on Loc.
(MARIO RAMIREZ)                   Y.AXWORTHY, G.HAYMAN
CAMERA COMBI        (4.45pm)      T.ROSS, J.DUNTON                     5.30pm on Loc.
(CARLOS VELEZ)
WARDROBE COMBI #1   (own Inst.)   B.RINGWODD, F.ANTONELLI, T.CASTALLINE, M.JONES
                                  A.INFANTE, G.JOHNSTONE (as per F.Antonelli's instructions)
WARDROBE COMBI #2   (own Inst.)   E.PERCIVAL, B.HIGGINS, K.ORR, C.STREETER, D.HARKNESS,
(CESAR CHAVEZ)                    R.WARD, M.LANG, (as per F.Antonelli's instructions)
MAKE-UP COMBI       (4.45pm)      G.DE ROSSI, M.DE ROSSI,              5.30pm on Loc.
JUAN CRUZ                         M.TAMAGNANI, L.ROCCHETTI
WHITE PICK UP       (8.00am)      R.DIAZ                               8.30am at Studios
(JUAN JARAMILLO)
APOGEE COMBI        (8.00am)      K.SWENSON, B.BEALMEAR, G.GUBI, J.DYKSTRA, J.BENJAMIN,
(J.VELAZQUEZ)                     M.KLINE, D.DORNEY, A.WHITLOCK        8.30am at Studios
SOUND COMBI         (4.45pm)      N.STOLL, H.HAPTAS.                   5.30pm at Loc.
(SELF DRIVEN)
SP/FX COMBI         (as per K.West) D.GALLIANO, A.BALANDIN, G, ZINC, A.PARRA
(DAVID RIOS)                      A.KELLY, J.HATT, J.CLIFFORD.
SP/FX WAGONEER      (as per K.West) J.BAKER
(D.CRUZ)
SP/FX WAGONEER      (as per K.West) D.KNOWLES, T.COX
(R.ALVARADO)
OWN ARRANGEMENTS    (as per K.West) Y.DE BONO, R.SKINNER, T.WOODS, J.STIRBER
PROPS DPT.COMBI                   L.ROMERO, R.DOWNING, M.BENSTEAD, G.SUMNER'S INSTRUCTIONS
(J.ERAIS)
OWN ARRANGEMENTS    (8.00am)      T.GIBBS, P.SHAW.                     8.30am at Studios
PRODUCTION COMBI    (4.45pm)      M.ANDERSON, E.GEORGE, G, WHITTEAR,.
(JUAN OLALDE)
PRODUCTION CAR      (2.00pm)      M.SCHIAVONE                          2.30pm on Loc.
(RICARDO CORTES)
2nd TRIP            (4.30pm)      J.MATTHEWS, R.LARNER                 5.00pm on Loc.
PRODUCTION COMBI    (4.45pm)      R.HUMPHREYS, K.YAMASUKI, A.PACANOWSKI,
(V.ROMERO)                        G.GOLDWIN, D.ELLIS, W.HARPER         5.30pm on Loc.

DUNE CREW BUS :                   FIRST TRIP : R.ABLANQUE, V.CONSOLI, M.LARSON, J.BOLAÑOS,
                                  A.DEL TORO, S.BARELLI, S.CATARINELLI, E.D'ACHILLE, A.MARTA,
H.ROYAL  :6.30am                  A.MARTA, V.MARTA, T.SERINI, D.HERCH
H.NIZA   :6.35am
H.ROYAL  :8.00am                  SECOND TRIP : J.M. ALARCON, K.PHIPPS

2 BUSES             5.00pm        Mexican Crew                         5.30pm on Loc.
1 BUS               5.00pm        Extras  (34)                         5.30pm on Loc.
1 COMBI             4.30pm        Stand-ins (5)                        5.00pm on Loc.

ARTIST CAR #1       5.00pm        ARTURO GARCIARUBIO    ATLIXCO 142B   then to
(L.PEDRAZA)         5.30pm        FRANCESCA ANNIS       HIDALGO 161    6.00pm on Loc.
                                                        CASA #2

ARTIST CAR #2
(G.CARO)            5.30pm        KYLE MacLACHLAN       S.AMBERES      6.00pm on Loc.
                    5.30pm        EVERETT McGILL        H.CENTURY      6.00pm on Loc.

ARTIST CAR #3       5.30pm        SEAN YOUNG            H.CENTURY(Rm.805)  6.00pm on Loc.
(G.LARA)            5.30pm        JUDD OMEN             H.CENTURY(Rm.804)  6.00pm on Loc

ARTIST CAR          STAND BY AT STUDIOS FROM 5.00pm AS PER A.D's DPT. INSTRUCTIONS .
```

First unit call sheet, April 19, 1983, page 3.

```
                      C A L L   S H E E T .           Production N°15.

PRODUCTION TITTLE : DUNE                    DATE : Wednesday April 20th, 1983
PRODUCER : RAFFAELLA DE LAURENTIIS          CREW CALL: 5.30pm at Studios (Mex.Crew)
DIRECTOR : DAVID LYNCH
                                            LEAVE HOTELS at 5.30pm
                       NIGHT SHOOTING       TO BE ON LOC at 6.15pm
```

SETS & SCENES NUMBERS :			D/N	LOCATION :	
EXT.FREMEN PLACE - DEEP DESERT .				TRASH DUMP / RED EAGLES	
TO COMPLETE : Sc. ,165,166,167			N	LAS AGUILAS ROJAS.	
168,210					

ARTIST	CHARACTERS	P/U	M/U	LINE UP	ON SET
FRANCESCA ANNIS	JESSICA			TO BE NOTIFY	
KYLE MacLACHLAN	PAUL			TO BE NOTIFY	
SEAN YOUNG	CHANI			TO BE NOTIFY	
EVERETT McGILL	STILGAR			TO BE NOTIFY	
JUDD OMEN	JAMIS			TO BE NOTIFY	
MARTIN LASALLE	FREMEN #1			TO BE NOTIFY	
HONORATO MAGALONE	FREMEN #2			TO BE NOTIFY	
RICHARD HUMPHREYS	STUNT COORDINATOR			6.15pm on Loc.	
DAVID ELLIS	STUNT DOUBLE for PAUL			6.15pm on Loc.	
WILL HARPER	STUNT DOUBLE for JAMIS			6.15pm on Loc.	

STAND-INS :			M-UP/WARD	
JOSEPHINE LOVELL	FOR JESSICA	at Studios at 5.30pm	6.00	6.15pm
GONZALO IRIGOYEN	FOR PAUL	" " "	6.00	6.15pm
A.N.OTHER	FOR CHANI	" " "	6.00	6.15pm
A.N.OTHER	FOR STILGAR	" " "	6.00	6.15pm
A.N.OTHER	FOR JAMIS	" " "	6.00	6.15pm

CROWD :				
30 FREMEN MEN (stillsuits)		at Studios at 5.00pm	5.30	7.00pm
4 FREMEN WOMEN (stillsuits)		at Studios at 5.00pm	5.30	7.00pm

PRODUCTION REQUIREMENTS :
PRODUCTION: Motorhomes for actors-honey wagon for shooting crew-tents for M-UP &
                  Wardrobe-Production tent with radio communication with Prod.Office-
                  coffee service on Dres.Rooms & Location-Security guards on entrance &
                  around location- 2 loud hailers-ambulance & Doctor on Set-labourers
                  on set - working lights .
              *   Caravanas para actores-honey wagon para equipo de rodaje-carpas para
                  vestuario y maquillaje-carpa de Produccion con comunicacion radio
                  con oficina Prod.-cafe en camerinos y Locacion-vigilancia en entrada
                  y alrededores de locacion- 2 alta voces-ambulancia y Doctor en Loc.-
                  peones en Loc.-luces funcionando-
CATERING :   Dinner for 200 people ready from 8.00pm /*Cena para 200 personas lista
                  desde las 8.00pm.
PROPERTY :   Crysknives for Fremen,for Chani,for Jamis-dummy knife-telescopic knife
                  Leto's signet ring-fremkit for Paul-still tents to cover Jamis'body-
                  dipsticks-thumpers-ropes-hooks-
              *   Crysknives para Fremen, Chani & Jamis-cuchillo truco-cuchillo teles-
                  copico-anillo de Leto-Fremkit para Paul-Still tienda para cubrir
                  cuerpo de Jamis-varillas musicales-golpeadores-cuerdas-ganchos-
SET DRESSING :   Small bushes-cacti-tiny clump odd leaves-cones for dew collecting-
              *   Pequeños matorales-pequeñas plantas de hojas raras-conos para
                  recolección de rocío-

First unit call sheet, April 20, 1983, page 1.

                                                                Page #2

SP/FX :   Fremen SP/FX impacts on rocks- rig Jamis suit for water spill when killed
                 by Paul-/* Efectos especiales de impactos Fremen en rocas- preparar traje
                 de Jamis para que agua se derrame cuando le mata Paul-

MAKE-UP :   Jamis wound on chest-hand cut effect for Jamis- Make up take place on Loc.
              * Jamis herido en pecho-efecto de mano cortada para Jamis-el maquillaje
                 tendrá lugar en Locacion.

WARDROBE: Cloaks or blankets to warm up actors - Artists dressing will take place
                 on Location
              * Capas o mantas para calentar actores- el vestuario de actores se hará
                 en Locacion .

CAMERA :   As per F.Francis instructions /*Según instrucciones de F.Francis.

ELECTRIC :   5 D.C generators on Location ready from 2.00pm
                 1 D.C generator on Location ready from 2.00pm
                 Grips & Electric. Crew at 4.30pm at Studios/*Tramoyistas y Elect.4.30pm Stu
TRANSPORTATION :
                 Equipment trucks, vans & Combies as per each Dpt. request.
                 1 crew buses
                 1 bus for crowd
                 1 Combi or car for Stand-ins
                 4 Actors cars
                 1 Direction Dpt. combi

NOTE :   TO ALL CREW AND ARTISTIC PERSONNEL WEAR WARM,WIND PROTECTION, CLOTHES.
                 A TODO EL EQUIPO Y ACTORES , PROVEERSE DE ROPA CALIENTE, CORTA VIENTO.

ADVANCE SCHEDULE:

                 THURSDAY APRIL 21st, 1983
                 TO COMPLETE :
                 EXT.FREMEN PLACE- DEEP DESERT .   LOCATION:
                 Sc.:   ,165,166,167,168.210   (N)   TRASH DUMP/AGUILAS ROJAS
                                                                            RED EAGLES
                       NIGHT SHOOTING .

                                                      J.Lopez Rodero
                                                      Assistant Director .

First unit call sheet, April 20, 1983, page 2.

JUAN CLEMENTE
Production

CALL SHEET (SECOND CAMERA)

PRODUCTION TITLE: "DUNE"
PRODUCER: RAFFAELLA DE LAURENTIIS
DIRECTOR: FRED ELMES

DATE: WEDNESDAY, APRIL 20th, 1983.
*MIERCOLES
CREW CALL: 8.00am at Studios

SETS AND SCENE NUMBERS:	D/N	STAGE/LOCATION
PAUL'S ROOM-ARRAKEEN PALACE (To continue HUNTER-SEEKER PICK UPS) *Para continuar con PICK UPS DE CAZADOR- BUSCADOR Sc: 80pt.	D	STAGE #4

NOTE: NO CAST   *NOTA: SIN REPARTO

REQUIREMENTS:

PRODUCTION: Check details in all Departments involved-Coffee Service on Set.
   *Checar detalles en todos los Deptos. involucrados- Servicio de Café en Foro.

CAMERA: Mitchell Mark II - Lightflex - anamorphic lenses-MOY Gearhead.

SP/FX: As established by First Camera.
   *Según lo establecido por Primera Cámara.

GRIPS   )
PROPS   )   As established by First Camera.
ELECT   )   *Según lo establecido por la Primera Cámara.
ART   )

ADVANCED SCHEDULE:

      THURSDAY APRIL 21st, 1983.
      *JUEVES

INT. PAUL'S ROOM - ARRAKEEN PALACE -(D)   LOC:
(Complete) *(Completar)   STAGE #4
DYKSTRA (PART) Red Droplets *Gotas rojas.

SECOND UNIT (PART): Windows glow white light.
*SEGUNDA UNIDAD (PARTE): Ventanas brillan con luz blanca.
Sc: 78B pt.

Second unit call sheet, April 20, 1983.

```
                        CALL  SHEET.              Production N° 16


PRODUCTION TITTLE : DUNE                  DATE : Thursday April 21st, 1983
PRODUCER : RAFFAELLA DE LAURENTIIS        CREW CALL : 5.30pm at Stud.(Mex.Crew)
DIRECTOR : DAVID LYNCH                    LEAVE HOTELS :5.30pm
                         NIGHT SHOOTING.  TO BE ON LOC.:6.15pm


SETS & SCENES NUMBERS :          D/N        LOCATION:
EXT.FREMEN PLACE - DEEP DESERT .            TRASH DUMP/RED EAGLES
TO COMPLETE :  Sc.165,166,167,168,210   N   AGUILAS ROJAS .
```

ARTIST	CHARACTERS	P/U	M/U	LINE UP	ON SET
FRANCESCA ANNIS	JESSICA	TO BE CONFIRMED			
KYLE MacLACHLAN	PAUL	TO BE CONFIRMED			
SEAN YOUNG	CHANI	TO BE CONFIRMED			
EVERETT McGILL	STILGAR	TO BE CONFIRMED			
JUDD OMEN	JAMIS	TO BE CONFIRMED			
MARTIN LASALLE	FREMEN #1	TO BE CONFIRMED			
HONORATO MAGALONE	FREMEN #2	TO BE CONFIRMED			
RICHARD HUMPHREYS	STUNT CO-ORDINATOR	6.15pm on Loc.			
DAVID ELLIS	STUNT DOUBLE FOR PAUL	6.15pm on Loc.			
WILL HARPER	STUNT DOUBLE FOR JAMIS	6.15pm on Loc.			

```
STAND-INS :                                          M-UP/WARD
JOSEPHINE LOVELL    FOR JESSICA    at Studios at 5.30pm    6.00pm        6.15pm
GONZALO IRIGOYEN    FOR PAUL            "      "      "       "             "
A.N.OTHER           FOR CHANI           "      "      "       "             "
A.N.OTHER           FOR JAMIS           "      "      "       "             "
A.N.OTHER           FOR STILGAR         "      "      "       "             "


CROWD :
30 FREMEN MEN.(stillsuits)       at Studios at 5.00pm    5.30pm         7.00pm
 4 FREMEN  WOMEN (stillsuits)         "      "      "    5.30pm         7.00pm


PRODUCTION REQUIREMENTS :
PRODUCTION :        Motorhomes for actors -honey wagonfor shooting crew-tents for Ward.&
                    M-UP-Production tent with radio communication with Prod.office-
                    coffee service  in Dress.rooms &Location-Security guards on entrance &
                    around Loc.-2 loud hailers-ambulance & Doctor on set-labourers on set-
                    working lights.
                *   Caravanas para actores-honey wagon para equipo de rodaje-carpas para
                    vestuario y maquillaje-carpa de Prod.con communicacion radio con Oficina
                    de Prod.-cafe en camerinos y locacion-vigilancia en entrada y alrededores
                    de Locacion- 2 altavoces-ambulancia y Doctor en Locacion-peones en Loc.-
                    luces funcionando.
CATERING :          Dinner for 250 people ready from 8.00pm/*Cena para 250 personas lista
                    desde las 8.00pm .
PROPERTY :          Crysknives for Fremen,for Chani, for Jamis-dummy knife-telescopic knife-
                    Leto's signet ring-fremkit for Paul-still tents to cover Jamis'body-
                    dipsticks-thumpers-ropes-hooks-
SET DRESSING :      Small bushes-cacti-tiny clump odd leaves-cones for dew collecting-
                *   Pequeños matorales-cactus-paqueñas plantas de hojas raras-conos para
                    recolección de rocío-

SP/FX :             Fremen SP/FX impacts on rocks- rig Jamis suit for water spill when killed
                    by Paul- /*efectos especiales de impactos Fremen en rocas-preparar
                    traje de Jamis para derrame de agua cuando le mata Paul.
```

First unit call sheet, April 21, 1983.

```
                    C A L L   S H E E T  (SECOND CAMERA)
PRODUCTION TITLE: "DUNE"                    DATE: THURSDAY APRIL 21, 1983.
PRODUCER: RAFFAELLA DE LAURENTIIS                 *JUEVES
DIRECTOR: FRED ELMES                        CREW CALL: 8.00am at Studios.


SETS AND SCENE NUMBERS:              D/N          STAGE/LOCATION

INT. PAUL'S ROOM-ARRAKEEN PALACE      D           STAGE #4
(To continue HUNTER-SEEKER PICK UPS)
*(Para continuar con Pickups de CAZADOR-
                             BUSCADOR
   Sc: 80pt.


NOTE:  NO CAST                  *NOTA:  SIN REPARTO


REQUIREMENTS:

PRODUCTION: Check details in all Departments involved- Coffee service on Stage.
       *Checar detalles en todos los Departamentos involucrados- Servicio
        de Café en Foro.

CAMERA: Mitchell Mark II- Lightflex- Anamorphic lenses- MOY Gearhead.

SP/FX: As established by First Camera.
       *Según lo establecido por Primera Cámara.

GRIPS   )
PROPS   )   As established by First Camera.
ELECT   )   *Según lo establecido por Primera Cámara.
ART     )


ADVANCED SCHEDULE:
              FRIDAY APRIL 22nd, 1983.
              VIERNES

              INT. PAUL'S ROOM-ARRAKEEN PALACE (D)      LOC:
              (Complete) *(Completar)                   STAGE #4

              DYKSTRA SHOT (PART): Red Droplets *Gotas rojas

              SECOND CAMERA(PART): Windows glow white light.
              *SEGUNDA CAMARA (PARTE): Ventanas brillan con luz blanca.
              Sc: 78B
```

Second unit call sheet, April 21, 1983.

```
                    CALL SHEET.                    Production N° 17


PRODUCTION TITTLE : DUNE                       DATE :   Friday April 22nd, 1983
PRODUCER : RAFFAELLA DE LAURENTIIS             CREW CALL : 5.30pm at Stud.(Mex.Crew)
DIRECTOR : DAVID LYNCH                         LEAVE HOTELS : 5.30pm
                        NIGHT SHOOTING .       TO BE ON LOC.: 6.15pm


SETS & SCENES NUMBERS :                D/N            LOCATION:
EXT.FREMEN PLACE - DEEP DESERT .                      TRASH DUMP/RED EAGLES
TO COMPLETE : 165pt,166pt,167,168pt     N             AGUILAS ROJAS .
IF TIME PERMITS:  210

ARTIST              CHARACTERS          P/U       M/U      LINE UP       ON SET

FRANCESCA ANNIS     JESSICA             T.B.N
KYLE MacLACHLAN     PAUL                T.B.N
SEAN YOUNG          CHANI               T.B.N
EVERETT McGILL      STILGAR             T.B.N
JUDD OMEN           JAMIS               T.B.N
MARTIN LASALLE      FREMEN #1           T.B.N
HONORATO MAGALONE   FREMEN #2           T.B.N

RICHARD HUMPHREYS   STUNT CO-ORDINATOR     6.15pm on Loc.
DAVID ELLIS         STUNT DOUBLE FOR PAUL  6.15pm on Loc.
WILL HARPER         STUNT DOUBLE FOR JAMIS 6.15pm on Loc.
DEBBIE ELLIS        STUNT DOUBLE FOR JESSICA    "    "    "

STAND-INS :                                              M-UP/WARD
JOSEPHINE LOVELL    FOR JESSICA    at Studios at 5.30pm   6.00pm        6.15pm
GONZALO IRIGOYEN    FOR PAUL             "       "          "             "
A.N.OTHER           FOR CHANI            "       "          "             "
A.N.OTHER           FOR JAMIS            "       "          "             "
A.N.OTHER           FOR STILGAR          "       "          "             "


CROWD :
30 FREMEN MEN (stillsuits)         at Studios at 5.00pm    5.30pm       7.00pm
 4 FREMEN WOMEN (stillsuits)              "       "        5.30pm       7.00pm


PRODUCTION REQUIREMENTS :
PRODUCTION :          Motorhomes for actors -honey wagon for shooting crew-tents for Ward.&
                      M-UP-Production tent with radio communication with Prod.office-
                      coffee service in Dress.rooms &Location-Security guards on entrance &
                      around Loc.-2 loud hailers-ambulance & Doctor on set-labourers on set-
                      working lights.
                    * Caravanas para actores-honey wagon para equipo de rodaje-carpas para
                      vestuario y maquillaje-carpa de Prod.con communicacion radio con Oficina
                      de Prod.-cafe en camerinos y locacion-vigilancia en entrada y alrededores
                      de Locacion- 2 altavoces-ambulancia y Doctor en Locacion-peones en Loc.-
                      luces funcionando.
CATERING :            Dinner for 250 people ready from 8.00pm/*Cena para 250 personas lista
                      desde las 8.00pm .
PROPERTY :            Crysknives for Fremen,for Chani, for Jamis-dummy knife-telescopic knife-
                      Leto's signet ring-fremkit for Paul-still tents to cover Jamis'body-
                      dipsticks-thumpers-ropes-hooks-
SET DRESSING :        Small bushes-cacti-tiny clump odd leaves-cones for dew collecting-
                    * Pequeños matorales-cactus-pequeñas plantas de hojas raras-conos para
                      recolección de rocío-

SP/FX :               Fremen SP/FX impacts on rocks- rig Jamis suit for water spill when killed
                      by Paul- /*efectos especiales de impactos Fremen en rocas-preparar
                      traje de Jamis para derrame de agua cuando le mata Paul.
```

First unit call sheet, April 22, 1983.

PATSA PRODUCCIONES S.A.

MEMORANDUM

TO: David and Rafaella
FROM: Anatole and George
RE: The Video Documentary

Now that we have actually begun work, the full scope of our project is only now beocming apparent. If we are to produce the average of two or so hours of tape per day which was requested of us, a number of problems arise--specifically from the fact that there are only two of us working on the project. It has become clear to us that we simply won't have the time to view all the material we produce, let alone log it, and assemble it into usable form. Yet this must be done as we go along because the amount of material we accumulate will grow too large to be put into order at the end ot the job.

Further, as you know, neither of us is a video technician. Our equipment requires fairly frequent technical attention to keep it fully operational.

We would like to take the opportunity to make a proposal: that we be provided with backup personnel to deal with these matters. This additional crew would never become involved on the set, so David would not have to deal with any extra people on the set. And it would free us to do a better job.

There are currently two people on the Dune payroll in low level positions who would nicely fill these requirements and we would like you to consider assigning them to us if possible.

The first is Arturo Garciarubio, an assistant on the first unit. He has extensive experience in video, both as a cameraman and as a technician. As our video technician and technical advisor he would be invaluable-- and in his present position his capacities are being vastly underused.

The other is Doug Hersh, who works out of Vicente Escriva's office. He has video editing and effects experience and we feel he would be well qualified for keeping the mass of material we will produce in good order.

We should add that both these men joined the Dune project not just because they were looking for a job--in fact, both could make better money elsewhere--but rather out of a sense of excitement and personal interest in David's work. They are here as admirers more than employees.

We hope that you will seriously consider this proposal. Not only will it make our job easier to do--it will, we feel, result in us producing a more valuable record of the Dune produciton. This will be as much to your advantage as it will be to ours.

ESTUDIOS CHURUBUSCO AZTECA, S.A. ATLETAS No. 2 COL. COUNTRY CLUB 04220 MEXICO, D.F.

Our memo to David and Raffaella.

```
                    CALL  SHEET  (SECOND CAMERA)
PRODUCTION TITLE: "DUNE"                    DATE: SATURDAY APRIL 23, 1983
PRODUCER: RAFFAELLA DE LAURENTIIS                 *SABADO
DIRECTOR: FRED ELMES                        CREW CALL: 8.00am at Studios.
```

SETS AND SCENE NUMBERS:	D/N	STAGE/LOCATION
INT. PAUL'S ROOM-ARRAKEEN PLACE (To continue HUNTER-SEEKER PICKUPS) *(Para continuar con Pickups de CAZADOR BUSCADOR)	D	STAGE #4

So Sept.

NOTE: NO CAST   *NOTA: SIN REPARTO

REQUIREMENTS:

PRODUCTION: Check details in all Departments involved - Coffee service on Stage.
            *Checar detalles en todos los Departamentos involucrados - Servicio
             de Café en Foro.

CAMERA: Mitchell Mark II - LIGHTFLEX - Anamorphic lenses - MOY Gearhead.

SP/FX: As established by FIRST Camera.
       *Según lo establecido por PRIMERA Cámara.

GRIPS   )
PROPS :) As established by First Camera.
ELECT   ) *Según lo establecido por Primera Cámara.
ART   )

CATERING: Running Buffet ready from 12.00PM. (ONLY for shooting crew)
          *Snack listo desde las 12.00PM. (SOLO para personal de filmación)

Second unit call sheet, April 23, 1983.

Week 6: April 25–May 1, 1983

Monday, April 25: DAY THIRTY-SIX (9 hrs)

It'll be a very long day today. A car to the studio at ten. Shoot Judy Miller and the seamstresses. Look at what we shot last week. Maybe unpack the editing system. Meet with Raffaella. Supposedly meet with Anne Strick. Go to the location and shoot all night...

Not such a long day after all. We've been more or less designated the house video crew – home video for the producers. The meeting with Raffaella was quite friendly, seemingly open.

No more of this so closely following David. We'll shoot the first unit when it's starting on a new set or location, or when it's shooting something particularly difficult or interesting. Same with second unit. And in between, we have to do all the other stuff – the various departments and shops. Following a particular individual, shooting everything they do, everything that happens to them. In Raffaella's mind, I'm afraid we're firmly linked with Anne Strick; we're publicity.

Not what we came down here for. But we can still work to put together *our* film – which they can accept or refuse at the end; at least we'll have done it. But there will be limits; working Sundays to film someone's pool-side gathering doesn't appeal to me – and if they seriously want it, I may push for overtime.

The whole thing has become a *job*.

As for Raffaella's remark – "*if* you're going to be here for six months …" – well, maybe she was just flexing her producer's muscles. But if not, if we get terminated early – what about this famous twenty-five thousand? they could easily pull a number on us – "you were just getting a thousand a week, good-bye."

Yet we have been permitted Arturo's services for a few hours a week for camera maintenance. And they'll give us an assistant for logging tapes and general office work – and duping and rough assembly. (Not Doug though – and considering Anatol's antipathy to him, that's probably a good thing.)

And it's been cleared up with Paul Sammon – he has a very low position and anything he wants done has to go through Raffaella. (He wanted a copy of my article – he scanned it in the office [Doug had just returned it] and seemed highly appreciative; I mumbled negatively – I don't want him ransacking it for his own stuff.) (The article might serve me well here – judiciously circulated, it could raise me up by making David's work more accessible to people working on the film – because very few people seem to have taken the time to sit down and examine his work in that much depth.)

So – since we have four nights' worth of footage from Aguilas Rojas, we didn't have to go out there again tonight (for which I do not feel terribly sorry). Tomorrow night, though, both first and second units will be there – something big, so we'll go along.

But neither of us is terribly happy that we're being moved somewhat away from the centre, from David.

As this becomes just a job, our thoughts are being drawn more and more to a project of our own – the Paris thing, which is shaping up as a fairly off-the-wall *noir* piece (Anatol says that in the page-and-a-half synopsis I capture a feel for Parisian strangeness quite remarkable for someone who's never been there – also says that my *Eraserhead* article captures the feeling of what went on very faithfully, that reading it brings the whole experience back. Maybe I do have some kind of talent after all.) So maybe we can assuage our creative sides by developing that script (called "Café Universal") while doing Raffaella De Laurentiis' home movies over the next few months.

Meanwhile I've developed some kind of problem with my right leg. I thought at first it was just because I was suddenly over-using muscles left idle a long time. But instead of loosening up, it's getting worse. I walk with a limp and get extremely painful spasms in my thigh. Guess I'll have to see the doctor tomorrow – though from what I've heard, I don't hold much faith…

Tuesday, April 26: DAY THIRTY-SEVEN (16 1/2 hrs)

Didn't sleep much last night. Woke about five-thirty full of anxieties – I'm going to have to insist on having something in writing, some guarantee about this job.

The doctor – "Feelgood", as everyone calls him – took me out to his car in the parking lot, and opened the trunk to reveal large plastic bags full of samples of prescription drugs. He gave me some painkillers and muscle relaxants for the spasms in my leg (caused apparently by the way I brace myself when I'm holding the mic boom).

Meanwhile, the ideas for the script keep flowing.

Wednesday, April 27: DAY THIRTY-EIGHT (16 1/2 hrs)

A long day yesterday, and deadly dull on the set (still at the Aguilas Rojas location – doing close-ups and reaction shots; lots of set-ups, but almost no movement).

Obviously there are still major communications problems. Raffaella might have decided (with some prompting from Anne Strick) that we were spending too much time with the first unit, but when we got there yesterday evening we had a chance to chat with David and his first remark was "where the fuck were you guys last night?" A friendly tone, but it's apparent that he (like we) thought we came down to shoot a documentary of him making *Dune* – not that we came as a video PR unit.

We're supposed to shoot a little piece with him this evening, a substitute for Sammon's convention piece. None of us is too happy about it, but it's been arranged with Raffaella. David, reluctant to get into this kind of thing, said we'll just do something ourselves, present it to them, and if they don't like it that's just too bad. But there are likely to be dozens of people standing around watching...

But if the night was cinematically dull, it was still quite important for us. We met Jack Leustig, Kyle's agent. His wife (who's in casting) found Kyle – then got fired from the project because she tried to interfere with the lousy deal De Laurentiis offered him (a seven-year exclusive contract). Jack took Kyle on to help him against the pressure.

He seems like a very decent guy, telling us a bit about how Raffaella works (a good thing because Anatol has this annoying tendency of wanting to tell her all our plans right now before we know anything about her – he's already gone on a kick about getting her interested in the story we're developing, maybe setting up a small production unit on the side – I've been able to discourage him so far, but Jack's tales helped immensely to cool him off; she wouldn't give a shit about our plans and I wouldn't trust her with them – *if* we're cooking up something viable, we should protect it carefully).

Jack is also a writer and actor, so he seems much more sympathetic to the underdogs of the business than the legendary Hollywood agent. He talked at length with us about our *Dune* project and what kind of agreements we've got so far – and says he'll research it for us to see what kind of legal position we're in to protect our work. He'll be back here every five weeks for one week (Kyle needs the support) and next time he's down he'll try to have some information for us to help us finally negotiate a contract.

But on top of all this he's been married for twelve years to a French woman who's worked with biggies like Godard and who has good connections over there. And he's a little interested in getting into production. And seemed a little intrigued by our idea of a small film in Paris with David in a role (even made a note to check on access to Depardieu, Lino Ventura, and the punk in sunglasses from *Diva* – all of whom we can see in parts that are shaping up in the story). The whole thing is still a fairy tale, a dream – but we strangely keep running into pointers which keep us heading in this direction. If we can develop a tight script, maybe the project really would be feasible.

He's just played a part in the U.S. remake of Godard's *Breathless* (as the cop killed by the main character – Richard Gere in the Belmondo role). Which was directed by Jim McBride who did *Glen and Randa*, the lovely low-budget post-holocaust story of two teenagers searching a ravaged land for fabled Metropolis – which I've only seen once, about eleven years ago, in Newfoundland.

Anatol and I seem to be on some kind of streak – what we need keeps falling into our laps (he's been saying for weeks that we need someone we can trust, who knows the business, to take a look at our deal and advise us). In fact, it seems like *too* much. All these things coming together, from this job on – there must be some kind of hidden catch.

Thursday, April 28: DAY THIRTY-NINE (9 hrs)

A very long day yesterday, with many an up-and-down.

We went to the studio at two-thirty. The stunt coordinator, a guy named Richard Humphreys, had requested Tuesday night that we shoot them preparing a stunt on the backlot in the afternoon (a huge rock breaking away and a man plummeting off it). We said yes – because it does fall within the bounds of our job. Even though the guy had subjected us to a "joke" a little earlier: while our backs were turned he took my mike and boom so he could watch the panic when we discovered it missing. Ha. Ha. Those people who saw it seemed pretty disgusted – Humphreys thought it hilarious.

So we showed up a bit early, they weren't there. So we hurried away, not wanting to do it anyway. They found us a little later, so we did it after all. But Humphreys came on the director. He told Anatol exactly how he must shoot it, treated us like hired lackeys. But in the end, it worked out for us. When we returned to the office to show them the tape, we ran into Raffaella – our first big screening (even Kit West was there to see how the rock functioned). And Raffaella seemed thoroughly pleased with it.

She now calls me George, she jokes with us, she pats our faces – the whole bit. John Dykstra told us he overheard her telling someone that we're doing a very good job.

Yesterday evening we were to shoot David for the promo piece. All three of us were reluctant. We spoke to him just after we got to the dump. Agreed to do it later, after he was dirtied up. Anne Strick was hanging around, wanting to be there to see it done.

Just before supper I went to speak with David again, to suggest that we do it at the end of the night so as not to interrupt a particularly heavy shooting schedule. Raffaella was there. She stepped in. "No, no, no, George," she said, stroking my face several times with both hands. "He won't do it then. He'll say he's too tired. We'll do it right after dinner."

So after we ate, we prepared to take our equipment up onto the rocks to shoot him far from everybody. I went down into the ravine again to tell David we'd be ready in about fifteen minutes. We talked about the thing, what it was for, what sort of thing was necessary. Raffaella came over and jokingly said, "is this guy bothering you? If he is, he can be taken care of." David turned to her and said, "He's doing his job, and he's doing it very well."

We waited up on the rocks for a long time. It was the first time we'd been up there – the view was spectacular. We were climbing around like a couple of kids. Both of us sort of hoping David wouldn't come up. But he did finally.

It went badly. He was completely reluctant and we didn't have the resources to draw him out. The problem is, he doesn't want to talk about *Dune* or his work. We were there for more than half an hour as they set up the crane down below. It was quite uncomfortable. (When we looked at the tape this morning at the studio, I felt even worse; David is so horribly tense and unnatural.) He said we'll have to do it as an interview, come up with questions. But since he doesn't want to talk about *Dune*, what kind of questions am I supposed to ask? This thing is for *Dune* promotion, after all.

Jack read my article during the evening. His praise was fulsome, to say the least. He couldn't believe that I'd done it for almost nothing, for a small circulation magazine. Said it should be released as a book. While he's looking into the situation with our contract, he says he'll also check what my legal position is with the magazine.

Stage 2, Estudios Churubusco, Mexico City, 1983.

Anatol jumped the gun again. Trying to ease the tension with David before we shot, he blurted out what Jack had said (because David's planning an *Eraserhead* picture book – the one Ron Miller told us about). But David and Jack have been caught on two sides of the struggle between Kyle and De Laurentiis. So I don't know what chance there would be of getting me involved in the book. Probably very little in the first place (I'm sure David wants it to be *his* book); now even less.

It was a long night, ending as the sky got light just after six. The sequence went three days (nights) over schedule – and they'll probably have all kinds of continuity problems because of the dust.

They're still shooting nights (probably through next week – longer?), but at least we're out of the dump.

Friday, April 29: DAY FORTY (15 hrs)

A shorter day yesterday. We went to the studio at six-thirty, cleaned the camera, shot a cassette on Stage 2 where Dykstra has his transmission bluescreen, finally met Jurgen Prochnow (whose English seems flawless). After supper, everything moved to the backlot – Castle Caladan (the same scene as was shot in front of the bluescreen – different point of view).

David spotted Anatol's leather replica 'forties flight jacket – and is off on another jacket kick (it seems to be a kind of tension release – Kuki Lopez and Freddie joined in again, as they did for the other jackets; everything stopped for a few minutes and David wanted to radio Leslie, out at Aguilas Rojas with the second unit, to get her on it right away).

One of the first things Raffaella said was, why hasn't she seen us following people around yet? Apparently she wants us to work around the clock. And she'd forgotten already that we did the bit with the stunt guys yesterday – still seems to think we're having fun. Or maybe not. Maybe it's just her producer's manner, keeping people on edge all the time.

So, since they were only doing one scene last night and we'd already covered it – and we were tired anyway – we left earlier (two-thirty, three), so we could go back to the studio earlier this afternoon. But we still feel a little as if we're deserting David who really seems to appreciate us being around.

I suggested to Anatol that we make Raffaella our first subject – plant ourselves in her office and shoot her all day – whatever she does, whoever she sees, until she says enough, go back to David. But of course she wouldn't.

So we'll probably spend a week or so, shooting shit around the studio, ending with a couple of hours on set in the evening each day. Raffaella's big point is that in six months we'll accumulate a huge mass of boring stuff behind the camera.

Little realizing that no matter *what* you're shooting, if you do it continuously for six months, you'll wind up with a great boring mass. So if we can quickly show her an accumulation of boring behind-the-scenes stuff, maybe she'll ease off on this insistence that we spend most of our time away from the set.

Anatol's insufficient grasp of English can be a nuisance. Last night while chatting with David, we mentioned our problem with Anne Strick, that she wants to appropriate us to publicity. I said, she doesn't seem to have a clear idea of why we're actually down here. I started to add that Raffaella doesn't either, but Anatol cut in to say that Raffaella has a very clear idea of why we're here – leaving David with the impression that everything's okay between us and Raffaella. I thought he did it to prevent me saying anything negative about her in front of David. But what he meant was that she has a very clear idea of her own about what we're doing – i.e. boring house video.

He annoyed me more than once yesterday evening. He's gone off on a thing about Sean Young now; she's interested in video, in being behind the camera – says if they paid her she'd like to stay on here after her role is done. Now he'd like to whip off a video movie with her. We were wandering about the dark backlot – a wonderfully eerie place – saying what a great location it is, and he said we should shoot something with Sean there and send it to the States for TV showing. He was speaking as if it was something we could do over the next few weeks. I said it's not that easy to bang out a two-hour script. He said it doesn't have to be good (I've told him before I don't like writing crap – at least not deliberately). I said you still have to come up with an idea. And he almost snapped back, "Well, that's your problem and you'd better solve it." As if I have some massive flaw which is detrimental to him. As if I'd better have the script ready by this weekend or the next at the latest. Never mind that there's very little time for writing – and I'm supposed to be working on the Paris thing.

The man has a problem thinking things through. He'll get an idea suddenly and he'll want it fulfilled on the spur of the moment – and if you can't do it for him, you've let him down.

Sunday, May 1: DAY FORTY-TWO (7 hrs)

Friday was a good day – long, but good. We went to the studio in the afternoon. Didn't actually do much – but showed a pile of stuff to Anne Strick. She liked it all, whatever it was, however dull. Said she'd tell Gordon what a fine job we're doing.

Friday night was the best session since we started shooting. On the backlot, with huge fans, the rock wall, and a big crane dolly. It was interesting to watch and the dust (which we expected to be dreadful – mixed with fine sand) wasn't anything near as bad as at Aguilas Rojas; it was an open space, and the wind was more easily directed. But I do wonder how the people in the residential area just over the wall felt about the lights, the dust, and the noise (the fans were equipped with old aircraft engines).

Back at the hotel about six yesterday morning.

Arturo had said he'd be going in Saturday to tune the camera. I felt we should be there – he's a nice guy and he started helping us just out of friendship. Anatol now seems to think of him just as an employee.

I called Anatol at one-thirty in the afternoon. He was still asleep, uninterested in going to the studio. For someone who claims to need little sleep, he seems to have more trouble than I do getting going. I think he's actually quite a drinker.

So I grabbed a cab and went alone. Arturo was already there at work. The place was deserted – it was an official day off – except for a fête on the lawns by the TV studio (Children's Day).

We were there until almost nine. A good thing I went (Anatol never did show up) because I got to see what the problems are (a number of them, though they can be dealt with) – and also got to see that Arturo really does know what he's doing.

I got back here at nine-fifteen, after dropping Arturo off. Called Anatol. Called Fred. No one home. No messages. Fuck him, I thought. Read a while, went to bed. I didn't eat all day.

I got up at noon, went for a bad breakfast at Denny's up the block. I took my book up to the penthouse pool at the Royal and sat reading and drinking beer. A few familiar faces out in the sun, but I kept to myself. Raffaella showed up, said *bon jour* and asked where Anatol was. I said I hadn't seen him and she went away.

A while later he showed up. "I've been worried. Did you go to the studio?" I'd told him when I called him Saturday afternoon that I was going. He was so worried he didn't even leave a message. But before I could answer, he was off to chat with Raffaella (I got the impression he'd gone out with her among others yesterday evening).

When he came back, I told him what I'd learned yesterday. And he said we're invited up to Raffaella's this evening – Strick is cooking dinner. I figure if Raffaella can't invite me when she speaks to me, but just adds me on when she asks him I can do without it. I'm not some appendage who has to go along with Anatol...

Finished King's *Christine* at last. A bit better than *Cujo*, but not much. A short story idea blown out of all proportion. A poor book, which would obviously make a fairly good horror movie.

Arturo is an interesting character. Wide experience as a news cameraman, stationed in Spain. Learned to be a technician in the field. When the economy collapsed here and Televisa couldn't afford to keep its overseas office anymore, he and some other staff members formed their own company in Madrid. Fifteen months ago, he married a Spanish woman. He came back here a while ago to return his mother's body for burial. He and his wife hate Mexico City – but he stayed on here just to work on this film. When it's over, they'll go back to Spain.

Kyle moved out of the Amberes this afternoon – got himself a house not far from the studio. I helped load the Jeep with his stuff, but there wasn't room to go along. I might move up to his suite – will, if I can get it. Third floor front – away from the air conditioner, and with more light.

It's quite possible that I've made a big mistake, deciding not to go upstairs for supper. But it would have been a bigger mistake to show up on the doorstep, saying "hi, Raffie, where's the grub?" if she only invited Anatol – which is quite possibly the case.

If she brings it up tomorrow, I'll just point out that she didn't invite me – and tell her to ask me herself next time instead of treating me like a subspecies of Anatol.

As it is, I went for a long walk – west along Reforma to a large war memorial park (crowded with people, mostly huge families with countless small children, with a large proportion of young couples necking, quite intensely), then back east, just past Insurgentes. I cut back to Copenhagen, where I ran into Bob and his wife just sitting down to eat at a little outdoor café. I was invited to join them, so I did – had a small, light meal, pleasant company. And came back here only to see Strick, all dressed up, waiting at the elevator. She almost saw me – but I escaped. Came up and took a shower. Now I'll read a while (Orwell) and get to bed early.

Bob has been offered the job of line producer on a low-budget film in L.A., beginning mid-June, to last ten weeks (a youth/car picture, budgeted at one-and-a-half million). He might take time off from *Dune* to do it – depending on which credit seems more important...

Nine-fifteen: someone knocked at the door, and a few seconds later the phone rang. I ignored both, lying in bed reading. Thinking: maybe I should have gone, considering Anatol's habit of saying the wrong thing, or simply saying too much. Maybe he shouldn't be alone with Raffaella and Strick – he could get us both in a mess.

Week Six Documents

```
                                            DATE: TUESDAY APRIL 26, 1983.
                                                  *MARTES
                    FILMACION NOCTURNA      CREW CALL: 5.30pm at Studios.
                    NIGHT SHOOTING

SETS AND SCENE NUMBERS:                     D/N        STAGE/LOCATION
1) INT. PAUL'S ROOM-ARRAKEEN PALACE          D         STAGE #4
   (HUNTER SEEKER PICKUP SHOTS) -COVER SET
  *(PICKUPS DE CAZADOR BUSCADOR)
   Sc: 80pt.
2) EXT. FREMEN PLACE- DEEP DESERT            N         TRASH DUMP/RED EAGLES
   TO COMPLETE: Sc: 165pt., 167, 168pt.               *AGUILAS ROJAS
   and 210.

        ARTIST            CHARACTERS


       2)AS ESTABLISHED BY FIRST CAMERA    2) *COMO LO ESTABLECIO PRIMERA
                                                                  CAMARA


REQUIREMENTS FOR 1):
PRODUCTION: Check details in all Departments - Coffee Service on Stage.
           *Checar detalles en todos los Departamentos- Servicio de café en
                                                                       Foro.
CAMERA: Mitchell Mark II - LIGHTFLEX - Anamorphic lenses- MOY Gearhead.
SP/FX: As established by FIRST CAMERA.
      *Según lo establecido por PRIMERA Cámara.
GRIPS   )
PROPS   )  As established by First Camera.
ELECT   ) *Según lo establecido por Primera Cámara.
ART     )

REQUIREMENTS FOR 2): NOTE: SECOND CAMERA will incorporate to
                           FIRST CAMERA'S call at RED EAGLES/TRASH DUMP
                           LOCATION for NIGHT SHOOTING.
                    *NOTA: LA SEGUNDA CAMARA se incorpora al llamado de
                           la PRIMERA CAMARA en la LOCACION AGUILAS ROJAS
                           para rodaje de noche.

ATTENTION/TRANSPORT: SECOND CAMERA Personnel to leave Studios at 8.00pm to
                     go to RED EAGLES LOCATION. Camera Combie for LOC. same time.
                    *El personal de SEGUNDA CAMARA saldrá de los Estudios a
                     las 8.00pm rumbo a la LOCACION AGUILAS ROJAS. Combie para cá-
ATTENTION/CATERING:  SECOND CAMERA Personnel will have dinner on LOCATION
                     at 8.30pm.
                    *El personal de SEGUNDA CAMARA cenará en LOCACION a las
                     8.30pm.
CAMERA: Mitchell Mark II- Standard Lightflex - ZOOM lightflex - Anamorphic
        lenses- MOY Gearhead - 2 Tripods *2 Tripiés.
ATTENTION: SP/FX: Andrew Kelly and John Halt to come to STAGE #4 at 11.00am
                  for rigging of Sc: 80pt.
                 *Andrew Kelly y John Halt venir a FORO #4 a las 11.00am para
                  preparar Sc: 80pt.
```

Second unit call sheet, possibly mis-dated April 26, 1983.

```
                    CALL  SHEET (SECOND CAMERA)
PRODUCTION TITLE: "DUNE"
PRODUCER: RAFFAELLA DE LAURENTIIS            DATE: TUESDAY APRIL 26, 1983.
DIRECTOR: FRED ELMES                              *MARTES
                                             CREW CALL: 7.30 am at Studios
```

SETS AND SCENE NUMBERS: D/N   STAGE/LOCATION

EXT. ROCK OUTCROPPING-DEEP DESERT   D   BACKLOT (EMILIO)
*EXT. ROCA SALIENTE-DESIERTO PROFUNDO.
Sc: 256

    NOTE: NO CAST   NOTA: SIN ACTORES

REQUIREMENTS:
PRODUCTION: Check details in all Departments - Coffee Service on Set.
          *Checar detalles en distintos Departamentos- Servicio de café en Set.
CAMERA: Mitchell Mark II - Lightflex - 5:1 Zoom 35mm lens Anamorphic lenses-
        MOY Gearhead- High Speed MOTOR *MOTOR de Alta Velocidad.
EMILIO: Miniatures *Miniaturas.
SP/FX: Dust, wind, BLACK SMOKE effects (and other techniques).
       *Efectos de polvo, viento y HUMO NEGRO (y otras técnicas).
GRIP: POROFLEX Reflectors already established for Sc: 256.
      Reflectores POROFLEX ya establecidos para Sc: 256.
ELECT: Contact line (AC) for Camera. Check adequate power at Backlot.
      *Línea de contacto (AC) para Cámara. Checar energía adecuada en Backlot.
ART: Fix shade in area indicated to José Luis Barreras.
     *Fijar sombra en área indicada a José Luis Barreras.
TRANSPORT: Standby car for Personnel- Camera Combie- Pickup truck for equip-
           ment transport.
          *Auto pendiente para Personal - Combie para cámara - Camioneta Pickup
           para transporte de equipo.

    NOTE/TRANSPORT: Pickup Fred Elmes at 7.30am at Amberes Hotel to come
                    to Studios.
                    Pickup Leslie Werner at 7.30am at Century Hotel to
                    come to Studios.
                   *Recoger a Fred Elmes a las 7.30am en Hotel Amberes
                    para venir a los Estudios.
                    Recoger a Leslie Werner a las 7.30am en Hotel Century
                    para venir a los Estudios.

NOTE: If Single Frame Motor is available, a TEST SHOT will be made today STAGE#4
      for Sc: 25A - INSERT-FILMBOOK-(PLANETS AND GALAXIES MOVE).
*NOTA: Si el MOTOR DE CUADRO POR CUADRO está disponible se hará un SHOT DE PRUE-
       BA, hoy mismo, para la Sc: 25A - INSERT-LIBRO/PELICULA (PLANETAS Y GA-
       LAXIAS SE MUEVEN) en el FORO #4.

ADVANCE SCHEDULE: WEDNESDAY APRIL 27, 1983. *MIERCOLES
                  1) INSERT-FILMBOOK (Planets and Galaxies move)
                     Sc: 25A   LOC: STAGE #4.
                    *INSERT-LIBRO/PELICULA (planetas y galaxias se mueven)
                     Sc: 25A   LOC: FORO #4.

        (COVER SET) 2) INT. PAUL'S ROOM- ARRAKEEN PALACE (HUNTER-SEEKER PICKUPS)
                       Sc: 80pt.   LOC: STAGE #4
        *(COVER SET)   INT. CUARTO DE PAUL-PALACIO ARRAKEEN (PICKUPS DE CAZADOR-
                       Sc: 80pt.   LOC: FORO #4   BUSCADOR)

Second unit call sheet, possibly mis-dated April 26, 1983.

```
SETS BEING STRUCK AND BUILT AS OF TUESDAY, APRIL 26th

STAGE 1
        Interior Hallway, Caladan has been struck
        Interior Paul's Room, Caladan has been struck

STAGE 4
        Interior Jessica's Room, Caladan has been struck

STAGE 5
        The Emperor's spaceship & steel tent is in the middle
        of construction
```

Set construction memo, April 26, 1983.

```
                    C A L L   S H E E T .              Production N°21

PRODUCTION TITLE : DUNE                      DATE :Thursday April 28th,1983
PRODUCER : RAFFAELLA DE LAURENTIIS           CREW CALL: 5.30pm at Studios
DIRECTOR : DAVID LYNCH                       LEAVE HOTEL at 5.00 pm
                         NIGHT SHOOTING .

SETS AND SCENES NUMBERS:                     LOCATIONS:
1) CLIFF WALL-CASTLE CALADAN  Sc.:28b pt,141pt (N)   STAGE #2 (BLUE BACKING)
2) EXT.CLIFF WALL- CALADAN    Sc.:26a, 28   (N)      CASTLE CALADAN in BACK LOT

ARTIST           CHARACTERS         D/R      P/U      M/U       WARD    ON SET
                                             from 4.00pm to 5.00pm rehears.w/dog
JURGEN PROCHNOW  DUKE LETO          203      3.30pm   4.00pm             6.00pm
KYLE MacLACHLAN  PAUL               218      5.00pm   5.30pm             6.00pm
FRANCESCA ANNIS  JESSICA            217      T.B.N for voice recording
STAND-INS :
GONZALO IRIGOYEN  FOR PAUL                            5.00pm             5.30pm
A.N.OTHER         FOR DUKE LETO                         "                  "

CROWD:
6 ATREIDES GUARDS (CALADAN) (black Caladan uniforms)  7.00pm             8.00pm
```

PRODUCTION REQUIREMENTS:
PRODUCTION: Security guards in Stage #2 and Back Lot-coffee service in Dress-
                    Rooms ,Stage #2 and Back Lot-A.D's desk rig to Stage light,bell &
                    telephone-working lights along the way to the Back Lot-mosquitoes
                    repellent-
                  * Vigilancia en Foro #2 y Back Lot-cafe en Camerinos ,Foro #2 y en
                    Back Lot- mesa de Asst.Dir.conectada a luz de Foro,campana y telefono
                    luces de trabajo en el camino del Back Lot-locion anti mosquitos-
CATERING :   Dune's restaurant open from 8.00pm- snacks from 1.00am(Ballesteros)
                  * Restaurante de Dune abierto desde las 8.00pm-snacks desde la 1.00am.
PROPERTY :   Atreides banner-Duke Leto's ring-guns for Atreides Guards
                  * Bandera Atreides- anillo de Leto- armas para Guardas Atreides.
LIVESTOCK/PROPERTY: Duke Leto's dog available for rehearsal at 4.00pm
                  * Perro de Leto preparado para ensayo a las 4.00pm.
SP/FX :   Wind-midst-rain in pool's of light./* viento-bruma-lluvia estraña
                    en Caladan.
WARDROBE: Water from rain in actors costumes-/* agua de lluvia en trajes de
                    actores.
CAMERA :   As per F.Francis instructions/*Según instrucciones de F.Francis.
                    Portable blue backing &vistavision Camera-/*pantalla azul portatil &
                    vistavision camera.
ELECTRIC: Stand by generator rigg to Stage #2-generators for Back Lot.
                  * Generador conectado al Foro #2 estar preparado-generadores para B.Lot
SOUND :   Recording session for inner voices of Jessica & Paul-
                    Recording room for session from 5.00pm. Sc.:78,80,90,92 .

                                                      J.Lopez Rodero
                                                      Assistant Director.
ADVANCE SCHEDULE:
              FRIDAY 29th,1983 NIGHT SHOOTING - BACK LOT-
              EXT.ROCK CLIFF-DEEP DESERT- Sc.:151a pt,152,153a,153b,155,156 (N)

              "B" CAMERA : EXT. FREMEN PLACE- TRASH DUMP- IF NOT COMPLETE .

              SATURDAY 30th,1983 NIGHT SHOOTING - STAGE #2-work with end at 11.30pm.
              INT.GENERATOR ROOM-ARRAKEEN PALACE - Sc.:73 (D)

              MONDAY MAY 2nd,1983 NIGHT SHOOTING -BACK LOT-
              EXT.ROCK CLIFF-DEEP DESERT- Sc.:156b,156c,159,160,161,162,163 (N)

First unit call sheet, April 28, 1983.

```
                    C A L L   S H E E T (SECOND CAMERA)

PRODUCTION TITLE: "DUNE"                DATE: FRIDAY APRIL 29, 1983.
PRODUCER: RAFFAELLA DE LAURENTIIS             *VIERNES
DIRECTOR: FRED ELMES                    CREW CALL: 5.30pm at Studios
               NIGHT SHOOTING  *RODAJE DE NOCHE


SETS AND SCENE NUMBERS             D/N        STAGE/LOCATION

EXT. CALADAN CASTLE                 N         BACK LOT
(Atreides Guards lower flag)
*EXT. CASTILLO DE CALADAN
(Guardias Atreides bajan bandera)
Sc: 52A


ARTISTS         CHARACTER        D/R      P/U    HAIR /WARD    ON SET


GUSTAVO GANEM   ATREIDES GUARD                   5.30pm        7.00pm
                CRYING *LLORANDO


CROWD
9 ATREIDES GUARDS (Black Uniforms)               5.30pm        7.00pm
                *(Uniformes Negros)


REQUIREMENTS:
PRODUCTION:Coffee services on Set-Dinner ready from 9pm to 10pm-Check details
        in all Departments.
          *Servicio de café en Set- Cena lista de 9pm a 10pm- Checar detalles
           en distintos Departamentos.
CAMERA:Mitchell Mark II- Anamorphic Lenses- 5:1 ZOOM (From FIRST CAMERA)
       *(De la PRIMERA CAMARA)- MOY Gearhead _Umbrellas*(Sombrillas) -
        Hustler Dolly- Lightflex.
PROPS: Black and green banner and pole-Guns and accessories for Guards as
       established.
       *Bandera negra y verde y asta de bandera - armas y utilería estable-
        cidas para Guardias.
SP/FX: Rain - "electronic" mechanism to lower flag - Cherry pickers (Same
       S/FX crew involved in this Sc.)- Wind.
       *Lluvia- mecanismo "electrónico" para bajar bandera- Cherry pickers
       (Mismo personal de SP/FX involucrado en esta Sc)- Viento.
ELECT: 2 DINOS or 3 10/K  Reflectors rigged on  SP/FX  Tower - Barn Doors.
       *2 DINOS o 3 Reflectores 10/K colocados en Torre de SP/FX - Aspas.
GRIPS: Rig SP/FX Tower (10 meters high) same place where it used to stand.
       *Levantar Torre de SP/FX (10 metros de altura) en el mismo sitio donde
        estaba colocada.

       NOTE ELECT/GRIPS: This rigging must be done by Personnel not from
       SECOND CAMERA during daytime.
       *NOTA: ELECT/GRIPS: Esta preparación deberá hacerla otro personal
        diferente al de la SEGUNDA CAMARA durante el día.
M/UP/WARD: Tears for Guard - Black Uniforms for Atreides.
         *Lágrimas para el Guardia- Uniformes Negros para Atreides.
ART: Standby during shooting. *Pendiente durante Filmación.
TRANSPORT: Combie for Camera - Standby Car for Personnel- Pickup truck
       for GRIPS/ELECT.
         *Combie de cámara - Auto pendiente para Personal - Camioneta Pick-
          up para GRIPS/ELECT.

ADVANCED SCHEDULE: MONDAY MAY 2nd  : INT. PAUL'S ROOM-ARRAKEEN PALACE
                  *LUNES              (Hunter-Seeker Pickup shots-TO COMPLETE)
                                    *(Pickup Shots de Cazador-buscador-PARA
                                      COMPLETAR) Sc: 80pt   LOC: STAGE# 4
                                            Jesús Marín
                                            Assisstant Director
```

Second unit call sheet, April 29, 1983.

Week 7: May 2-8, 1983

Tuesday, May 3: DAY FORTY-FOUR (14 1/2 hrs; 10 1/2 hrs)

Apparently I didn't miss much Sunday evening. There were quite a few people there, but it was pretty dull.

Saturday evening, Anatol was out with Fred – linked up with a bunch of crew people and Raffaella – wound up partying at Raffaella's suite until late. He couldn't figure out where I'd got to, he said. Even though I told him I was going to the studio, he thought I'd changed my mind and just disappeared. Logic isn't his strongest point.

David Lynch and producer Raffaella De Laurentiis. Photograph copyright Universal/De Laurentiis.

Yesterday was a long dull day. I was woken by a driver at nine-forty-five, sent for who knows what reason. Took a shower, called Anatol – no reply. So I grabbed a cab to the studio. He had taken the eight o'clock crew bus – not having slept Sunday night. He wound up sleeping on our office floor all afternoon. I just wandered around, talking to people (Giles [Masters] and Kevin [Phipps] in the art department – both English, with family backgrounds in film).

No backlash about Sunday evening. I explained what happened to Strick. It was all informal anyway.

The night's shooting was dull – just shots of Paul and Jessica at the rock wall. The Fremen extras had been called; a shot was lined up, they were all positioned; but it was decided that it didn't look right – so they were all sent home again (at what cost?) and a number of different shots set up. We didn't stick around. Left at one.

We talked to Maggie [Anderson], the dialect coach (a wonderful woman, a Scot who's lived most of her life in Rome and who's worked on some big Italian productions), about our Paris idea. She seemed quite taken with it.

Now if only I can find time to put together an at least functional script.

Which brings me to a sore point.

I don't want to do this party thing on Sunday. After six days of a heavy schedule, that one day off is desperately needed. We're always exhausted on weekends. To be told to give up our day off to shoot home movies of Tony Masters' party is unacceptable. And if they insist, it's obvious that they're not taking us seriously, don't consider what we're doing to be work. In which case, why the fuck are they wasting money on it?

The problem is Anatol has gone all wishy-washy about it. After being against it, he now says well, he'll do it one time, but if they start making a habit of it, he'll put his foot down. Which to me is dumb. Right now is the time to make them take us more seriously. It's a simple matter of establishing a professional attitude towards us. If we set a precedent by being party photographers on Sunday, it'll only be that much harder to straighten things out later on.

Fred's been having a hard time. His all-Mexican crew presents not only a language problem – they have a very slack attitude towards their work. For a couple of weeks he's been doing hunter-seeker inserts in Paul's room on Stage 4. A lot of painstaking shots – using glass, mirrors, wires, all kinds of techniques. Yesterday when they got to the set where a wire shot had been rigged a week ago, they found a lot of their lights removed, wires cut – a general mess. Several hours later, Leslie (doing continuity for second unit) discovered by accident that the assistant director, Jesus Marin, hadn't even bothered to make a report (in fact, doesn't even file routine A.D. reports).

If this film ever actually gets completed, it'll be something of a miracle.

Wednesday, May 4: DAY FORTY-FIVE (19 hrs)

We went to the Bank of America representative yesterday to take care of some business (I want to transfer to a high interest account) before going to the studio.

As usual, we were slower getting in than we'd planned. Had to show some more stuff to Strick and another guy from Universal (Leonard Morpurgo). Were then going to go shoot Fred at work. But there was a sudden change of plans. Strick talked to Armstrong. He wants Morpurgo to bring back some of our material when he flies out Friday morning. Anatol immediately went to Raffaella. She wanted to see our stuff yesterday evening... As it turned out, we're going to rush out a dupe of some of the material (an hour or so) for Raffaella and David to see Thursday - and they can pass it on if they approve.

When Anatol talked to her, Raffaella said, in effect, so what? they're paying for it. He asked her why she was just giving this stuff away. Maybe we'll eventually get her over to our side.

The further we go, the more of a joke our equipment seems to be. This stuff isn't meant to produce anything for long-term preservation. Anatol's complaints get louder and longer all the time - he still hopes he can push them to approve a 16mm/Nagra system. I really doubt it.

Thursday, May 5: DAY FORTY-SIX (4 1/2 hrs)

I got to the studio about nine yesterday morning (after less than six hours sleep) and fumbled around with our duping equipment. Impossible to do anything even resembling editing because we have no time-code readers, no time base correctors, nothing... By the time Anatol got there at about twelve, I had seven minutes of clumsy, shapeless mess duped.

So after lunch, we just began at the beginning and started going through the material chronologically. Since nothing has been duped yet, we had to scan everything, lifting a shot here, another there. With only one major break - about two hours to do some shooting on Stage 2 (the generator room) and eat some supper - we worked until just after four this morning, going through over fifty cassettes. I worked the machines the whole time - Anatol watched and commented, sometimes helpful, sometimes annoying. He burned out before the end - no energy, voice a slur. By the end of it all, my eyes were burning and I knew I didn't want to do this again; if Armstrong wants samples, he can send better equipment and a person who knows how to use it. Because the almost two hours of VHS we ended up with was a shitty mess.

We got thoroughly depressed by it all. We've just been pumping out a pile of dull, repetitious, generally uninformative material. This has nothing to do with what we wanted to do on David - something personal about him and his work (which I doubt he'd let us do anyway) - and the project (*Dune*) doesn't lend itself to more general coverage. It's very static. In fact, I'm becoming worried; it looks like a collection of stills, tableaux (maybe it looks different in dailies - but to us, there seems to be almost no movement). I have an awful feeling that it may simply be too big, may collapse back on David.

Both of us are at the point where we'd probably rather ship everything back to Armstrong and let him do what he wants with it – have nothing to do with the editing; I don't even want to think of looking at this stuff again.

We got to the studio at noon, checked that Raffaella had got the tape, spoke to Strick – and bumped into Bob (forget his last name), the Patsa Productions man on the film; he'd just received an application from a woman, fluently bilingual (Argentinian, lived in New York for years), with some video experience. Called her immediately. Anatol spoke to her – she seems to talk a *lot* – and she's interested in joining us – though, of course, not purely in a background capacity (it's the same with everyone). If she's really interested in being our assistant (logging, running the machines) – not really a full-time job – maybe we can offer her the position of interviewer as a sop to the desire for greater involvement. Mostly, I think, it depends on how much Raffaella is willing to pay (we had lunch with Bob's secretary – a twenty-four year old Swedish-American redhead resident here for quite a few years – and she only gets twenty-five thousand pesos a week, the same as our *allowance*, and her rent isn't paid either; and of course Arturo only gets two hundred dollars a month...).

Met and shook hands with Max von Sydow this afternoon – one of the few actors I know of whom I'd feel it a genuine pleasure to meet. A friendly, very gentlemanly man who will unfortunately only be here about three weeks.

Saturday, May 7: DAY FORTY-EIGHT (10 1/2 hrs, 7 1/2 hrs)

Anatol spoke to Armstrong yesterday. He expressed some concern for our health in this place. And also made it quite clear that we're not here to make a film about David Lynch – that we're to get off the set and shoot other things. Raffaella apparently, without even having seen any of our tapes, had complained to him. When Anatol told her this afternoon that we'd found very little on David when we went through it all on Wednesday, and that we'd be following her around for a day next week, she seemed to perk up. As Anatol says: what kind of person would want to be followed around all day by a video crew? would actively desire it? Christ...

We also learned this afternoon that Tony Masters was pissed off about the bit we did on Ron Miller – thought we were putting him above Masters... So we have to placate him and stroke his ego.

This whole thing is such a pain – what's the point of doing it?

Masters will no doubt be pissed off that we've managed to get out of filming his fucking party tomorrow.

We have to wait around here until we get a call from David – to go and interview him at his hotel; a priority. Strick of course seems to think that if we only do David tomorrow, we'll be at the studio first thing Monday morning to follow either Raffaella or Tony Masters around – never mind that the camera needs servicing. She's getting extremely pushy again.

We want to try to get a serious interview out of David tomorrow – the first of a series, we hope – because we're getting the distinct impression that he's deliberately being pushed into the background. This whole thing about being ordered to stay away from him, plus the fact that he scarcely gets a mention in the material given out to the local press... I'm now thinking that I should do something for *CFQ* to boost him a little. It's quite likely that De Laurentiis wants to get whatever is special about David without giving away any credit.

We don't think it was entirely accident that when Strick gave us a list of names, people we should follow about, she included hairdressers and makeup people but neglected to include David, Freddie Francis and Fred Elmes. Minor characters, of course, on a project like this.

When we got back to Zona Rosa yesterday evening, we went to the Bellinghausen, the pseudo-German restaurant we'd been to once before – a quite pleasant, plain place. A bottle of wine with the meal. And afterwards a walk.

Another slow day today. The awful thing is that both Anatol and I are bored with what's going on on the production – there's really nothing much to document – unless we start concentrating on the personalities. Things are getting very strained and there are bound to be explosions (Kuki Rodero, the A.D., seems to be nearing the breaking point – and he strikes me as the kind who might lash out in the end; there's bad feeling amongst the crew – the long, erratic hours and a certain lack of consideration from the producers; the extras and stand-ins tend to be treated very badly, like cattle, lumps of meat – the Mexicans in positions of low power tend to be unpleasant and dictatorial towards anyone under their command...). The atmosphere which seemed so good at the start is collapsing under the weight of poor management, the inefficiency endemic to Mexico, and the foul climate and pollution here (we're in the midst of a heat wave with the highest temperatures in a hundred years).

Bought a record this evening – even though I have nothing to play it on (maybe I can borrow David's system to tape it); Divine, star of John Waters' films – called *Jungle Jezebel*. Probably awful, but I couldn't resist. (I believe Edith Massey, "the egg lady", has a record too.)

Another dead Saturday night. Left it too late to make arrangements. Asked Debbie, an English woman in wardrobe, this afternoon. No go. Dozed off when I got back here – when I woke, tried Bob (not in), Greg (tied up unwillingly in a party for the Apogee crew thrown by some mysterious woman), Sean Young (not in).

The applicant for the position of our assistant quickly went sour. A pushy, overly talkative woman (actually of Peruvian parentage, born in the States), she obviously didn't know as much as she said she did and her manner was somewhat grating. Besides which she was turned down by the powers-that-be because she was American – they want a Mexican for paperwork reasons.

We're supposed to be seeing three more people on Monday (two coming through Carlos, assistant to Tony Gibbs and Penny Shaw in editing; one through Eric, on the second unit). I really doubt we'll find anyone suitable.

Sunday, May 8: DAY FORTY-NINE (3 hrs)

The best day we've had since we came here. We spent three hours with David this afternoon – just talking. We got a lot off our chests, told him about the order not to shoot David Lynch, discussed our position – and finally got him in front of the camera, with us on either side, and just conversed with him. He was relaxed, talkative. And I had none of the problems I had with, say, Ron Miller – with David it isn't interviewing, it's just conversation. And when he's relaxed he talks quite freely. Both Anatol and I were revitalized by the afternoon.

As far as David is concerned our place is primarily with first and second unit, watching the actual making of the film – all the behind the scenes stuff can be dealt with without cutting severely into that. He was to see Raffaella this evening, so perhaps he can talk to her about all this.

Other things came out of the afternoon too. "So," he asked, "are we going to do this *Eraserhead* book?" Using my text. That immediately cheered me up – it looks like a real possibility. Also, I may finally get to see the material excised from the film (none of it was included in the material selected for *CFQ*, but it will be in the book). So I told him of Anatol's idea of a book of the "Art of David Lynch" – paintings, drawings, and bits from the films. He loved it.

And he's going to let me read *Blue Velvet*, his '50s script (which he says needs heavy work on the last third).

As for our "Café Universal", he misplaced the brief outline, but seems intrigued by what we've told him; I'll develop it in more detail and show it to him when it's more presentable.

Best of all, he's agreed to have sessions like this fairly regularly during the production, an on-going journal on video. Perhaps we can get him together with Freddie, Fred, and others on occasion, to discuss what's going on. This is the sort of stuff we've been hoping to get.

Rainy day, Mexico City.

After all this, Anatol and I had a leisurely supper, talking about how things were looking up and tossing ideas back and forth for inclusion in the script. A good day. Which ended with the first rain – maybe the heat wave will break.

The rain has developed into a thunderstorm – lovely...

By the way, we're averaging over seventy hours a week (just over fourteen bucks an hour).

Among other things we talked about with David was music for the film. He's toying with all kinds of ideas (including rock groups – adapted to orchestra?). He favours massed Russian strings and choir to give it a soaring, ethereal quality. I mentioned Eno – and he said Eno is interested in the project and they'll probably be talking to him.

Also, it looks as if Anatol and I will be allowed to see some dailies...

Week Seven Documents

```
                           CALL SHEET                    Production No. 23

PRODUCTION TITTLE: "DUNE"                          DATE: Monday May 2nd. 1983.
PRODUCER: RAFFAELLA DE LAURENTIIS                  CREW CALL: 6:00pm at Studio
DIRECTOR: DAVID LYNCH                              LEAVE HOTEL: 5:30pm
                           NIGHT SHOOTING
                                                                J.LOPEZ RODERO
                                                                Assistant Director

SETS & SCENES NUMBERS:
(1) EXT. ROCK CLIFF-DEEP DESERT   Sc.160,161   (N)   LOCATION: BACK LOT
(2) EXT. ROCK OUT CROPPING-DEEP DESERT Sc.173  (N)              "       "
(3) EXT. ROCK CLIFF-DEEP DESERT   Sc.162       (N)              "       "
    EXT. CREVICE-DEEP DESERT      Sc.163       (N)              "       "
```

ARTIST	CHARACTERS	D/N	P/U	M/U	WARD	ON SET
FRENCESCA ANNIS	JESSICA	217	5:30pm	6:00pm		10:00pm
KYLE MacLACHLAN	PAUL	218	6:00pm	6:30pm		7:30pm
SEAN YOUNG	CHANI	208	6:30pm	7:00pm		10:00pm
EVERETT McGILL	STILGAR	207	7:30pm	8:00pm		10:00pm
MARTIN LASALLE	FREMEN #1	212		8:00pm		10:00pm
HONORATO MAGALONNE	FREMEN #2	214		8:00pm		10:00pm

STAND INS/DOUBLES:

JOSEPHINE LOVELL	FOR JESSICA			5:30pm		6:00pm
GONZALO IRIGOYEN	FOR PAUL			5:30pm		6:00pm
A.N. OTHER	FOR CHANI			8:00pm		8:30pm
A.N. OTHER	FOR STILGAR			8:00pm		8:30pm

CROWD:

4 FREMEN WOMEN				8:00pm		9:00pm
29 FREMEN MEN				8:00pm		9:00pm

PRODUCTION REQUIREMENTS:

PRODUCTION:	Security guards in Back Lot-A.D.'s Desk rig to lights and bell-campers for actors-honeywagon for company-Doctor & Ambulance on Set-coffee service on set and dress rooms-worklights along the way to the working area-goggles and dust masks for crew. * Vigilancia en Back Lot-mesa de Asst. Dir. conectada a luz & campana-caravanas para actores-honeywagon para equipo-Doctor y Ambulancia en el Set-cafe en camerinos y Back Lot-luces de trabajo en el camino al area de trabajo del Set-gafas y mascarillas para polvo para equipo.
CATERING:	Dune Restaurant open since 8:00pm-Snacks on Set at 1:00am (Ballesteros) * Restaurant Dune abierto desde las 8:00pm-snacks a la 1:00am en Set.
PROPERTY:	Fremenkits-weapons for Fremen-Dipsticks-Thumpers-Ropes-Leto's signet ring-wrapped dummy for Jamis./*Fremenkits-armas para Fremen-varillas mu golpeadores-sogas-Qnillo con insignis de Leto-fusil para Jamis
CONSTRUCTION:	Dig hole F/vista vision camera as discussed w/Dykstra/* Sanja para camara vista vision como acordado con Dykstra.
PROPERTY:	Poles-postes (leading to entrance)(señalando la entrada)
SP/FX:	Wind-yellow dust-lightning *Aire-polvo amarillo-rayos-
WARDROBE:	Blankets to cover actors & crowd/*Mantas para cubrir actores y equipo.
CAMERA:	As per Freddie Francis instructions-John Dykstra and crew to be on set at 5:00pm.-Vista vision camera./*Según instrucciones de Freddie Francis John Dykstra y equipo a las 5:00pm en set-cámara Vista vision.
ELECTRIC:	Stand by generators rigged to set lights/*generadores conectados a luces de set.
TRANSPORTATION:	All vehicles readdy to move company from Back lot to the production offices & Restaurant-Dune minibus to take crowd to the set./*todos los vehiculos para transportar a la compañia a oficinas de producción y Restaurante-Camión Dune para llevar a figurantes al set.

```
ADVANCE SHEDULE:  IF NOT COMPLETED:  EXT. ROCK CLIFF DEEP DESERT Sc.162(N)   BACK LOT
                                     EXT. CREVICE-DEEP DESERT    Sc.163(N)
                                     EXT. ROCK OUTCROPPING       Sc.173pt.(N)
              IF COMPLETED ABOVE:    INT. ATREIDES SHIP-SPACE Sc.55 (Space)   STAGE #4
   NIGHT SHOOTING                    EXT. ATREIDES SHIP-CALADAN Sc.52Cpt. (N)CINETECA PARKING LO
```

First unit call sheet, May 2, 1983.

```
                    C A L L  S H E E T (SECOND CAMERA)

PRODUCTION TITLE: "DUNE"                    DATE: MONDAY MAY 2nd, 1983
PRODUCER: RAFFAELLA DE LAURENTIIS                 *LUNES
DIRECTOR: FRED ELMES                        CREW CALL:8.30am at Studios


SETS AND SCENE NUMBERS:             D/N         STAGE/LOCATION

INT. PAUL'S ROOM - ARRAKEEN PALACE   D           STAGE #4
(To complete HUNTER-SEEKER PICKUPS)
*(Para completar     PICKUPS de CAZADOR-
                              BUSCADOR)
Sc: 80pt.


NOTE: NO CAST                       * NOTA: SIN ACTORES


REQUIREMENTS:
PRODUCTION: Check details in all Departmentd involved - Coffee Service on
                                                                   Stage.
           *Checar detalles en todos los Departamentos involucrados -
            Servicio de Café en Foro.
CAMERA: Mitchell Mark II - Lightflex - Anamorphic lenses - MOY Gearhead
SP/FX: As established by First Camera.
      *Según lo establecido por Primera Cámara.
  GRIPS   )
  PROPS   )
  ELECT   )  As established by First Camera.
  ART     )  *Según lo establecido por Primera Cámara.


NOTE: Tests will be made with both SINGLE/FRAME motor and the FRIESS High
      Speed Motor during the day.
       *Se harán pruebas con los motores de CUADRO POR CUADRO y FRIESS de
        Alta Velocidad., durante el día.



                                                           Jesús Marín
```

Second unit call sheet, May 2, 1983.

```
                    C A L L   S H E E T  (SECOND CAMERA)

PRODUCTION TITLE: "DUNE"              DATE: TUESDAY MAY 3rd, 1983.
PRODUCER: RAFFAELLA DE LAURENTIIS           *MARTES
DIRECTOR: FRED ELMES                  CREW CALL: 8.30am at Studios.


SETS AND SCENE NUMBERS:          D/N       STAGE/LOCATION

INT. PAUL'S ROOM-ARRAKEEN PLACE   D        STAGE #4
(To complete HUNTER-SEEKER PICKUPS)
*(Para completar PICKUPS de CAZADOR-
                         BUSCADOR)
Sc: 80pt.


NOTE:  NO CAST                    *NOTA: SIN ACTORES


REQUIREMENTS:
PRODUCTION: Check details in all Departments involved- Coffee Service on
                                                                    Stage.
          *Checar detalles en todos los Departamentos involucrados-
           Servicio de Café en Foro.
CAMERA: Mitchell Mark II - Lightflex - Anamorphic lenses - MOY Gearhead.
SP/FX: As established by First Camera.
       *Según lo establecido por Primera Cámara.
GRIPS     )
PROPS     )     As established by First Camera.
ELECT     )     *Según lo establecido por Primera Cámara.
ART       )


ADVANCED SCHEDULE:     WEDNESDAY MAY 4th, 1983.
                       *MIERCOLES

                       INT. PAUL'S ROOM-ARRAKEEN PALACE (D)
                       (To complete HUNTER-SEEKER Pickups)
                       *(Para completar PICKUPS de CAZADOR-BUSCADOR)
                       Sc: 80pt.          STAGE: #4


                                              Jesús Marín
                                            Assistant Director
```

Second unit call sheet, May 3, 1983.

```
                    C A L L    S H E E T  (SECOND CAMERA)
PRODUCTION TITLE: "DUNE"              DATE: WEDNESDAY MAY 4th, 1983.
PRODUCER: RAFFAELLA DE LAURENTIIS          *MIERCOLES
DIRECTOR: FRED ELMES                  CREW CALL: 8.30am at Studios


SETS AND SCENE NUMBERS:              D/N          STAGE/LOCATION
INT. PAUL'S ROOM- ARRAKEEN PALACE     D            STAGE #4
(To complete HUNTER-SEEKER PICKUPS)
*(Para completar PICKUPS de CAZADOR-
                        BUSCADOR)
Sc: 80pt.


NOTE: NO CAST                          *NOTA: SIN ACTORES


REQUIREMENTS:

PRODUCTION: Check details in all Departments involved-Coffee Service on Stage.
           *Checar detalles en todos los Departamentos involucrados- Servi-
            cio de café en Foro.
CAMERA: Mitchell Mark II - Lightflex - Anamorphic lenses - MOY Gearhead.
SP/FX: As established by FIRST Camera.
      *Según lo establecido por PRIMERA Cámara.

GRIPS   )
PROPS   )    As established by FIRST Camera.and indications by Director.
ELECT   )    *Según lo establecido por PRIMERA Cámara, e indicaciones del
ART     )                                                      Director.


ADVANCED SCHEDULE:    THURSDAY MAY 5th, 1983.
                     *JUEVES
                      NOTE: This day ALL PERSONNEL from SECOND CAMERA will
                            join FIRST Camera's Call. -CHECK CALL.
                      *NOTA: Este día TODO EL PERSONAL de la SEGUNDA CAMARA
                             se unirá al Llamado de la PRIMERA CAMARA.
                             CHECAR LLAMADO.


                                                    Jesús Marín
                                                    Assistant Director
```

Second unit call sheet, May 4, 1983.

```
                    C A L L    S H E E T  (SECOND CAMERA)
PRODUCTION TITLE: "DUNE"              DATE: THURSDAY MAY 5th, 1983.
PRODUCER: RAFFAELLA DE LAURENTIIS           *JUEVES
DIRECTOR: FRED ELMES                  CREW CALL: 8.30am at Studios.

SETS AND SCENE NUMBERS:               D/N            STAGE/LOCATION
1) INSERT-FILMBOOK-PLANETS AND GALAXIES   X          STAGE #4
   MOVE.
  *INSERT-LIBRO/PELICULA-PLANETAS Y GALA-
   XIAS SE MUEVEN.
   Sc: 25A
2) INT. PAUL'S ROOM-ARRAKEEN PALACE       D          STAGE #4
   HUNTER-SEEKER Pickup shots-TO COMPLETE
  *PICKUPS de CAZADOR-BUSCADOR
   Sc: 80pt.

NOTE: NO CAST                   *NOTA: SIN ACTORES

REQUIREMENTS (General):
PRODUCTION: Check details in all Departments -Coffee Service on Stage.
           *Checar detalles en distintos Deptos.-Servicio de Café en Foro.
REQUIREMENTS FOR 1):
CAMERA: As per Fred Elmes' instructions. *Según instrucciones de Fred Elmes.
GRIP/PROPS/ELECT: As per Fred Elmes' instructions.
                 *Según instrucciones de Fred Elmes.
ART: Art Work/ PLANETS.  *Trabajo de Arte /PLANETAS.


REQUIREMENTS FOR 2):
CAMERA: Mitchell Mark II - Lightflex - Anamorphic lenses-MOY Gearhead.

SP/FX: As established by FIRST Camera and Director's indications.
      *Según lo establecido por PRIMERA cámara e indicaciones de Director.
GRIPS  )
PROPS  )   As established by FIRST Camera and indications by Director.
ELECT  )  *Según lo establecido por PRIMERA Cámara e indicaciones del
ART    )   DIRECTOR.


ADVANCED SCHEDULE:    FRIDAY MAY 6th, 1983.
                     *VIERNES
                      NOTE: This day ALL PERSONNEL from SECOND CAMERA will
                      join FIRST Camera's Call -CHECK CALL.
                     *NOTA: Este día TODO EL PERSONAL de la SEGUNDA CAMARA
                      se unirá al llamado de la PRIMERA CAMARA- CHECAR LLA-
                      MADO.




                                                       Jesús Marín
                                                       Assistant Director
```

Second unit call sheet, May 5, 1983.

```
                    C A L L   S H E E T  (SECOND CAMERA)
PRODUCTION TITLE: "DUNE"              DATE: SATURDAY 7th MAY, 1983.
PRODUCER: RAFFAELLA DE LAURENTIIS           *SABADO
DIRECTOR: FRED ELMES                  CREW CALL: 8.00am at Studios.

SETS AND SCENE NUMBERS:               D/N          STAGE/LOCATION
(NEW TEST) INSERT-FILMBOOK-PLANETS AND X           STAGE #4
GALAXIES MOVE
*(NUEVA PRUEBA) INSERT-LIBRO/PELICULA-
 PLANETAS Y GALAXIAS SE MUEVEN
Sc: 25A

NOTE: NO CAST                 * NOTA: SIN ACTORES

REQUIREMENTS:
PRODUCTION: Check details in all Depts.- Coffee Service on Stage.
            *Checar detalles en distintos Deptos.- Servicio de Café en Foro.
CAMERA: Mitchell Mark II- Single/Frame Motor *Motor de Cuadro por Cuadro-
        Back-Wards Motor (Churubusco Studios) *Motor de Reversa - 16mm Pro-
        jector(with Projectionist)*(con Proyeccionista) - 16mm Material for
        this Sc. *Material de 16mm para esta Sc.- plus any other indication
        by Fred Elmes *MAS cualquier otra indicación de Fred Elmes.
ART: Art Work / PLANETS.  *Trabajo de Arte/PLANETAS.
PROPS: Filmbook.  *Libro-película.
GRIP/ELECT: As per Fred Elmes instructions. *Según indicaciones de Fred Elmes.
SP/FX: As discussed by Fred Elmes and Andrew Kelly.
        *Según lo discutido entre Fred Elmes y Andrew Kelly.
CATERING: SNACK ready from 11.00am for 35 people.
          SNACK listo desde las 11.00am para 35 personas.

ADVANCED SCHEDULE:    MONDAY 9th MAY,1983.
                      INT. RESERVOIR-SIETCH TABR- (N)  LOC: WAREHOUSE
                      Sc: MONTAGE, 179A, 31pt.              *BODEGA


                                                    Jesús Marín
                                                    Assistant Director
```

Second unit call sheet, May 7, 1983.

Week 8: May 9-15, 1983

Tuesday, May 10: DAY FIFTY-ONE (13 hrs, 8 hrs)

Max Von Sydow as Dr. Kynes flies an Atreides 'thopter over the desert with Duke Leto (Jurgen Prochnow), Paul (Kyle MacLachlan) and Gurney Halleck (Patrick Stewart) as passengers. Photograph copyright Universal/De Laurentiis.

We went to the studio yesterday afternoon, after a late breakfast with Fred – still pale and weak from a bout of some bug (the strain of this situation is wreaking havoc on his health).

Right away, we discovered that the first cassette from Sunday afternoon was ruined; the camera was receiving a strong FM signal, at times about as loud as David. For some reason it faded out on the second and third cassettes. Still, we got some excellent stuff from that conversation.

We had a guy from Apogee, an electronics man named Steve, look at the camera, and Arturo came in later. They opened it up, removed the recorder – but there's apparently not much you can do with the FM problem (like CBs on your TV or stereo). As for the hissing problem we've been getting, they couldn't help because we were never sent the manual for the recorder.

Then when we were getting ready to go, we kept getting the servo red light – meaning the recorder wasn't getting a sync signal and wouldn't record. I cleaned the connections and that seemed to help. But the time-code generator isn't working. We're getting more and more pissed off.

Raffaella told Anatol we missed a lot of good material by not following her around yesterday. I heard a little later what the good material pertained to when I spoke to Maggie on Stage 1. I told her about our Sunday afternoon, how good it had been for the three of us, and she said she was glad because Monday was very bad for David, he was feeling lousy because they'd had to fire Aldo Ray because of his drinking problem. When I heard that, I found myself fuming. If that's the kind of thing Raffaella wants us to catch on tape – her being the big producer as seen in someone else's humiliation – she can fuck herself. If anything like that does come up when we follow her around, I told Anatol, I'm shutting off the mike and walking away. And if she wants to fire me for that, okay.

We won't be doing her today because she'll be spending most of her time phoning around for a replacement.

We still haven't got an assistant, though we met a guy yesterday who looks very promising – named Pablo, the friend of Eric Krohnengold. Apparently Carmen, the woman last week, never even spoke to Raffaella; she talked to Vicente Escriva (more or less the office manager) who told her what a dry, dull, boring job it was and that most of the time she'd have nothing to do. Hiring our assistant has nothing to do with him in the first place – and for him to be trying to discourage our applicants is really just a bit too much.

But the day ended well; shooting a scene in the studio parking lot – the entrance to a Harkonnen ship on the Arrakeen landing field – with a crowd of Harkonnen soldiers (superbly evil looking creatures in their oily suits) and Max von Sydow (Dr. Kynes), beaten and half dead, being abused by Paul Smith (Rabban), a huge, magnificently maniacal villain. It was the first scene that actually excited us, looking truly epic – we hope to see the dailies of it.

We didn't stay long today – left the studio about nine; we've got a bunch of stuff to do tomorrow (starting with Tony Masters at nine in the morning).

After yesterday evening's intensity, it settled back to the slowness we've come to know so well.

But yesterday! What we shot is incredible – everything came together – we caught the excitement of what was happening and it's visually dynamic. The first stuff we're actually happy with (and really want to show to David and Freddie Francis).

Pablo joined our crew today. He seems intelligent, polite, very attentive – I hope he works out okay.

Anatol and I rode back to the Zona Rosa with Debbie and Roz from wardrobe this evening. Debbie's going to the coast this weekend with a few other people. Roz is going to New York Thursday – doing a wardrobe fitting with Sting – too bad it's not possible for us to go along – just to get away from here for a couple of days.

Pablo Ocampo Pinan and Anatol Pacanowski.

I may have to leave the Amberes. It appears that my jacket has been stolen. And for two days there's been no hot water for my shower…

Wednesday, May 11: DAY FIFTY-TWO (9 1/2 hrs)

If I don't get a break soon, a chance to catch up on some real rest, I think I'll collapse. It's impossible to get a full night's sleep, what with the heat and the lack of oxygen – and last night a bout of what Bob calls "the Hershey squirts". This fucking place is impossible.

We shot some stuff with Tony Masters this morning. Apparently he's been dying to get on camera – he made up his own interview essentially – was so eager to start, he was going before we were quite ready.

After that, we were too exhausted by our stomach problems and general tiredness to do much of anything. We had to screen some stuff for Strick. And were given an order for this five-to-seven minute convention promo thing – to be ready next week. Good luck. First Armstrong refuses to give us editing capability – then we're expected to start editing on the spot. Of course what we're supposed to put into this thing is the kind of shit we don't like (such as Tony rambling on).

Luckily we have Pablo – and Ellie, a connection with Mexican TV working for the *Dune* effects people. She put us in touch with the head of Pronarte, the government video facility at Churubusco – so we went to see him at five-thirty.

An old university friend of Pablo's works there too. So, within half an hour we had facilities booked for a couple of hours Friday morning for transfer of our material to 3/4" and subsequent assembly (we'll send Armstrong twenty or thirty minutes which he can edit as desired in L.A.).

Of course all this is subject to approval by David and Raffaella – and they haven't even looked at the dupe we made last week.

Problems: Strick seems to think that this can all be knocked out quickly Friday morning and sent to the States Monday. She doesn't understand that it may be technically complicated. Even less does she seem to realize that it'll take hours to locate the necessary shots (we haven't logged anything yet, remember). So she's already listing all the things we should do tomorrow (Raffaella again – she's more eager than Masters, it seems).

But the main thing is this: this stuff is not what we were hired for (remember the one-hour documentary? a lot of people seem to forget). This is extra work – and a lot of trouble (because we were hamstrung at the beginning as far as editing is concerned). And further, it's taking us away from the job we are supposed to be doing – covering the *Dune* production. This is publicity. Armstrong told us we weren't doing that. So we figure we should be paid extra for this. But Anatol, despite his penchant for flying off the handle, is reluctant to "stir up trouble" because we aren't really in a firm position. I think that if we don't set it straight right now, it'll be too late afterwards; we mustn't set a precedent that all this extra stuff is free.

Pablo seems like a real find – intelligent, competent, and well-connected.

This morning when I again asked at the desk about my jacket, the manager happened to be there. The jacket was waiting here when I got back this evening.

And Christina Espinoza is getting on to them about moving me to a suite upstairs – she says *only* talk to the manager. Everyone else is useless.

We've been invited to a party Saturday – actually invited. Not because of our equipment. In fact when Penny Shaw (assistant editor) gave us the invitation this afternoon (it's at her and Tony Gibbs' place) and we pleaded for her to refuse having it videotaped, she seemed surprised, thought it a ridiculous idea. So we're safe there.

Egos: Masters made no mention of Ron Miller during his spiel – even though he showed us some of Miller's paintings. And Strick pointedly told us to avoid Miller's interview when we put this promo thing together. Heads of departments only, please…

Met Dean Stockwell (Dr. Yueh) this afternoon. Friendly, apparently willing to be of service to us.

Friday, May 13: DAY FIFTY-FOUR (15 hrs, 4 1/2 hrs)

Some important occurrences yesterday.

I got the script of *Blue Velvet* from David (he again mentioned that the last third needs a complete reworking – I think he may really be asking for my suggestions).

We shot the old women sewing Jessica's cloak again in the morning – a pointless exercise, we felt, but it went better this time: Pablo was there to draw them out – and more importantly Anne Strick stayed away.

In the afternoon, we did a brief interview with John Dykstra – a lot of fun (though bad lighting spoiled the video); he's easy to interview – give him a reasonable question and he'll give a long, animated, interesting answer with a scattering of humour and anecdote.

A big scene in the evening, in the Great Hall in Arrakeen with Paul Smith (Rabban – he was the prison commandant in *Midnight Express* and did some action comedies in Italy, plus the Burt Lancaster *Moses* and *Masada*; huge as he is, he seems decent, sensitive and full of humour – obviously relishes the part of a villain). It was the first time I've seen David mishandle an actor – a Mexican who didn't speak enough English to be able to handle his lines (badly injured, he staggers in to report on the battle to Rabban); it was obvious very early that he would have to be dubbed, so his pronunciation really didn't matter – but his physical movements and his expression and tone were perfect. Yet David kept on drilling him in his lines – in front of everyone – until he was so upset and flustered that he lost the structure of them, let alone the pronunciation. He fell apart and it was obvious that everyone was losing patience with him. Finally they redesigned the whole shot, dropped the lines. Now Rabban grabs him, bellows, crushes his head in anger and throws him down – really threw him down. The poor guy bounced off the floor for about four takes. His terror, confusion, and pleading tone were all too real – and I felt that the grin he gave at the end of it all was a defensive one. The thing is, he was a nice guy but he never should have been cast because he couldn't handle the English lines. I felt bad about the whole thing – most of the other people there seemed to treat it all as a joke.

For most of the scene Pablo and I were alone. He's very good (he lit the bit with the woman and the cloak very well), seems able to handle the camera (I tried it again myself for a few minutes – it's really horribly difficult to hold it steady, let alone put a shot together).

Because Anatol went to show Raffaella the sample tape we put together (and one master from Monday). He said she was thoroughly enthused. She's going to call Armstrong ("that asshole Armstrong," she called him in front of

Strick) in *Cannes* today to tell him to ship us an editing system (a few weeks ago, Anatol asked her why she was just giving all this material away – apparently the idea sank in yesterday evening). She also came up with a fairly simple concept for this promo tape, so we don't have to try to be advertising men ourselves (I can't think that way) and told Anatol what material we can use in it. So our position might be secure now.

A bad rumour going around (I heard it from Doug Hersh): after having piled everything onto second unit and having refused to give Fred a decent crew, they're saying he's just a film-school kid who can't handle a professional job and he's on his way out. If true, it's an appallingly shitty deal and it'll generate a *lot* of very bad feeling, because everyone who knows Fred knows the impossible situation he's in.

A bad sign: Anatol mentioned that we've unfortunately been ignoring second unit until now and Raffaella replied, "Ignore them."

Another bad sign: when they were talking of this promo thing, the idea of a commentary came up. Raffaella turned to Strick and said she'd better get to work. So what am I? chopped liver? Armstrong hired me (supposedly) as a writer. Admittedly I don't want to write promo shit, but I should get first refusal.

Christina Espinoza got on the phone to the Amberes yesterday, spoke to the manager. This morning I moved to the fifth floor – lots more light, the sounds of the city replacing the air conditioner – and, unfortunately, due to the height, more radio interference on my stereo.

Sunday, May 15: DAY FIFTY-SIX (3 1/2 hrs)

We went to a party Friday evening – thrown in honour of the birthday of a woman we don't know. In a two-storey penthouse apartment with a terrace from which there was a wide view of the city. We arrived in our more or less usual gear – to find the place full of men in jackets and ties, young executive types. After a few hours it got really crowded (a lot of people from Churubusco) and Anatol got totally drunk (amplified by a lot of grass) – a condition in which he's fairly tedious.

Also at the party was the man who had such a rough time on Thursday evening in the Great Hall (also in a suit and tie) – a nice guy whose English is actually quite good. He was just inexperienced and nervous.

We went to the studio about eleven yesterday morning – due to shoot a training session with Kyle and Kiyoshi. We had trouble finding a place to do it. Finally went to the Y and got a yoga room – very light, but a lot of traffic noise (how people could possibly meditate there, I can't imagine) and simple anatomical charts on the wall showing digestive tract and male and female reproductive organs.

It was quite interesting to watch the Japanese sword training – Kyle has a brown belt in karate, so he's a very quick study. But Anatol wasn't in particularly good shape and approached it badly, not interested in a boring training film but rather in a "psychological study" – that is, he caught almost none of the action but went for interminable, repetitive facial closeups which show absolutely nothing of what's going on. He's got some very peculiar ideas as a cameraman…

We returned to Zona Rosa in the afternoon, needing to catch up on rest. But I wound up reading David's *Blue Velvet*. Parts of it are excellent (like the opening), but it has an unfinished feel to it, needs elaboration. The story of a young man whose life gets turned upside down, it contrasts a sunny world of young love and family life and crisis with a brutal underworld into which the guy's curiosity draws him. Parts of it have a kind of *Eraserhead* strangeness (it occasionally slips into a microscopic world), but the normal world it depicts is a little too ordinary, a little cliched while the darker underworld is a bit too predictable – I wanted the whole thing to shift more into strangeness, unreality, which is the direction the early part promises. But all that would require a complete rethinking of the script's world.

After reading it, I sat down and started outlining my own script in some detail, getting two-and-a-half pages done before I had to leave for another party – thrown by Tony Gibbs and Penny Shaw. Pablo drove us there, somewhere in the south of the city, an old area of narrow cobbled streets and large houses in high-walled gardens. Tony and Penny's place is gorgeous, loaded with art, high-ceilinged rooms, narrow winding staircases, a rooftop patio, large back garden in which a kind of pavilion had been set up – some Mexican caterers were making excellent food and there was an almost unending flow of wine and other liquid refreshment. It was a huge party, but not crowded and impossible like the one on Friday – I spent the night talking to all kinds of people, drinking vast quantities of wine, and opening up really for the first time since I came here. It was the most fun I've had in ages.

Speaking of Pablo: to our surprise (and a little embarrassment) we learned yesterday at the party that he's made a couple of documentaries (with Eric, from second unit, who apparently is a writer) which have won prizes in Mexico and Brazil. We'll try to set up a screening (one is in 16mm, the other Super-8).

Went up to the pool on top of the Royal this afternoon. Freddie Jones was up there – met him informally. He's exactly the same person as he is on screen.

Reread *Blue Velvet*. Made some notes on how I would change it (requiring alterations beginning on page twenty-three – not just in the final third as David said). I'll return the script, but I won't say anything unless he specifically asks. If he does ask, I might just give him my notes as the basis for later discussion.

Had supper with Greg and talked away half the evening – actually, he did most of the talking – a little bit like a book by Henry Miller – bizarre and amusing sexual escapades. Actually, I like Greg a lot – he's very open and straightforward and whatever he talks about, it doesn't come across as boasting.

By the way, Patsa – the Mexico City-based company which put together the facilities, etc. for *Dune* – has apparently gone belly-up. Dino has taken over completely, I understand (well, sort of; Universal is not just distributing, it's co-producing).

I suppose this might mean that Marie, the Swedish redhead to whom I sold my remaining U.S. dollars last week, might not be coming back when she returns from her trip to L.A. (She was the assistant to the Patsa liaison on *Dune* who has now, of course, departed our offices.)

Week Eight Documents

```
                    C A L L    S H E E T  (SECOND CAMERA)
PRODUCTION TITLE: "DUNE"              DATE: MONDAY MAY 7th, 1983.
PRODUCER: RAFFAELLA DE LAURENTIIS          *LUNES
DIRECTOR: FRED ELMES                  CREW CALL:8.00am at Studios.


SETS AND SCENE NUMBERS:           D/N         STAGE/LOCATION
(NEW TEST) INSERT-FILMBOOK- PLANETS    X         STAGE #4? or X
AND GALAXIES MOVE
*(NUEVA PRUEBA) INSERT-LIBRO/PELICULA-
PLANETAS Y GALAXIAS SE MUEVEN
Sc: 25A


NOTE: NO CAST                   *NOTA:   SIN ACTORES

REQUIREMENTS:

PRODUCTION: Check details in all Depts- Coffee Service on Stage.
           *Checar detalles en distintos Deptos - Servicio de Café en Foro.
CAMERA: Mitchell Mark II - Single Frame Motor *Motor de Cuadro por Cuadro-
        Backwards Motor *Motor de Reversa (Churubusco Studios) -16mm Projec-
        tor (With Projectionist)* (Con Proyeccionista)- 16mm Projector for
        this Sc. *Material de 16mm para esta Sc. - PLUS any other indication
        by Fred Elmes *MAS cualquier otra indicación de Fred Elmes.
ART: Art Work /PLANETS  *Trabajo de ARTE/PLANETAS.
PROPS: Filmbook  *Libro-película.
GRIP/ELECT: As per Fred Elmes instructions.   *Según instrucciones de Fred
                                                                    Elmes.
SP/FX: As discussed by Fred Elmes and Andrew Kelly.
      *Según lo discutido entre Fred Elmes y Andrew Kelly.


ADVANCED SCHEDULE: TUESDAY 10th, MAY, 1983.
                   INT. RESERVOIR-SIETCH TABR - (N)   LOC: WAREHOUSE
                   Sc: MONTAGE, 179A, 31pt.                *BODEGA


NOTE/PRODUCT: Standby Projectionist and Editing Assistant to check material
              as per Director's indications.
             *Pendientes Proyeccionista y Asistente de Edición para checar
              material según indicaciones de Director.




                                                    Jesús Marín
                                                    Assistant Director
```

Second unit call sheet, May 8, 1983 (mis-dated).

```
DUNE PRODUCTIONS LTD
PATSA PRODUCCIONES S.A.

                        MEMO

DE:  VICENTE ESCRIVA                May 9, 1983

A:   TODO EL PERSONAL

RE:  CAMBIOS EN EL PLAN DE RODAJE DE HOY, DIA 9 Y MAÑANA DIA 10 DE MAYO.

     EL COVER SET (INT. TUNNEL-LANDING PAD) previsto para hoy cambia por
     INT. ATREIDES SHIP - Stage 4 - sc. 55.

     Si disponemos de tiempo después de completar el rodaje en el Int.
     GURNEY'S ROOM en el foro 6, se se rodarán insertos en la habitación
     de Paul en Caladan.

     Para mañana 10 de Mayo:
     INT. TUNNEL, LANDING PAD - Stage 5 - sc. 93,93b y EXT. ATREIDES
     SHIP - Parking Lot - sc. 52 c. (noche).

     ─────────────────────

     CHANGES IN SCHEDULE SHOOTING FOR MAY 9 AND 10.

     COVER SET - INT. TUNNEL LANDING PAD scheduled for today, changes
     for INT. ATREIDES SHIP - Stage 4 - sc. 55.

     If disposing of time, on completition of INT. GURNEY'S ROOM - stage
     6, pick up on Paul Caladan's bedroom should be try.

     May 10.-

     INT. TUNNEL, LANDING PAD - Stage 5 - sc. 93, 93b and EXT. ATREIDES
     SHIP - Parking Lot - sc. 52 c. (night shooting).
```

Schedule changes, May 9, 1983.

```
CALL SHEET (SECOND CAMERA)

PRODUCTION TITLE: "DUNE"                    DATE: TUESDAY 10th, MAY 1983.
PRODUCER: RAFFAELLA DE LAURENTIIS                 *MARTES
DIRECTOR: FRED ELMES                        CREW CALL: 8.30am at Studios.


SETS AND SCENE NUMBERS                      D/N        STAGE/LOCATION

(NEW TEST) INSERT-FILMBOOK -PLANETS          X         STAGE #4
AND GALAXIES MOVE
*(NUEVA PRUEBA) INSERT-LIBRO/PELICULA-
PLANETAS Y GALAXIAS SE MUEVEN
Sc: 25 A


NOTE: NO CAST                               * NOTA: SIN ACTORES

REQUIREMENTS:

PRODUCTION: Check details in all Depts. - Coffee Service on Stage.
            *Checar detalles en distintos Deptos. - Servicio de Café en
                                                                    Foro.

CAMERA: Mitchell Mark II - Single/Frame Motor *Motor de Cuadro por Cuadro-
        Backwards Motor *Motor de Reversa (Churubusco Studios) -16mm Pro
        jector (With Projeccionist) *(Con Proyeccionista)- 16mm Film Ma
        terial for this Sc. *Material Fílmico de 16mm para esta Sc. -
        PLUS any other indication by Fred Elmes. *MAS cualquier otra in
        dicación de Fred Elmes.

ART: Art Work /PLANETS. *Trabajo de ARTE/ PLANETAS.

PROPS: Filmbook.  *Libro-película.

GRIP/ELECT: As per Fred Elmes instructions. *Según instrucciones de Fred
                                                                    Elmes.

SP/FX: As discussed by Fred Elmes and Andrew Kelly.
       *Según lo discutido entre Fred Elmes y Andrew Kelly.

TRANSPORT: Pick up Fred Elmes and Leslie Werner at respective Hotels at
           8.00am to come to Studios.
           *Recoger a Fred Elmes y Leslie Werner en Hoteles respectivos
           a las 8.00am para venir a Estudios.

NOTE/PRODUCTION: Standby Projeccionsit and Editing Assistant to check
                 material as per Director's indications.
                 *Pendientes Proyeccionista y Asistente de Edición para
                 checar material según indicaciones de Director.

NOTE/GRIP: Have ready 4 boards (1.20 by 2.40mts.) covered by BLACK velvet
           as per Andrew Kelly's (SP/FX) instructions.
           *Tener listos 4 bastidores (1.20 por 2.40mts) forrados con
           terciopelo NEGRO según instrucciones de Andrew Kelly (SP/FX).


ADVANCED SCHEDULE:      ? ? ?
```

Second unit call sheet, May 10, 1983.

```
                    C A L L   S H E E T  (SECOND CAMERA)

PRODUCTION TITLE: "DUNE"                    DATE: THURSDAY 12th, MAY, 1983.
PRODUCER: RAFFAELLA DE LAURENTIIS                 *JUEVES
DIRECTOR: FRED ELMES                        CREW CALL: 8.30am at Studios.
```

SETS AND SCENE NUMBERS | D/N | STAGE/LOCATION
INT. PAUL'S ROOM-ARRAKEEN PALACE | D | STAGE #4
(TO COMPLETE HUNTER-SEEKER PICKUPS)
*(PARA COMPLETAR Pickups de CAZADOR-BUSCADOR)

NOTE: NO CAST   *NOTA: SIN ACTORES

REQUIREMENTS:
PRODUCTION: Check details in all Departments-Coffee Service on Stage.
    *Checar detalles en distintos Deptos.- Servicio de Café en Foro.
CAMERA: Mitchell Mark II- Lightflex- Anamorphic lenses-MOY Gearhead.
SP/FX: As established by FIRST Camera and indications by Director.
    *Según lo establecido por PRIMERA Cámara e indicaciones del Director.

GRIPS   )
PROPS   )   As established by First Camera and indications by Director.
ELECT   )   *Según lo establecido por Primera Cámara e indicaciones del
ART   )   Director.

TRANSPORT: Pick up Fred Elmes and Leslie Werner at respective Hotels
           8.00am to come to Studios.
           *Recoger a Fred Elmes y Leslie Werner en Hoteles respectivos
           a las 8.00am para venir a Estudios.

ADVANCED SCHEDULE: FRIDAY 13th, MAY 1983.
                      INT. PAUL'S ROOM-ARRAKEEN PALACE   LOC: STAGE #4
                      (Paul opens Filmbook and activates
                      it) (D)
                      *(Paul abre un libro-película y lo
                      activa)
                      Sc: 78A Pt.
NOTE: Check with Fred Elmes and John Dykstra details for this Scene.
    *Checar con Fred Elmes y John Dykstra detalles para esta Escena.

                      SATURDAY 14th, MAY 1983.
                      INT. AUTOPSY ROOM-ARRAKEEN PALACE (D) LOC: METROPO-
                      INSERT-MONITOR- Yueh's hand picks   LITANO HOSPITAL
                      cylinder from Harkonnen's stomach.
                      *INT. CUARTO DE AUTOPSIA-PALACIO ARRAKEEN
                      Insert-Monitor- La mano de Yueh hurga
                      el estómago del Harkonnen para sacar
                      el cilindro.
                      Sc: 97A
NOTE: This Scene (97A) will First be Recorded in Video at Hospital and then be
      filmed at Studios.
    *Esta Escena (97A) será Grabada en Video en el Hospital primero, y
      posteriormente filmada en Estudios.

Second unit call sheet, May 12, 1983.

```
CALL SHEET (SECOND CAMERA)
PRODUCTION TITLE: "DUNE"                    DATE: FRIDAY MAY 13th, 1983.
PRODUCER: RAFFAELLA DE LAURENTIIS                *VIERNES
DIRECTOR: FRED ELMES                        CREW CALL: 8:00am at Studios.


SETS AND SCENE NUMBERS                D/N         STAGE/LOCATION
INT. PAUL'S ROOM-ARRAKEEN PALACE       D          STAGE #4
(TO COMPLETE Hunter-Seeker Pickups)
*(PARA COMPLETAR Pickups de Cazador-
 Sc: 80pt.                  BUSCADOR)


NOTE: NO CAST               *NOTA: SIN ACTORES

REQUIREMENTS:
PRODUCTION: Check details in all Depts-Coffee Service on Stage.
            *Checar detalles en distintos Deptos.- Servicio de Café en Foro.

CAMERA: Mitchell Mark II- Lightflex- Anamorphic lenses-MOY Gearhead.

SP/FX: As established by FIRST CAMERA and indications by Director.
       *Según lo establecido por Primera Cámara e indicaciones del Director.

GRIPS:   )
PROPS    ) As established by First Camera and indications by Director.
ELECT    )*Según lo establecido por Primera Cámara e indicaciones del Direc
ART      )                                                              tor.

TRANSPORT: Pick up Fred Elmes and Leslie Werner at Respective Hotels at
           7.30am to come to Studios.
           *Recoger a Fred Elmes y Leslie Werner en Hoteles respectivos a
            las 7.30am para venir a Estudios.

ADVANCED SCHEDULE:    SATURDAY MAY 14th, 1983.
                      *SABADO
                      INT. AUTOPSY ROOM-INSERT (D)LOC: HOSPITAL METROPOLITANO
                      (Yueh's hand picking cylinder
                       from Harkonnen's stomach)
                      *INT. CUARTO DE AUTOPSIA-INSERT
                      (Mano de Yueh saca cilindro de estómago
                       de Harkonnen)
                      Sc: 97A

NOTE: Standby Projeccionist to check material in the morning (8.30am)
      *Pendiente Proyeccionista para checar material en la mañana (8.30am).
```

Second unit call sheet, May 13, 1983.

```
                    CALL  SHEET              Production N° 33

PRODUCTION TITLE: "DUNE"                     DATE: Friday May 13th, 1983.
PRODUCER: RAFFAELLA DE LAURENTIIS   Half hour CREW CALL: 11:30 A.M. at Studio
DIRECTOR: DAVID LYNCH               later     LEAVE HOTEL: 11:00 A.M.
                                    1/2 hora tarde
```

Handwritten: "Half hour later 1/2 hora tarde"

SETS & SCENES NUMBERS :				LOCATION:			
1) INT. SUB BASEMENT PASSAGEWAY ARRAKEEN PALACE	Sc. 118	(N)		STAGE #6			
2) INT. SUB BASEMENT PASSAGEWAY ARRAKEEN PALACE	Sc. 115	(N)		STAGE #6			

ARTIST	CHARACTERS	D/R	P/U	M/U	WARD	ON SET
JURGEN PROCHNOW	DUKE LETO	203	11:00			11:30
DEAN STOCKWELL	DR. YUEH	205	11:00			11:30
LINDA HUNT	SHADOUT MAPES	216	11:00			11:30
			A LINE UP WILL TAKE PLACE BEFORE MAKE UP			

STAND-INS :					
A.N. OTHER	FOR DUKE LETO		11:00		11:30
A.N. OTHER	FOR DR. YUEH		11:00		11:30
A.N. OTHER	FOR SHADOUT MAPES		11:00		11:30

PRODUCTION REQUIREMENTS:

PRODUCTION:	Security guards in Stage #6-AD'S desk rigged to Stage lamp, bell and telephone-cofee service on stage and dress rooms *Guardias de seguridad en Foro #6-Mesa de Asst. Dir. conectada a luces campana y telefono-servicio de cafe en Foro y camerinos
CATERING:	DUNE Restaurant open from 1:00 PM.*Restaurant DUNE abierto desde la 1:00 PM.
PROPERTY:	Leto's ring-shield belt for Leto (Sc.118) /* Anillo de Leto-Cinturón escudo para Leto (Sc.118)
PROPERTY/ART:	Pin on Paul's door-Symbol on Paul's door /* Seguro en puerta de Paul-Simbolo en puerta de Paul
SP/FX:	Dart shot in Leto's shoulder/* Tiro de dardo en el hombro de Leto
MAKE UP & HAIR:	False tooth being place-2 teeth for Leto /* Diente falso siendo colocado-2 dientes para Leto
CAMERA:	As per Freddie Francis instructions /*Segun instrucciónes de Freddie Francis
ELECTRIC:	Lights going darker-Stand by generator rigged to Stage #6 *Luces apagandose - Planta generadora conectada a Foro #6
SOUND:	As per Nelson Stoll instructions /* Según instrucciones de Nelson Stoll

ADVANCE SHEDULE:

SATURDAY MAY 14th, 1983	TO COMPLETE:		
	INT. SUB BASEMENT PASSAGEWAY ARRAKEEN PALACE	Sc. 118,115	STAGE #6

First unit call sheet, May 13, 1983.

```
                    CALL  SHEET.    FOR VISTAVISION UNIT.

PRODUCTION TITTLE :  DUNE                     DATE : Friday May 13th, 1983
PRODUCER  :  RAFFAELLA DE LAURENTIIS          CREW CALL:  8.00am at Studios
DIRECTOR  :  DAVID LYNCH                      LEAVE HOTEL : 7.30am then to Studios


SCENE & SETS NUMBER :                         LOCATION :  WAREHOUSE- IZTAPALAPA
1) INT.RESERVOIR-SIETCH TABR-   Sc.: 179a (N)             BODEGA.
   (Paul's P.O.V water.)
2) INT.RESERVOIR-SIETCH TABR.   (montage)
   (tracking shot)


CROWD .                         AT STUDIOS    WARD.ON LOC.    ON SET

2 WATERMASTERS                  8.00am        8.30am          9.00am
4 FREMEN                        8.00am        8.30am          9.00am
  ISABELLE CLEMENTE             8.00am        8.30am          9.00am


PRODUCTION REQUIRMENTS:
PRODUCTION :          2 security guards on Loc.-coffee service on set-Doctor on Set-
                      radio communication W/ Prod.Office-5 mirrors to be broken.
                   *  2 guardias de seguridad en Loc.-cafe en Loc.-Doctor en Loc.-
                      comunicacion radio con Oficina de Prod.-5 espejos para romper.
CATERING :            Lunch ready from 12.30 noon for 60 people /* comida lista desde
                      las 12.30  para 60 personas .
SP/FX :               Dolly-water drop effect./* dolly-efecto de gota de agua-
WARDROBE :            Alfonso Govea & Horacio Martinez to attend crowd (8.00am at Studios)
                   *  Alfonso Govea y Horacio Martinez atender figuracion (8.00am en Estud.)
MAKE UP  :            Magdalena Eriz,Agripina Lozada & Humberto Escamilla (8.00am at Stud.)
                      Make up will take place on Loc./*se maquillara en Loc.

GRIPS :               6 pieces of wood + 6 triplay + 1 saw
                   *  6 tablones + 6 triplay + 1 sierra.

CAMERA :              As per J.Dykstra's inst./* según inst. de J.Dykstra.
ELECT.                Moving glow globe (Macarrone)/* globo brillo moviendose(Macarrone)
                      1 AC generator (2.000WTS) ready on Loc. at 8.00am.
                      2. DC generator (1.200WTS) ready on Loc. at 8.00am.
                      1 Macarrone Assistant & cable for Camera/*1 asst. de Macarrone & cable
PROPS :               Water containers-weapons for Fremen-water rings-dipsticks- water
                      meter (stand by)- 2 metal trays.
                   *  Contenedores de agua- armas para Fremen-anillos de agua-varillas
                      musicales-medidor de agua (estar preparado)-2 bandejas de metal.
TRANSPORTATION:

APOGEE COMBI                  7.30am    J.DYKSTRA & CREW
CAMERA COMBI   (at Stud.) 8.00am        For equipment
1 BUS          (at Stud.) 8.00am        For Crew & Crowd
1 COMBI        (at Stud.) 8.00am        For Make up & Wardrobe Crew (+ equipment + costumes)
1 TRUCK        (at Stud.) 8.00am        For facilities
1 PROP TRUCK   (at Stud.) 8.00am        Props equipment
1 PRODUCTION CAR    "     8.00am        For any emergency.
```

VistaVision unit call sheet, May 13, 1983.

```
         C A L L    S H E E T  (SECOND CAMERA)
PRODUCTION TITLE: "DUNE"              DATE: SATURDAY MAY 14th, 1983.
PRODUCER: RAFFAELLA DE LAURENTIIS           *SABADO
DIRECTOR: FRED ELMES                  CREW CALL: 8.00am at Studios.


SETS AND SCENE NUMBERS                D/N          STAGE/LOCATION
INT. PAUL'S ROOM-ARRAKEEN PALACE      D            STAGE #4
(TO COMP. HUNTER-SEEKER Pickups)
*(PARA COMP. pickups de CAZADOR-
                       BUSCADOR)
Sc: 80pt.


NOTE: NO CAST                    *NOTA: SIN ACTORES


REQUIREMENTS:

PRODUCTION: Check details in all Depts- Coffee Service on Stage.
           *Checar detalles en distintos Deptos - Servicio de Café en Foro.
CAMERA: Mitchell Mark II- Lightflex- Anamorphic lenses- MOY Gearhead.
SP/FX: As established by FIRST Camera and Director's indications.
      *Según lo establecido por PRIMERA Cámara e indicaciones del Director.
GRIPS   )
PROPS   )  As established by FIRST Camera and indications by Director.
ELECT   ) *Según lo establecido por PRIMERA Cámara e indicaciones del
ART     )  Director.
CATERING: SNACK ready from 11.00am for 30 people.
         *SNACK listo desde las 11.00am para 30personas.


ADVANCED SCHEDULE:    ?  ?  ?



TRANSPORT: Pick up Fred Elmes and Leslie Werner at respective Hotels/ 7.30am
           to come to Studios.
          *Recoger a Fred Elmes y Leslie Werner en Hoteles respectivos a
           las 7.30am para venir a Estudios.

   NOTE: Standby Projeccionist to check material in the morning(since 8am.
        *Pendiente Proyeccionista para checar material en la mañana desde
         las 8.00am.
```

Second unit call sheet, May 14, 1983.

Week 9: May 16-22, 1983

Monday, May 16: DAY FIFTY-SEVEN (9 1/2 hrs)

Things changed a little today. As we were driven to the studio this morning, Anatol explained an idea he had: rather than waste Pablo we should make maximum use of him – that is, not shut him away in our office. He could record sound as Anatol shot – and I could act as line producer, keeping a running log as we shoot, pointing them in the right direction, keeping track of what's going on. So we tried it.

Actually, it's quite easy to keep a rough, but fairly detailed record of what's being shot as it's shot. In all, it worked out quite well – we suddenly found ourselves more coordinated, moving around a lot more but not getting so exhausted.

At breakfast we learned in passing from Doug that they're building the spice miner on the backlot (Strick hasn't been keeping us up on things at all, so we'll just shut her out – she's of no use). So we went to get that (a beautiful piece of work, still under construction). Happened to notice something else going on behind the rock wall – a vast set for the Hall of Rites (about two-hundred feet long, it's to be magnified vastly by an Al Whitlock glass painting). So we got all that.

Then we got a little in Giorgio's set decoration shop. Spoke to Aldo Puccini and discovered that they're building the bridge across the gorge at Aguilas Rojas. So we went there after lunch, caught some of that, and got a little interview with Aldo (a marvellous character who started at Cinecitta in his late teens, worked with Fellini, and has made films all over the place) – though we were told it would be almost impossible to get him to talk, he's actually very articulate and very willing.

Then we returned to the studio and finally shot Fred and his unit on Stage 4, doing a hunter-seeker wire shot. He's still having trouble – three times in the last two shooting days, the film has run out during a take – because the guy responsible "forgets".

Things are looking up, then. I just hope to keep abreast of what's going on and push Anatol a little to get him to shoot things he may not be all that interested in personally. As for Pablo, he seems to be very good, just has to get used to what he's doing – as it is, he seems able to anticipate what is necessary – he doesn't have to be pushed.

We asked Raffaella this afternoon if it would be possible to get one of her spare Nagras from the States (Nelson is going to help us set up a better sound

Giorgio Desideri's set decoration shop, Estudios Churubusco.

system, using a Nagra as a pre-amp so Pablo can regulate the sound going into the recorder on the camera) – she immediately had Golda get on the direct line to New York – and we're going to get it. All in a matter of moments. She seems to be very favourable towards us now.

I saw David in the corridor at lunch, spoke to him. Said I'd read *Blue Velvet*. He asked how I liked it. I said parts of it were very good. But it needs work, he said. I said I'd made notes on how I'd alter it – but maybe he'd be offended. Very, he joked. Said we'd get together to talk about it later. But I don't really know how much he wants to hear my suggestions – not too much, I suspect.

Bought some cassettes this evening: Orff's *Carmina Burana* and *Catulli Carmina*; Beethoven's Sixth and Ninth; and ABC's *Lexicon of Love*. Very cheap – sixteen, seventeen dollars for all five – but probably with quality to match.

We hope to have Eric come along on the picnic next Sunday because what before seemed a vague and impracticable idea now appears quite plausible – to make a short film here in Mexico City. Both Pablo and Eric have experience (those documentaries) and Eric is a writer.

We envision a short (at most one hour) piece in which a poor, illiterate man leaves his village (a pastoral scene) and comes to the city in hopes of finding a means of survival. It would be a phantasmagorical descent into an urban hell – all the things we dislike about the city – the crowding, the pollution, the poverty, the false sense of westernized progress. The man would be sucked in and destroyed, left dead in a dump somewhere (pulling back to a panoramic helicopter shot of the vast city which devoured him).

Fremen Great Hall set, backlot, Estudios Churubusco.

If we can work out a fairly simple script, we'd try to make enough spare time to produce it.

Wednesday, May 18: DAY FIFTY-NINE (8 1/2 hrs, 9 1/2 hrs)

Fairly slow day yesterday. The Universal executives who flew in Monday evening didn't bring *any* of our equipment (not even the wide-angle lens) which has been sitting around at Bexel for three weeks. They want us to do a good job, but they won't lift a finger to help (no one told them about the stuff, they said – although one of them was here a couple of weeks ago and heard about it then).

So we weren't too well disposed to jump up and shoot them on their tour of the studio. Luckily, as always, there wasn't enough light on the sets for our camera. But in the afternoon we followed them to the backlot – an excruciating experience; they know nothing about movie-making (will the huge half spice miner braced with all kinds of wood framing actually roll around the sand?). And they gave off a constant stream of absolutely witless "jokes". We eventually fled – along with George [Whitear], the stills photographer.

Speaking of George, I get along with him quite well (as I do with most of the English), though he looks like a debauched old satyr (whose facial twitches and nasal problems hint at long-time use of certain chemical powders). But it's becoming very difficult not to believe that he's actively interfering with us on the set – certainly, there are only a few really good vantage points from which to catch the action – but time and again, he jams his bald patch right in front of our lens, a few inches to either side simply will not do – so shot after shot is ruined by his gleaming dome. Why? Maybe he considers us competition – ridiculous, but possibly true.

Raffaella ran around excitedly yesterday afternoon and shipped us off to Azteca Stadium. The big VistaVision shot of twenty-five hundred soldiers originally scheduled for yesterday was pushed back a week – but someone failed to tell someone else – and the army arrived early yesterday afternoon, all ready to go. So we had to go out there and tape the scene – unfortunately, not being a news crew, we didn't think until afterwards that we should have interviewed some of them – so we've got a bunch of pointless shots of soldiers with no explanation. But maybe we can grab a few next week and get them to talk about it.

We heard later that the major who had taken the cancellation message has been arrested.

It's going to take me a while to get used to on-the-spot logging. When the shoot is slow (as at Azteca), I can get most of the shots, checking with Anatol as we go along. But when it gets fast (as on stage in the evening as they rushed to get a shot finished – the crew have refused to work such long hours), I obviously can't be very detailed. I tried and it was a mess.

But it may work out.

At supper yesterday evening, I told Anatol another of my story ideas – one I've been trying to develop on and off for years (ever since seeing that huge unfinished spaceship set in Fellini's *8 1/2*). And he liked it immediately – better than the Paris one.

And speaking of Paris, we're beginning to think it might be a good idea to take a, say, two-week break in the middle of this job and hop over to Europe – scout some locations as it were around the middle of July (Bastille Day, the two-hundredth anniversary of hot-air ballooning…). I could even take a quick side-trip to England, and Anatol could drop in on his ex-wife in Brussels. For the first time in my life I can actually contemplate such a thing without worrying about the money.

Thursday, May 19: DAY SIXTY (7 hrs)

Didn't shoot much yesterday – a bit in the 'thopter cave, Stage 5. Had to put off the interview with Max again – he was exhausted by the heat and on-set line changes.

It turned out to be a pity that we didn't shoot more of those executives – as George predicted, it was the funniest thing we've done yet – they're such total idiots … like an old-time comedy team.

Max Von Sydow as Dr. Liet Kynes, planetary ecologist. Photograph copyright Universal/De Laurentiis.

Some of our test equipment apparently arrived on Saturday – customs called yesterday. There was no prior notification, no copy of the manifest – we had to call L.A. to find out what had been sent. Anatol also spoke to Armstrong – saying how excellently everything is working out. Both he and Anne told him that I'm now acting as line producer – I'm not sure that's such a good thing.

Friday, May 20: DAY SIXTY-ONE (8 1/2 hrs)

An odd day yesterday. So much has changed so radically that it sometimes hits me with a shock – in the midst of it, I'm generally not aware of the difference.

Three months ago, tell me that I would spend half an hour interviewing Max von Sydow and that I'd come away with something pretty good – and it would have been inconceivable. Yet I did it yesterday with scarcely a qualm. And with decent results. (Anatol and Pablo say they think I'm a good interviewer – I don't say much but I can key the victim and get him talking about things that interest him.)

Not to mention that I'm running around, talking to people, arranging things – me, who used to hate dealing with new people. (Anatol pointed out something I hadn't really been aware of: on Wednesday when we got news of the shipment, I went straight into Strick's office, said what had happened and that we had to call L.A. immediately to find out what had been sent – and she picked up the phone immediately and put through three calls – like a secretary; Anatol says I've begun acting like a producer.)

I visited Bob and Greg on Stage 8 in the afternoon, where they're setting up the second front projection screen – the backing is up, the reflector has to be applied now – from a scaffold which goes up forty-five feet. It's about five feet

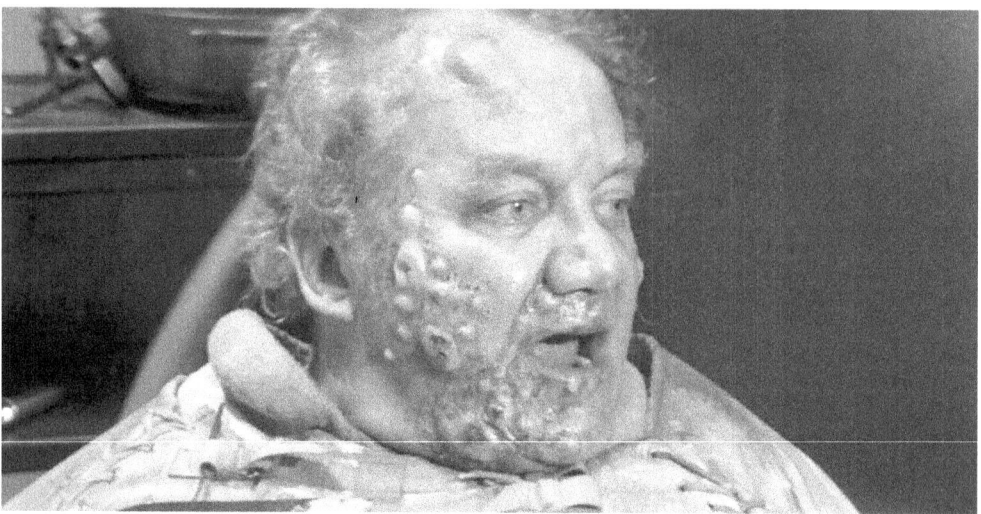

*Kenneth McMillan as the pustulent Baron Vladimir Harkonnen.
Photograph copyright Universal/De Laurentiis.*

wide and ten, twelve feet long and on wheels. Greg got me to climb it. I was scared shitless. But afterwards I followed him up to the stage catwalks, sixty feet up – I was terrified – but I went through with it for some reason – Greg deliberately applying the necessary peer pressure (we discussed it as we did it).

We left the studio early – four – in Pablo's VW Rabbit (or Caribe as they're called here). Went looking for humidifiers. I bought one for a hundred bucks. (We got our per diem a day early) – a Sharp, made in Japan. Also some tapes – Anatol got [Jean-Michel] Jarre's *China Concerts* for eight hundred pesos, the last copy they had. Looked in on a bookstore, drove around. A pleasant change of pace.

Pablo lives in a beautiful residential area near here. Obviously from our situation – existing just between the Zona Rosa and Churubusco – we have no real concept of the city at all.

Not too bad of a day. We shot a test of the Baron's flying rig this morning – with Ken McMillan in his fat suit. It looked very good. But we didn't get a chance to talk to McMillan before the test – I was a little worried about that.

So at lunch I introduced us to him and invited him to come and see the tape – so he did, right after lunch, with Bob Ringwood (in charge of the wardrobe department – and thus the fat suit), plus a whole bunch of other people (including Golda). It went over very well – and once again we've proved our usefulness (the effects people in charge of the rig also want to see it).

David had visited with Dino and Raffaella to check the rig out, so we got a little footage of them. Then Dino looked into our room just in time to see his own face on screen – all grainy and smeared at eighteen dBs amplification. Said something unintelligible to Ken McMillan, then left. The closest we've come to actually meeting him.

Visited the model and miniatures shops on the backlot this afternoon – not much happening. Most of it was all done before shooting started.

The spice harvester on the backlot dunes is looking very impressive – bigger all the time, and being given a fine corroded finish.

Before leaving this evening, I went over to first unit to ask Max to sign a release. He was very nice about it (I hated to hand him the thing). We shook hands; I said what a pleasure it had been and I hoped we'd meet again. He wished us luck on our project ...

Made a dupe of Jarre's *China Concerts* in the office today. Don't know why I didn't do it before I left home.

Saturday, May 21: DAY SIXTY-TWO (8 hrs)

Missed Fred shooting inserts for an autopsy scene today.

The picnic tomorrow has been cancelled – Pablo's wife has gone to visit a friend in another town and he'll join her there tonight.

So another dull weekend for yours truly (it's about eight now and I'm all alone in my room – as usual everyone else already had plans and disappeared for the evening). Wrote a long letter to Peter – and a brief card to Tim.

Might have a late supper with Fred –

Sting isn't the only actor flying in tomorrow – Jack Nance is due to arrive too.

I asked David if we could get together to talk about *Blue Velvet*. Sure – when *Dune* is finished with. He can't think about anything else at this stage ...

Huge thunderstorm this evening with some spectacular flashes of lightning above the city.

Spent the evening watching Alexander Mackendick's *Sammy Going South* on TV, a film I always enjoy (an awful image – TV here is technically lousy).

Fred called halfway through – didn't feel like supper – so I haven't eaten. Might as well just go to bed.

Sunday, May 22: DAY SIXTY-THREE

Slept until sometime after eleven. Walked over to the Royal (saw Sting on the street with a few other people, including Golda). Had breakfast by the pool, did some writing – beginning a more detailed outline of the early part of the Paris script.

Raffaella was very friendly towards me for some reason – chatted a little, called me George a number of times (she was reading a new version of *Conan II*).

Wrote, drank beer, chatted on and off with a few people. Got some sun.

Visited Greg in his room, had a couple of drinks, talked a while about writing, future plans, women…

Had to eat by myself (a tough steak at Denny's).

Should try to write a bit more before going to bed…

Week Nine Documents

```
CALL   SHEET.                    Production N° 37

PRODUCTION TITTLE :  DUNE                        DATE :  Wednesday May 18th,1983
PRODUCER  :  RAFFAELLA DE LAURENTIIS              CREW CALL:   8.00am at Studio.
DIRECTOR  :  DAVID LYNCH                          LEAVE HOTEL :7.30am .

SET & SCENES NUMBERS :                           LOCATION :
INT.TUNNEL-ARRAKEEN PALACE .    Sc.: 93pt, 93b pt. (D)       STAGE #5
```

ARTIST	CHARACTERS	D/R	P/U	M/U	ON SET
KYLE MacLACHLAN	PAUL	218	7.30am	after line up	8.00am
JURGEN PROCHNOW	DUKE LETO	203	"	"	"
MAX VON SYDOW	DR.KYNES	204	"	"	"
PATRICK STEWART	GURNEY	208	"	"	"

STAND-INS :
GONZALO IRIGOYEN	FOR PAUL		7.30am	8.00am
JERRY TEAGE O'HEA	FOR LETO		"	"
ANDRES B.ZBROWCZEK	FOR KYNES		"	"
ENRIQUE RODRIGUEZ	FOR GURNEY		"	"

STUNTS : R.HUMPHREYS,W.HARPER,K.YAMASUKI stand by at Studio from 8.00am.
          R.HUMPHREYS,W.HARPER wardrobe fitting at 10.00am at Studio.

CROWD :
12 ATREIDES GUARDS (Arrakeen uniform)   8.00am   9.00am
11 FREMEN GUARDS (stillsuits)   8.00am   9.00am

PRODUCTION REQUIREMENTS:
PRODUCTION : Security guards in Stage #5-keep out all particular use vehicles from
              the front of Stages #3,#4,#5,#6-A.D's desk rigged to Stage #5 lights
              bell & telephone-mobile dress rooms for actors- coffee service .
            * Vigilancia en Foro #5- dejar entrada de Foros #3,#4,#5,#6, libre de
              todos carros particulares- mesa de Asst.Dir.conectada a luces,campana
              y telefono de Foro #5-camerinos moviles para actores- cafe como usual

CATERING :   Dune's Restaurant open from 1.00pm/*Restaurante de Dune abierto
              desde la 1.00pm.
PROPERTY :   Device to activate ornithopter wings-weapons for guards-Fremen crys-
              knives /* aparato para activar alas del ornithopter-armas para
              Fremen- cuchillos para Fremen-
SP/FX /ART: Last part of the wings opening -/*ultima parte de las alas abriendose
              Tunnel door rigged to open /* puertas tunel conectada para abrir
CAMERA :   As per F.Francis inst./*Según inst. de F.Francis.
ELECTRIC.:   Stand by generators rigged to Stage #5 /generadores preparados conec-
              tados a Foro #5.
SOUND :   As per N.Stoll inst./*según N.Stoll inst.
NOTE :   John Dykstra to supervise thopter opening./*John Dykstra supervisar
              apertura del thopter.

                                                       J.Lopez Rodero
                                                       Assistant Director.

ADVANCE SCHEDULE :   Thursday May 19th,1983.
                     TO COMPLETE :
                     INT.TUNNEL -ARRAKEEN PALACE.   Sc.:93pt,93bpt(D)   STAGE #5

                     Friday May 20th ,1983
                     INT.GURNEY'S ROOM-ARRAKEEN.   Sc.:109 (N)   STAGE #6
```

*First unit call sheet, May 18, 1983.*
```

```
                    CALL SHEET (SECOND CAMERA)
PRODUCTION TITLE: "DUNE"                    DATE: WEDNESDAY MAY 18th, 1983
PRODUCER: RAFFAELLA DE LAURENTIIS                 *MIERCOLES
DIRECTOR: FRED ELMES                        CREW CALL: 8.30am at Studios.


SETS AND SCENE NUMBERS                      D/N          STAGE/LOCATION
INT. PAUL'S ROOM-ARRAKEEN PALACE             D            STAGE# 4
(TO COMP. HUNTER-SEEKER Pickups)
*(PARA COMP. Pickups de CAZADOR-
                    BUSCADOR)
Sc: 80pt.


NOTE: PICKUPS WITHOUT ARTISTS/SOUND
NOTA: PICKUPS SIN ACTORES Y SIN SONIDO


REQUIREMENTS:
PRODUCTION: Check details with allDepts- Coffee Service on Stage.
           *Checar detalles en distintos Deptos-Servicio de Café en Foro.
CAMERA: Mitchell Mark II- Lightflex-Anamorphic lenses- MOY Gearhead.
SP/FX: As established by First Camera and Director's indications.
      *Según lo establecido por Primera Cámara e indicaciones del Director.
GRIPS:   )
PROPS    ) As established by First Camera and indications by Director.
ELECT    ) *Según lo establecido por Primera Cámara e indicaciones del
ART      )  Director.

TRANSPORT: Pick up Fred Elmes and Leslie Werner at respective hotels/8.00am
           to come to Studios.
          *Recoger a Fred Elmes y Leslie Werner en hoteles respectivos a las
           8.00am para venir a Estudios.
NOTE: Standby Projectionist and Editing Assistant to check material.
     *Pendientes Proyeccionista y Asistente de Edición para checar material.

   NOTE: TEST will be done with 16mm Projector interlocked to 35mm Camera.
        *Se hará PRUEBA con el Proyector de 16mm amarrado a Cámara de 35mm.


ADVANCED SCHEDULE:     COVER SET:  STAGE #4
                   1) INT. PAUL'S ROOM-ARRAKEEN PALACE (D)
                      (TO COMP. HUNTER-SEEKER PICKUPS)
                      *(PARA COMP. Pickups de CAZADOR-BUSCADOR)
                      Sc: 80pt.
                   2) INT. PAUL'S ROOM-ARRAK. PALACE (D)
                      (Paul opens filmbook and activates it)
                      *(Paul abre un libro-película y lo activa)
                      SHOT with John Dykstra
                      *SHOT con J. Dykstra
                      Sc: 78A pt.
                   3) INT. PAUL'S ROOM-ARRAK. PALACE (D)
                      SECOND CAMERA SHOT (PART)
                      (Windows glow white light)
                      *(Ventanas brillan con luz blanca)
                      Sc: 78B pt.
```

Second unit call sheet, May 18, 1983.

```
           C A L L   S H E E T  (SECOND CAMERA)
PRODUCTION TITLE: "DUNE"                DATE: THURSDAY MAY 19th, 1983.
PRODUCER: RAFFAELLA DE LAURENTIIS             *JUEVES
DIRECTOR: FRED ELMES                    CREW CALL: 8.00am at Studios.

SETS AND SCENE NUMBERS                  D/N       STAGE/LOCATION
INT. PAUL'S ROOM-ARRAKEEN PALACE         D        STAGE #4
(TO COMP. HUNTER-SEEKER Pickups)
*(PARA COMP. Pickups de CAZADOR-
                       BUSCADOR)
Sc: 80pt.

NOTE: PICKUPS WITHOUT ARTISTS/SOUND
*NOTA: PICKUPS SIN ACTORES Y SIN SONIDO

REQUIREMENTS:
PRODUCTION: Check details in all Depts-Coffee Service on Stage.
     *Checar detalles en distintos Deptos-Servicio de Café en Foro.
CAMERA: Mitchell Mark II-Lightflex-Anamorphic lenses- MOY Gearhead.
SP/FX: As established by first Camera and Director's indications.
     *Según lo establecido por la Primera Cámara e indicaciones del Di-
                                                                rector.
GRIPS    )
PROPS    ) As established by First Camera and indications by Director.
ELECT    )*Según lo establecido por Primera Cámara e indicaciones del
ART      )                                                    Director.

TRANSPORT: Pick up Fred Elmes and Leslie Werner at respective hotels at
     7.30 am to come to Studios.
          *Recoger a Fred Elmes y Leslie Werner en hoteles respectivos a
           las 7.30 am para venir a Estudios.
NOTE: Standby Projeccionist and Editing Assistant to check material.
     *Pendientes Proyeccionista y Asistente de Edición para checar material.




ADVANCED SCHEDULE:       COVER SET:  STAGE#4
                    1) INT. PAUL'S ROOM-ARRAKEEN PALACE (D)
                       (TO COMP. HUNTER-SEEKER Pickups)
                      *(PARA COMP. Pickups de CAZADOR-BUSCADOR)
                       Sc: 80pt.
                    2) INT. PAUL'S ROOM-ARRAK. PALACE (D)
                       (Paul opens filmbook and activates it)
                       SHOT with John Dykstra
                      *(Paul abre un libro-película y lo activa)
                       SHOT con John Dykstra
                       Sc: 76A pt.


SATURDAY  MAY 21st, 1983:
*SÁBADO                    INT. AUTOPSY ROOM-ARRAK. PALACE -INSERT
                           (Yueh picks cylinder from dead Harkonnen's
                            stomach)
                          *(Yuen hurga cilindro en estómago de Harkonnen
                            muerto)
                           Sc: 97A     LOC: HOSPITAL METROPOLITANO
NOTE: THIS SC. will be recorded in Video at Hospital, and later on Filmed
      at Churubusco Studios.
     *Esta SC. será grabada en Video en el Hospital y posteriormente FILMADA
      en los Estudios Churubusco.

                                                  Jesús Marín
                                               Assisstant Director
```

Second unit call sheet, May 19, 1983.

\	"D U N E" SHOOTING SCHEDULE FOR THE WEEK FROM 23rd THRU MAY 30th,1983. FIRST CAMERA .			May 20th,1983.
DATE	SETS	SCENE N°	LOCATION	CAST
MONDAY 23rd MAY TUESDAY 24th MAY	INT.TRAINING ROOM – CASTLE CALADAN .	Sc.25 (N) 25b 25c	STAGE #1	PAUL GURNEY DR.YUEH THUFIR Crowd : 15 Atreides guards
WEDNESDAY 25th MAY	1) INT.TRAINING ROOM – CASTLE CALADAN. Stand by : 2) INT.OBSERVATION ROOM – ARRAKEEN PALACE .	Sc.25c (N) to complete Sc.84,87(D)	STAGE #1 STAGE #4	PAUL GURNEY DR.YUEH THUFIR Crowd : 15 Atreides guards PAUL DUKE LETO GURNEY THUFIR Crowd : 8 Atreides generals 6 Atreides sub-lieutenan
THURSDAY 26th MAY	INT.OBSERVATION ROOM – ARRAKEEN PALACE .	Sc.84,87 (D)	STAGE #4	PAUL DUKE LETO GURNEY THUFIR Crowd : 8 Atreides generals 6 Atreides sub-lieutenan
FRIDAY 27th MAY	INT.PASSAGEWAY-OBSERVATION ROOM ARRAKEEN PALACE . INT.OBSERVATION ROOM – ARRAKEEN PALACE .	Sc.131c (N) Sc.133 (N)	STAGE #4 STAGE #4	DUKE LETO DR.YUEH FEYD Small parts: 2 Large Sardaukars 6 Harkonnen soldiers BARON PITER YUEH DUKE LETO Double for Baron
SATURDAY 28th MAY	INT.OBSERVATION ROOM – ARRAKEEN PALACE . INT.PASSAGEWAY-OBSERVATION ROOM- ARRAKEEN PALACE . INT.VESTIBULE-OBSERVATION ROOM-ARRAKEEN PALACE .	Sc.133 (N) to complete Sc.136,139b (N) Sc.137(N) Sc.139c	STAGE #4	BARON PITER YUEH DUKE LETO FEYD NEFUD Crowd : 4 Harkonnen soldiers Double for BARON
MONDAY 30th MAY	TO COMPLETE THE ABOVE MENTIONED SCENES.			

Weekly shooting schedule First Camera, May 23–30, 1983.

				Page 3
	RED CAMERA IN CONJUNCTION WITH BLUE CAMERA .			
DATE	SETS	SCENE N°	LOCATION	CAST
MONDAY 23rd MAY	INT.RESERVOIR -SIETCH TABR.	Sc.179c retake : tracking shot .	Warehouse Iztapalapa	
TUESDAY 24th MAY	1) EXT.GROUNDS,ARRAKEEN PALACE.	Sc.284pt (DUSK) MATTE	PARKING LOT/ STADIUM	Crowd : 25 FREMEN (in costume) 2500 ARMY (no ward.request)
	2) EXT.STEEL TENT DOOR,ARRAKEEN GROUNDS.	Sc.274pt (N) MATTE		
WEDNESDAY 25th MAY	REST DAY AFTER NIGHT WORK			
THURSDAY 26th MAY	EXT.HARVESTER -DESERT .	Sc.105, Sc.106pt (D)	BACK LOT	SPICE MINER #1 SPICE MINER #2 Crowd : 24 Spice miners
FRIDAY 27th MAY	INT.TRAINING ROOM- CASTLE CALADAN . (fight,robot,blue backing, plates, pick ups)	Sc.25pt 25b pt 25c pt (N)	STAGE #1	Stunt Double for PAUL Stunt double for GURNEY
SATURDAY 28th MAY MONDAY 30th MAY	INT.TRAINING ROOM - CASTLE CALADAN .	to complete Sc.above mentioned.		

Weekly shooting schedule Red & Blue Cameras, May 23–30, 1983.

	GREEN CAMERA .		Page 4	
DATE	SETS	SCENE N°	LOCATION	CAST.
MONDAY 23rd MAY TUESDAY 24th MAY	INT.PAUL'S ROOM - CASTLE CALADAN . Hunter seeker	Sc.80pt	STAGE #4	
WEDNESDAY 25th MAY	INT.PAUL'S ROOM - CASTLE CALADAN.	Sc.78a (filmbook) Sc.78b (glowing window for dropplets)	STAGE #4	
THURSDAY 26th MAY	INT.TRAINING ROOM - CASTLE CALADAN . Filmbook	Sc.25pt	STAGE 1	PAUL
FRIDAY 27th MAY	INSERTS : Filmbook. Harkonnen machine . Kynes' stillsuit torn.	Sc.113a(D) 113b(D) 85pt(D) 145pt (N)	STAGE #5	Dead Harkonnen Double for Dr.KYNES
SATURDAY 28th MAY MONDAY 30th MAY	INT.SUB BASEMENT PASSAGEWAY- ARRAKEEN PALACE . (dart on Duke Leto's dropping high speed.)	Sc.118pt (N)	STAGE #6	Double for : Shadout Mapes (T.B.C.)

Weekly shooting schedule Green Camera, May 23-30, 1983.

Week 10: May 23-29, 1983

Thursday, May 26: DAY SIXTY-SEVEN (7 hrs, 13 hrs, 8 hrs, 7 1/2 hrs)

Anatol ran into Jack [Nance] with Fred Sunday evening, told him I was down here. Monday, I introduced myself to him in the office – he didn't make the connection at first. He hadn't read the article (I lent him a copy Monday evening – yesterday he said he'd started reading it and liked it so far).

Fremen Great Hall, backlot, Estudios Churubusco.

We were testing our wireless mic Monday morning when Cristina Monterubio came upstairs and said David wanted to see us on set. That's never happened before – so of course I got paranoid about it. When we got there, he was talking to Jack – he asked us to show him over the production. So we wound up giving Jack a guided tour of the stages, the backlot, and – after lunch – Aguilas Rojas. He was impressed – and for us it was great, since we've become so used to it all, to see it again with fresh eyes.

We didn't shoot anything that day and left the studio early. I wrote for a couple of hours (the Paris outline), then called Jack to invite him to supper. I went up to his room at the Century (the single most obnoxious hotel I've encountered – for some reason all the rooms are round, with round beds and round baths). He'd told us earlier he was on the wagon, but he had several beers at lunch – and when I got there he'd already had quite a bit of booze. He continued to drink at supper and afterwards, back in his room. After two dry years, he's suddenly hitting it again, hard.

He's very intense, often elliptical. I find his conversation hard to follow at times – and his soft voice doesn't help. He was quite passionate about Mexico and the state it's been driven into. When I left, he was quite pissed.

As I was wasting away by myself Sunday evening, Anatol was at Raffaella's with John Dykstra and Marty. From there, they went to La Pergola, where he got drunk. He said she was impressed to see me working Sunday afternoon on my script – and he told her I was the best writer he's met in ten years (he keeps telling people that). So he started talking again of trying to get her to back our project.

Sting makes his entrance as Feyd Rautha, stepping out of the shower.
Photograph copyright Universal/De Laurentiis.

By the way, she approves of Pablo, and gave the okay for Arturo to work with us.

Tuesday we shot another flying test with Ken McMillan – on a different set with a different kind of rig. We met Sting, who seemed quite friendly. Asked him for an interview – he seemed agreeable. But subsequently he's been avoiding it. So I'm not going to push it. As a pop star, he really doesn't impress me.

Tuesday afternoon at Azteca Stadium was boring. A lot of soldiers running around – but the shots weren't much. We were bothered a couple of times by the army liaison, an old guy (once with Pepe Lopez, once with Anuar Badin). Pablo pointed out later that he was fishing for a bribe – we ignored him.

We were joined in the evening by Marie, the Swedish-American redhead Anatol is after. She's really quite nice and seems interested in our project and future plans.

At supper, to our surprise, we were joined by Tony Masters. He's been called in connection with *2010: Odyssey Two* – it seems that Fox has got it (they wanted Spielberg to direct). And they asked Tony if he still had the original drawings from Kubrick's film – and maybe the models too. Pretty tacky.

We left the stadium about nine-thirty, the studio around ten. We went to Pablo's place – a very nice, spacious townhouse sort of thing. Marie, who lives next door, joined us. We talked and drank wine until sometime after two. A very pleasant time – it helped make this fucking city seem a little more human.

Yesterday morning, when we got in, Strick told us she wanted to shoot a group of Atari video game people having lunch. I ask you... We didn't, due to a lack of light and the sound of rain on the roof. But it's getting to the point where she seems to think we're here to record the doings of the publicity department. (She even had the gall to call us "her crew".)

Leonard Morpurgo brought some more stuff down for us from Bexel. The idiots, instead of sending the sponges for the shotgun, sent us a new shotgun plus zeppelin – two, we don't need. And the wide-angle lens which has been sitting there for a month waiting to be sent, was wrongly wired, so it doesn't work on our camera – and they didn't send a manual with it, so it'll be difficult for Arturo to re-wire it.

And today Morpurgo came over at lunch and told us that Armstrong is sending down a script. Now, the communication might be garbled – but it sounded as if it's for the sixty-minute documentary. If so, what the fuck am I doing here? And how can you write a documentary script before you've collected the documentary material?

There may be a screening of *Eraserhead* tomorrow evening at the studio.

Jack told us at supper last night (at La Pergola, with Pablo) that David was invited to Moscow to screen *Elephant Man* a couple of years ago. He went to Berlin, visited the Wall, climbed up for a view – saw a soldier looking back, a signal – and is convinced he was hit with microwave radiation, that it's still working inside him. He left quickly and refused to go to Russia.

Saturday, May 28: DAY SIXTY-NINE (9 hrs, 5 1/2 hrs)

While having breakfast at the studio yesterday morning, Catherine Coulson walked into the *comedor* with a friend – an attractive woman in her thirties, Jenny Sullivan. She's down here to have a look around – see if maybe there's a niche she can squeeze into (ordinarily, she would have worked with Fred – but Raffaella wouldn't allow him any Americans...). It'll probably never happen, but we're going to see if it's possible to get a second camera on our project (since

Jack Nance as Henry Spencer, the iconic image of Eraserhead. *Photograph copyright David Lynch.*

they want us to do a ridiculous amount of work) – she'll check Armstrong out when she goes back to L.A. Perhaps.

Shot a bit of Dykstra yesterday. And Giannetto De Rossi putting the makeup on Ken McMillan – a rather noxious, pustulant design.

In the evening, *Eraserhead*. A rather disappointingly small audience – but enthusiastic. It was the first film I'd seen in two months(!). So my mind, having fasted, was clean and fresh – the film hit me all over again. There are so many beautiful shots, so many extraordinary moments...

And to be able to walk up to David afterwards and shake his hand and say that I'd fallen in love with it all over again – I actually found myself choking up.

Strick was there, of course, putting in an appearance and saying how brilliant it all was. Unfortunately, when she asked about something, David pointed at me and told her she should read my article. She's suddenly realized that something special is going on here and that I'm connected. She wants me to make sure that *she's* the first to get a copy when the people who are reading them now are finished. Of course, I don't want her to read it – she'll ransack it for her own bloody purposes. Besides which, more important people are already waiting (Nelson and John, Kyle, Catherine, Marie...).

We went back to Pablo's for wine and cheese afterwards – with Marie, Eric and Geraldo (a friend of Pablo's from L.A., down to install a computer for Marie's boss). Talked about this and that – and *Eraserhead*. Both Anatol and I were all tensed up by it, so it took a while for us to settle into any conversation.

We're hoping Eric (an amazingly sharp guy – his wit in English is so rapid-fire, it's hard to believe it's not his first language) can come up with a script to be shot here (on video) quite quickly and cheaply.

Didn't do a thing all day – there's no energy left by Saturday. We just wandered around, talked to Catherine, poked about. Saw the Baron's first on-camera flight – it looked marvellous, but was in such a tight space we couldn't do anything with it.

There are some parties tonight, but I don't know if I'll go – don't really feel like it.

Penny Shaw, by the way – the assistant editor – is the daughter of Robert Shaw, by his first marriage.

She worked on *Heaven's Gate* – lasted from beginning to end, unlike most people.

Learned today that David had to marry his first wife, Peggy, because their daughter was on the way – makes the origins of *Eraserhead* that much clearer.

Went to one of the parties – Cristina Espinoza's birthday. Turned out quite well.

Eric came up with a script idea, which we immediately liked when we heard it this morning – an absurdist piece revolving around a writer who is kidnapped by mistake by some inexperienced terrorists. Suddenly at the party we spotted a woman who exactly fits the bill as the main female terrorist – a Mexican who speaks perfect English with a very English accent (having lived ten years in London) – who looks a little punk, a mix of glamour and sleaze. Who's a dancer and actress (worked last week in Michael Douglas' *Romancing the Stone*). Then met another woman who also turned out to be interested – whose husband is apparently a producer. We're supposed to meet at this woman's house tomorrow at six to talk (we want to get hold of Eric tomorrow and have him join us).

It all sounds wild and improbable, but...

I mentioned it to Bob Bealmear and it turns out he has a friend in New York who buys stuff for cable – with world-wide connections...

Unfortunately, as the evening progressed, and Anatol smoked a bunch of grass, he sounded more and more like a bullshit artist with big empty plans which he was using to hit on women. I got embarrassed and finally left. I don't like being associated with something which sounds phony. Far out, improbable – okay. But not phony. The guy often drinks too much – and when he smokes dope he starts to look a bit of a fool. After a good start to the evening, I wound up with my usual cynical disbelief – we'll never put it together – and we'll end up looking bad...

Week Ten Documents

```
                    C A L L   S H E E T  (GREEN CAMERA)
PRODUCTION TITLE: "DUNE"              DATE: THURSDAY 26th, MAY 1983.
PRODUCER: RAFFAELLA DE LAURENTIIS           *JUEVES
DIRECTOR: FRED ELMES                  CREW CALL: 8.00am at Studios.
```

SETS AND SCENE NUMBERS   D/N   STAGE/LOCATION
INT. PAUL'S ROOM-ARRAKEEN PALACE   D   STAGE #4
(TO COMP. HUNTER-SEEKER Pickups)
*(PARA COMP. Pickups de CAZADOR-
                 BUSCADOR)
Sc: 80pt.

NOTE: PICKUPS WITHOUT ARTISTS/SOUND
*NOTA: PICKUPS SIN ACTORES Y SIN SONIDO

REQUIREMENTS:
PRODUCTION: Check details in all Depts- Coffee Service on Stage.
         *Checar detalles en distintos Deptos-Servicio de Café en Foro.
CAMERA: Mitchell Mark II- Lightflex- Anamorphic lenses- MOY Gearhead.
SP/FX: Andrew Kelly and John Hatt. As established by First Camera and indica-
       tions by Director.
GRIP/PROPS/ELECT/ART: As established by First Camera and indications by
                 Director.
         *Según lo establecido por Primera Cámara e indicaciones
          del Director.
TRANSPORT: Pick up Fred Elmes and Leslie Werner at respective hotels at
       7.30am to come to Studios.
       *Recoger a Fred Elmes y Leslie Werner en hoteles respectivos a
        las 7.30am para venir a Estudios.
NOTE: Standby Projeccionist and Editing Assistant to check material.
     *Pendientes Proyeccionista y Asistente de Edición para checar mate-
       rial.   *VIERNES

ADVANCED SCHEDULE: FRIDAY MAY 27th, 1983.
             1) INT. PAUL'S ROOM-ARRAKEEN PALACE (D)   LOC: STAGE #4
               (Window glow white light)
              *(Ventana brilla con luz blanca)
               Sc: 78B pt.
REQUIREMENTS:
ELECT: Arc light - Dimmer - Molevators.*Luz de arco-Persiana- "Molevators".
             2) INT. PAUL'S ROOM- ARRAK. PALACE (D)   LOC: STAGE #4
               (PAUL opens filmbook and activates it)
              *(PAUL abre libro-película y lo activa)
               Sc: 78A [SHOT with John Dykstra]
REQUIREMENTS:
ARTIST: PAUL or PAUL'S DOUBLE-T.B.C. *PAUL o DOBLE de PAUL-PARA SER CONFIRM.
PROPS: Filmbook and accessories established for this Sc.
     *Libro-película y accesorios establecidos para esta Sc.

       IF POSSIBLE: 3) INT. SUB BASEMENT PASSAGEWAY-   LOC: STAGE #6
*SI ES POSIBLE: ARRAK. PALACE (N)
                (Dart for Duke Leto falling-
                 HIGH SPEED)
               *INT. CORREDOR SUBSOTANO-
               PALACIO ARRAKEEN
               (Dardo al Duque Leto cayendo-
                ALTA VELOCIDAD)
               Sc: 118pt.
REQUIREMENTS:
ARTISTS: DOUBLE for Shadout Mapes. *DOBLE para Shadout Mapes.
SP/FX: Dart. *Dardo.
CAMERA: High Speed motor. *Motor de alta velocidad.

Second unit call sheet, May 26, 1983.

6.

CAMERA DEPARTMENT CONTINUED:

GREEN CAMERA OPERATOR (Union)	LEOBARDO SANCHEZ		Av.Vasco de Quiroga N°1531,Mexico D.F 12 570-33-82
GREEN CAMERA FOCUS (Union)	PEDRO VAZQUEZ		Lago Maracaibo 30 Col.Argentina Tacuba,Mexico D.F 17 527-10-18
GREEN CAMERA CLAPPER LOADER (Union)	TOMAS PASTEN IBAÑEZ		Cascada 708-1. Col. Bandijal Mexico D.F 522-23-58

PUBLICITY DEPARTMENT

PUBLICIST	ANNE STRICK	1911 La Mesa Drive Santa Monica Cal.90402 213-394-3861	H.Century # 129
STILLS PHOTOGRAPHER	✓GEORGE WHITTEAR	2 Maxwell Road Ashford, Middx. England 7842-56972	Tokio 12, Apt.6 Zona Rosa, Mexico D.F 511-47-12
PUBLICIST ASSISTANT	ALISON KLARFELD	1,Old Forge Close Stanmore,Middx. 01-954-3523	Suites Amberes #23
STILLS PHOTOGRAPHER (Union)	ANGEL CORONA		Ermita Iztapalapa 440 Mexico D.F 582-39-57/582-29-72
VIDEO CREW	ANATOL PACANOWSKI	P.O Box 102 San Rafael Cal.94915 415-457-8378	H.Krystal #1201
VIDEO CREW	GEORGE GODWIN	P.O Box 1116 Neepawa Manitoba Roj Iho Canada	Suites Amberes #53
VIDEO CREW ASSISTANT	PABLO CAMPO PEÑON		Pirineos 525 Lomas de Chapultepec Mexico D.F 520-13-76
DIALECT COACH	✓MAGGIE ANDERSON	Flat 6 85, Cornwall Gardens London,S.W.7-4AY 589-3554	

Page 6 of the official Dune crew list puts us in our place.

```
                           C A L L   S H E E T

PRODUCTION TITLE: "DUNE                        DATE: Saturday May 28th, 1983.
PRODUCER:   RAFFAELLA DE LAURENTIIS            CREW CALL: 8:00am
DIRECTOR:   DAVID LYNCH                        LEAVE HOTEL: 7:30am

                   * RED & BLUE CAMERA * (PICKUP SHOTS WITHOUT DIALOGUE)
```

SETS & SCENES NUMBERS:		LOCATION:
1) INT. TRAINING ROOM - CASTLE CALADAN	Sc. 25c pt (N)	STAGE #1
2) INT. DUKE LETO'S QUARTES - CASTLE CALADAN (STANDBY SCENE)	Sc. 42pt. (N)	STAGE #5

ARTIST	CHARACTERS	D/R	P/U	M/U	WARD	ON SET
JURGEN PROCHNOW	DUKE LETO	203	T.B.N			

PRODUCTION REQUIREMENTS:

PRODUCTION: Security guards on Stage #1 & #5 - Coffe service, water, & soft
               drinks on Stage #1 & #5 - KEEP CLEAR the front & access to Stages
               for production & artist cars /* Guardias de seguridad en Foros #1
               y #5 - Servicio de cafe, agua y refrescos en Foros #1 y #5 - DEJAR
               LIBRE el frente y acceso a los Foros para coches de producción y
               artistas.
CAMERA: BL Camera as per J.Davis instructions - Vistavision Camera if Sc.
               25B not completed /*Cámara BL según instrucciónes de J.Davis -
               Cámara Vistavision si no se termina Sc. 25B
PROPERTY: Weirding Modules - Shield belts - table as per continuity -writting
               machine -cylinders sealing-parchment   /* Módulo misterio-
               so (Sonoro) - cinturón escudo - mesa según continuidad - máquina
               de escribir - cilindro sellado - pergamino.
SP/FX: Mechanism to activate robot ready - 2 spotlights rigged to come
               down with robot /* Mecanismo para activar robot listo - 2 luces
               "spot" conectadas para bajar con robot
ART DEPT: Ring on Robot side ready /* Ring en lado de Robot listo.
WARDROBE: As per this Sc./* Según esta Sc.
CATERING: Restaurant as per Saturdays /* Restaurant según todos los Sábados
               SNACK ready from 11.30am for 35 people at Stage #1.
               *SNACK listo desde las 11.30am para 35 personas en Foro#1.

ADVANCE SCHEDULE:

INT. TRAINING ROOM - CASTLE CALADAN   Sc. 25c pt.   STAGE #1
(Robot fight)

TRANSPORTATION:

PRODUCTION CAR	(own instructions)	J.DAVIS		
PRODUCTION CAR	7:00am	V. ALBARRAN	at home	7:30am at Studio
APOGEE COMBI	(own instructions)			

                                        Victor Albarran
                                        Assistant Director

First unit call sheet, May 28, 1983.

Week 11: May 30-June 5, 1983

Tuesday, May 31: DAY SEVENTY-TWO (8 hrs, 9 1/2 hrs)

The job moves smoothly on. Good words from Armstrong. I'm on good terms with Paul Sammon who just came down for two days (it helped me to see just how much confidence I've gained).

But he brought down a new book (one of three) which contains a lengthy piece on *Eraserhead*. Depressed me a bit.

I learned that Catherine brought down the first batch of pictures (half the total). They'll go off to *CFQ* as soon as the rest arrive. David told me to keep on his case about it (we spoke on stage; I made a mock strangling motion and said, "David, you're destroying my career" – Anatol, I'm afraid, caught it on tape).

Thursday, June 2: DAY SEVENTY-FOUR (9· hrs, 5 1/2 hrs)

Exhausted. I only got a few hours sleep last night.

At lunch yesterday, Jack came in, took my hand across the table and couldn't quite express what he felt. He sat beside me, ignoring everyone else, and told me how moved he was by the article. He'd finished it the previous night at one and had wanted to phone me. So many times, he said, he had looked at David over those years and said, "They'll never know. They'll never have any idea" – and along comes George Godwin and now they'll know. He said he had had to keep stopping because some little detail or other brought back a rush of memories and the tears flowed...

I've never had a response anything like it to my writing before – *I* started to get choked up.

So I called Jack in the evening when I got back here and we went to Pergola for supper. And the memories flowed. He talked about Herb Cardwell, regretting that no one had told me more about him... He talked about his marriage to Catherine (a real knock-down, drag-out hitting match)... He was enormously entertaining, acting out his stories. I realized the source of his intensity and felt more comfortable with him than ever before – he's incredibly sentimental, so much feeling that it spills over into everything...

After supper, he took me to a little place just up Amberes – a bar-cum-gallery which just opened last week. There were two pictures he wanted to buy. Already known to the owner and staff, he was warmly greeted – and introduced

Mexico City at night.

to the artist himself – a marvellous character named Oscar Rodriguez whose paintings are, to me, wonderful, gorgeous surreal pieces.

We also met another artist, Helen Bickham, an American who has lived here twenty years. So with them and the inhabitants of the place, we had a lengthy session, much beer, lots of good conversation. I said I'd try to arrange for the two artists to see what's going on at Churubusco – and to get in next time *Eraserhead* is screened (I cleared it with David and Kuki today).

We lingered after the place was closed. Then went on to Oscar's place – a huge old apartment, every inch of which was loaded with stunning paintings and sculptures (his own and other people's). In the middle of a conversation I caught sight of a small painting which just grabbed me – I wanted it. Not for sale, I was told – unless I could talk his wife out of it (a rather formidable New Englander). I'll have to see what I can do.

We stayed till nearly four, having a great time, talking and drinking mescal (from a plastic gallon jug, like anti-freeze; "here we pay for the mescal, not the bottle," said Oscar).

I can't remember ever having such an evening. It was great.

On the way home, Jack and I stopped for a bite at Denny's. We both fell in love with Oscar's work, couldn't stop talking about it.

I finally got to bed just after five.

We didn't shoot today (thank god) because the tubes are scarred. Had to try to clear them. So I came back here this afternoon for a sleep. The maid had stripped the bed, left her bucket and mop, and then obviously gone for a siesta. I crashed, having bolted the door. At one point I was woken by the phone – no doubt the desk wanting me to let the maid in. I ignored it. The mess will have to remain until tomorrow.

A letter from Jack, Kyle's agent. He's really researched our situation, outlined the areas we should be concerned about. Also looked into my position on the article – would be sticky if they won't go along with renegotiating the terms, giving me the book rights (because it was a commissioned work).

He's also sounding out U.S. and French contacts about the Paris film!!! The guy's amazingly active. So of course Anatol's immediate reaction is to distrust him. For myself, I see no reason to.

Friday, June 3: DAY SEVENTY-FIVE

Didn't go to work today – sleeping off this damned cold. Got up around two and wrote all afternoon – the bloody thing's getting so complicated I keep forgetting who characters are. But it's kind of fun – I've never put so much effort into a plot before. And I'm terrified that when it's done, someone will look at it and find it simplistic – that the complexity is just in my head.

Francesca Annis as Lady Jessica, consort of Duke Leto (Jurgen Prochnow) and mother of Paul (Kyle MacLachlan). Photograph copyright Universal/De Laurentiis.

Sunday, June 5: DAY SEVENTY-SEVEN (4 hrs)

Went to the studio yesterday, but there was nothing going on. No shooting. Shut down to prepare for whatever's to be done next. It seems that they used Francesca's accident (a stove blew up in her face giving her some minor burns) to take a breather for which the insurance company would pay. Even though she wasn't actually scheduled to shoot.

So we came back here, bought some bread, cheese, ham and beer and had a light lunch, listening to music (I've now chosen two songs for the Paris film's soundtrack – Honeymoon Killers' *L'heure de la sortie* and Kate Bush's *All the Love*).

Called Jack. He came over. And we went off in search of a bar at about two. Sat drinking in the Galeria Plaza all afternoon, stopped for some chicken and tacos up the road. Visited Fred, planning to go on with him for the evening. We split up to take care of various bits of business. I passed out in my room. Jack called at ten-thirty – he'd passed out too. So I just went to bed.

A friend of Pablo and Eric's, hired a couple of weeks ago to take stills on *Dune*, turns out to have a finished screenplay which sounds quite interesting – more sombre than Eric's idea. If it looks good, we might film it – giving Eric a lot more breathing space to develop his script, which (if finished) we might knock out in the week or two following the wrap on *Dune* in September.

Anatol annoyed me yesterday. We passed El Corral, the little bar-cum-gallery, and stopped in. He took a brief look. And later dismissed Oscar out of hand as a talented amateur, but not a real painter. When I said he'd hardly seen the guy's work, he said he didn't need to – one or two prints are enough to tell: the only good thing the guy does is the headless bodies.

Napkin doodle by Oscar Rodriguez: June 1, 1983.

Week 12: June 6-12, 1983

Monday, June 6: DAY SEVENTY-EIGHT

Didn't go to work today. Hardly slept all night – had the runs (mostly water). In between shitting, vomiting violently (almost dry), and almost passing out, I finished outlining the Paris story. A bit thin I'm afraid – but it can be fleshed out in the writing. Talked to Jack up on the Royal yesterday afternoon – he seems quite seriously to think we can get the money we need in Texas (it's gearing up for film production there). "So are we going to make a deal for this movie?" he asked. Maybe it will happen...

Saturday afternoon as we were getting drunk, Jack told us stories – he's a great story-teller, even with Anatol interrupting with non sequiturs (he doesn't have my habit of listening). Family history and their connection with the Kennedy assassination. And the tale of a Texas gangster who survived nine attempts on his life in the Forties before being blown up by a rural mailbox – "if there's one film I want to make, this is the one," Jack said. He wanted to know if I liked it (I did) – and I realized that I'm getting to a position where my writing abilities are coming into demand (Anatol – Jack – maybe David with regard to *Blue Velvet*...). A weird feeling.

Jack mentioned something else: a new angle on *Ronnie Rocket* (which he says is very perverse) – since the main character becomes a rock star, it offers the possibility of a soundtrack album. And A&M are interested. As with certain other movies, even if the film isn't a success, the money can be recouped from record sales...

Arturo Garciarubio as a second-stage Navigator; Jack Nance as Nefud [left]. Photograph copyright Universal/De Laurentiis.

With these days off, I haven't missed much. We haven't shot anything since last Wednesday. Last week we were trying to clean spots off the tubes. And Saturday, while Arturo was servicing the camera, a transistor burned out. They got a replacement today.

Wednesday, June 8: DAY EIGHTY (8· hrs, 8 hrs)

Crawled into work yesterday only to discover that the camera wasn't operational. Had a three-and-a-half hour lunch at the studio's Mexican restaurant (vastly superior to the *Dune* place) – after which I recouped a lot of energy (I was thoroughly drained all morning).

Went out in the evening with Anatol and Marie – some drinks, a late supper (midnight), back here. They stayed until two-thirty.

We missed quite a bit the last few days – they're getting into Geidi Prime, lair of the Baron – a bizarre, slimy, pustular, decadent sort of place – gloriously perverse. Today, with the camera operational, we caught a bit before being kicked off set by Freddie and Kuki. Not only is the Baron covered with awful sores – Rabban eats the juice of a little rat-like creature, and the slaves have their ears sewn shut – and some of them their eyes (the females).

I made the mistake of joking with David about it – he didn't get it, Anatol didn't get it – I looked like a fool (I just said "this is getting weird, David, you've got no sense of proportion" – and truthfully I think it is so weird that it might outweigh the more normal worlds of the film). David was, I think, offended – and I realized (with some prompting from Anatol) that I'm really not in a position to banter with him – he's the director of *Dune* after all, a major figure, and even though he's helped me out I still exist within certain formal bounds – we're not "buddies" in other words. I've got to cool it with the familiarity.

We caught another nice little bit with Aldo this afternoon. He's a wonderful character, and seems to like letting us in on things.

Anatol had an idea for raising extra money the night before last: we do twenty-five half-hour profiles on major (or just interesting) people on the production for sale to TV (at a thousand dollars a minute, it comes to three-quarters of a million). It'll mean extra work, but it'll give us a focus when we do the interviews – and provide a sense of purpose more or less lacking up to now. (I've sketched a brief proposal for the idea.)

The "script outline" arrived from Gordon yesterday. A dreadful piece of rubbish, unsigned (but probably the work of Sammon – it starts with his Moses thing…). But it's on the stationary of Kaleidoscope Films Ltd – who or what the fuck that is, I'd like to know.

We're going to have to straighten things out when Armstrong gets here in a couple of weeks – make sure he doesn't leave without us having something in writing.

Sunday, June 12: DAY EIGHTY-FOUR (11 hrs, 11 hrs, 7 hrs)

An interesting evening yesterday. Jack and I went for supper together (at the Bellinghausen), had a decent meal. Then Jack suggested a cab ride, since it was still early. We grabbed a VW taxi and went to the Zocalo, the main square – with the Presidential Palace, Cathedral, and National Pawn Shop. It's a whole other city. Massive European architecture, cobbled streets. We walked back into the streets – not the slightest taste of North America – a completely different culture. Fascinating.

We were standing on a corner, looking at a big church. A man came along, dropped his trousers across the street, facing the church, took a juicy shit, pulled up his trousers and continued on his way. The children playing in front of the church took no notice.

We went inside the Cathedral. Opulent, with people coming and going, crossing themselves – a little Indian girl scooped up some holy water in a plastic baggie. A wedding was in progress. Jack – baptized a Catholic – was very moved by the whole business.

We took a cab back to Zona Rosa and went for a couple of drinks at the Geneve (an old hotel in which, I was told, the Europeans and Americans took refuge during the revolution) and just talked. Jack's a fascinating character – I like him enormously. Maybe I should do some detailed interviews with him and write something about him...

The job drags on.

Anatol loved the Paris outline, only had a couple of minor suggestions.

Kyle's agent, Jack Leustig, is back. He read the outline – also likes it – also had some suggestions, valid ones; mostly to remove the suggestions of *Diva*,

Mexico City at dusk.

plus make a change in the ending to increase the dramatic impact. He says he's sounded out some people in France (through his French wife) and money is available for co-productions.

I'm inclined to trust Jack – so far he's been very helpful in getting information for us and quite open about his intentions (so far it's all free because he's found it interesting – not just the Paris film, but the *Dune* documentary and the book – he'd like to be officially involved in the film and the book, but if we find another route it's okay with him – if he is involved, of course, he'll get his share). Anatol however keeps making little negative remarks – he doesn't trust the guy. Because he's being too helpful; what does he want? Well, obviously he's seen something promising and would like to be in on it – I find that reasonable and comprehensible – there's no need to look for something ulterior.

Speaking of Anatol – I'm not sure our relationship will survive in the long run. He can be too much of a pain in the ass. There's more friction than I'm comfortable with (even though it is only occasional). He talks a lot about "we must do this, do that", then gets annoyed when I try to move it because he doesn't feel like doing it right now. At the moment, he's so bloody concerned with trying to get laid that he spends a lot of time on set hitting on women (Marie, the doctor...). Yesterday some interesting stuff came up – the Geidi Prime cable car fouled up, holding up a shot which had to be got quickly (the extras were suffocating) and Kit West became active coordinating the situation. Now, we're supposed to be doing something on Kit but we've got very little material on him yet. I pointed it out to Anatol. He said sure, okay – and went back to talking to Marie. Now I'm getting a little pissed off that I'm supposed to be assuming the responsibilities of a line producer – but have none of the authority. Particularly because other people are now accepting me in that position; Kuki now always talks to me as if I can control what Anatol does – yet I can only suggest. And yesterday Kuki was justifiably pissed off at all the spectators who wander onto the set. So he came to me and asked who the hell Marie was (she was standing there checking her lottery numbers). Because she comes in and Anatol talks to her for a long time, she becomes associated with the video crew; since I'm supposed to be line producer, in charge, Kuki holds me responsible for her presence; but since I have no authority I can't do anything about it. This whole business pissed me off. I found my patience with Anatol flagging. I spoke to him at one point in a fairly sharp tone (I'd asked a question – had he caught something? – so I could put it on the log sheet, and as too often happens, he didn't answer the question but started saying something else; so I interrupted and repeated the question more pointedly) – he snapped my head off.

It's all very well to be free and equal partners – but on the job we each have specific functions – and if the job is to be done we should fulfill those functions.

Yet he only listens to me when he feels like it. He's got a fairly unprofessional attitude. The stuff we've got so far is almost all very general – we lack details, inserts, cutaways. Yet every time I bring it up, he says that's all just boring industrial video – and he doesn't want to do it. The same with interviews: I know a full interview is boring to watch – but it's just raw material – you cut out expressions and use the voice with other material. It *has* to be done. He now agrees. But every time I push for an interview, he drags – and I have to push harder.

In the end we'll have a mess of material, most of which won't be much use for anything.

For myself, at this point I've virtually given up on the thing altogether. Just hang on until the end of the shoot, then forget about it – I don't even want to be involved in the editing. If Armstrong takes it away, I'll be happy.

I am both furious and disgusted. I arranged a meeting with Jack Leustig for this afternoon – with Anatol and myself – to talk about the information he's obtained on the "making of ..." project. I called Anatol at ten-thirty this morning – sure, he'd join us. But he didn't bother to show up.

Jack has invested time and money in checking this out. And Anatol doesn't have the decency to at least talk to him. I was thoroughly embarrassed. And for the first time I spewed out all my negative feelings about Anatol to someone else (what I wrote above – in spades). Because I'm tied to the man, I'm going to go down with this project if he won't pull himself together. Sucking up to Armstrong (even if he is a decent guy) will kill us – you don't get respect for kissing ass (which is why Strick keeps pushing harder and harder – Anatol let her in). We'll never get a decent deal out of Armstrong because Anatol is going to agree to whatever he says.

All I can do is hope to get out alive.

As for the Paris film – Jack is going to continue looking into financing possibilities – but, he says (and I can only agree with him), he'll never be able to work with Anatol (and frankly, seeing the way Anatol works, I don't have any faith in his ability to direct – he has no sense of responsibility to the job he's being paid to do) – so if Jack puts something together and produces my script (he likes the outline and thinks it has great possibilities), it'll have to be with another director. I can't argue with that.

This whole afternoon (I was with Jack for two-and-a-half hours) I got nothing but good feelings for him – I trust him. And I'm glad to say we seem to have established a positive relationship despite the present situation. At least he's still interested in the script and in the *Eraserhead* book. But as for the documentary – he says he could never work for us on that now because of Anatol's attitude – I can't blame him.

Week Twelve Document

```
                         C A L L    S H E E T
   PRODUCTION TITLE: "DUNE"              DATE: FRIDAY JUNE 10th, 1983
   PRODUCER: RAFFAELLA DE LAURENTIIS           *VIERNES
   DIRECTOR: DAVID LYNCH                 CREW CALL: 8.00am
                                         LEAVE HOTEL: 7.30am
                                         CAMERA/ELECT. GRIP: 7.30am

                         RED  &  BLUE CAMERA
                       (PICKUPS without Dialogue)


   NOTE: SATURDAY JUNE 11th WILL BE WORKED AS A NORMAL WEEKDAY (8.00am to
                                                                7.00pm)
   *NOTA: EL SABADO JUNIO 11 SERA TRABAJADO EN HORARIO NORMAL (8.00am a
                                                                7.00pm)
```

SETS AND SCENE NUMBERS	D/N	STAGE/LOCATION
INT. TRAINING ROOM-CASTLE CALADAN	N	STAGE #1
(RETAKES On Gurney-Paul fight)(TO CONT.)		
*(RETOMAS de pelea entre Gurney y Paul)		
VISTAVISION. Sc: 25B Pt.		
INT. SUB BASEMENT PASSAGEWAY-ARRAK. PAL.	N	STAGE #6
(Duncan sliding down)*(Duncan deslizándose)		
Sc: 128 (TO COMPLETE) *(PARA COMPLETAR)		

ARTISTS	CHARACTER	D/R	P/U	M/U	ON SET
KYLE MACHLACHLAN	PAUL	218		T.B.N.	
PATRICK STEWART	GURNEY	212		T.B.N.	

```
STAND INS:
                    FOR PAUL                              T.B.N.
                    FOR GURNEY                            T.B.N.

DOUBLES/STUNTS:              *TIMES depending on M-UP's schedule
                                   with 1st CAMERA.
RICHARD HUMPHREYS   Made up like Paul           7.00am    *8.00am
WILL HARPER         Made up like Gurney         7.00am    *8.00am
K. YAMASAKI         FIGHT SUPERVISOR                       8.00am

CROWD:
11 ATREIDES GUARDS (Green Caladan)                        T.B.N.


REQUIREMENTS:
PRODUCTION: Security Guards on Stages 1 & 6 - Bell and Red light rigged to
            Stages # 1 & 6- Coffee Service on Stages 1 & 6 and actors' dress
            rooms- KEEP CLEAR entrance to Stages 1 & 6 for Generators and
            Prod. cars.
           *Vigilancia en Foros 1 & 6 - Campana y luz roja en Foros 1 & 6-
            Servicio de Café en Foros 1 & 6 y camerinos de actores- DEJAR
            LIBRE entrada a Foros 1 & 6 para Generadores y Coches de Prod.
CAMERA: VISTAVISION and BL as per J. Devis' and J. Dykstra's instructions.
       *VISTAVISION y BL según instrucciones de J. Devis y J. Dykstra.
PROPERTY: Sc: 25B Pt.-Gurney's knife- Paul's knife- Shield belts- Baliset.
              *Cuchillo de Gurney- Cuchillo de Paul- Cinturones es-
               cudo- Baliset.
SP/FX: Sc: 25B Pt. - Rain effect on window. * Efecto de lluvia en ventana.
       Sc: 128- Smoke. *Hump Sliding effect for Duncan, ready. *Efecto de
                deslizamiento de Duncan, listo.
SET DRESSING: Large table, chairs and books. *Mesa grande, sillas y libros.
ELECT: Lights dimming. *Luces apagándose.
M-UP:Sc: 25B Pt.-Doubles to be made up like Paul and Gurney.
                Dobles maquillados como Paul y Gurney.
```

Red & Blue Camera call sheet, June 10, 1983.

Week 13: June 13-19, 1983

Tuesday, June 14: DAY EIGHTY-SIX (11 1/2 hrs, 10 1/2 hrs)

Ups and downs, crises and annoyances, problems and what have you.

Anatol just "missed us" on Sunday – but he doesn't trust Jack anyway. And Gordon's a nice guy – he promised we'd do well on this deal, and so there's no reason to think he won't do well by us...

I'm beginning to wonder about my judgment; why do I feel comfortable with Jack? David doesn't like him, doesn't want him anywhere near the book.

I think I'm going to wind up stiffed on the article, stiffed on this video project, lost as far as the book is concerned – Jack seemed like a security blanket – but everyone I'm involved with shuns him.

If Jack does manage to put together a production deal on my script, *he* won't be able to work with Anatol (and frankly I have nothing now but doubts about Anatol's abilities) and there would be no way to get David involved because of Jack's involvement. I could end up alienating a bunch of people (with Anatol it wouldn't matter so much – with David, I'd be sorry).

Jack asked me Sunday who I'd like to direct the script if he could find financing (a known director would offer more security of course than Anatol could). Yesterday, after some brief thought (more or less off the top of my head) I gave him two names: Franc Roddam and Bertrand Tavernier. I can't believe I'm considering things like this.

Yesterday, Pablo was sick and Anatol was drunk (he was up boozing until four in the morning). We sent Pablo home, and Anatol slept in the office. I spent the day waiting for Jurgen Prochnow to become available for an interview. He was incredibly decent, doing it after seven in the evening – a good one too. We had to get it because he was scheduled to have part of his beard shaved off this morning for his final shot (the Baron rips open the Duke's cheek and poisonous smoke comes out from the tooth implanted by Dr. Yueh).

That shot was got to this evening. All set up. Jurgen on the table, a tube running into the prosthetic on his cheek. Something went wrong on the take – too much smoke. Even before Ken McMillan tore the cheek, the yellow smoke spewed out (a broken seal?) engulfing Jurgen. He broke away from the table, tearing off the prosthetic – tearing the newly shaved cheek which was burned by the smoke. A bad end to the day – a lousy way to finish his work on the film which he yesterday said was a great pleasure...

Saturday, June 18: DAY NINETY (9 hrs, 10 hrs, 8 1/2 hrs, 2 hrs)

Not a good week at all. For a while Anatol was absolutely impossible – Thursday he was like a raving lunatic, whatever I said to him he became furious, refusing to understand me ... it got to the point where I just came out and said "I can't work like this – we'd better call Gordon and tell him to find someone else to replace me" and Anatol angrily agreed. By the end of the afternoon he was back to what for him is normal. But by now, both Pablo and myself have no respect for him – he's a self-made failure, obviously doesn't know how to do this job and has no sense of responsibility. Pablo and I have agreed to push him as much as possible to shoot what's necessary – and if he gets awkward again to shoot it ourselves.

Meanwhile, the atmosphere on *Dune* has lost much of the friendly tone it once had. Raffaella doesn't know how to treat people decently. Everyone feels used and abused on the production. The hours have grown longer again. And still no one seems to have signed a contract (even Dykstra). The Apogee people are all gloomy because David doesn't have a practical idea of what's involved in the effects work and Raffaella doesn't want to pay for what they're asking Apogee to deliver.

Wednesday evening I had supper with Jack Nance at his hotel, after which we went to a sleazy little nightclub on Insurgentes. An amazing place with a continuous show – a live band, strippers, singers, a comedy group whose skits included religious satire. We stayed until the joint was closing up – around three-thirty.

It struck me there that it would be a good idea to make a film of Malcolm Lowry's *Under the Volcano* with Jack as the minor diplomat who drinks himself to death ... should check that out.

Helen Bickham, the artist, visited the studio yesterday – Oscar Rodriguez was supposed to come too, but he didn't make it.

If we could find transport, she'd act as guide tomorrow on a trip to Tepoztlan (one of the towns studied in my Mexico course last fall). Though Jack, who'd like to go, finds her chatter intolerable.

I took Maggie Anderson, the dialect coach, to supper yesterday (Bellinghausen) – she's a marvelous character – I definitely want to keep in touch with her (she's leaving early next month).

Sunday, June 19 DAY NINETY-ONE

Only spent a couple of hours at the studio yesterday – to shoot one of the artisans in Giorgio's shop.

Went to supper with Maggie again – an odd thing. I'd taken a nap in the afternoon. Helen and her stepson dropped by. After they'd gone, I took a walk around the area, came back here about eight. I tried to call Fred to see if he'd like to go eat – and found myself talking to Maggie, who'd just called here to speak to Pier Luigi Basile – a crossed line. She recognized my voice asking for room 21 and asked if I'd like a "return engagement". So we went to a Chinese restaurant on Niza – not too bad.

Giorgio Desideri's set decoration shop.

We talked about David – he is not, she insists, either a painter or a writer. He expresses himself graphically through his fingers, carried by instinct, intuition. As for writing, she says the script is dreadful (it does lack the central thread of character development necessary to carry the story – the weight of that has to fall on Kyle).

As she sees it, he's typically American – he carries no past with him, no cultural baggage. Her metaphor is that he was born in the caul and still hasn't escaped it – he's grown in the womb. But his instinct is so powerful that it throws up a lot of things which do work – yet nothing so complete because nothing is thought (the problem with *The Elephant Man*).

We also talked about Anatol – she too sees him as someone not really going anywhere (though he'll get jobs because he can charm people like Raffaella). She rather surprised me, after asking about the genesis of the Paris script, by saying I should go on to something else because if I've decided not to do it with Anatol he'll steal it from me...

After supper I introduced her to El Corral, which she loved.

It's a pity she's not thirty years younger – she's the best date I've ever had.

Week Thirteen Document

```
                              CALL SHEET
PRODUCTION TITLE: "DUNE"                    DATE: Wednesday, June 15th, 1983
PRODUCER: RAFFAELLA DE LAURENTIIS           CREW CALL: 6:30am at studio
DIRECTOR: FRED ELMES
```

GREEN CAMERA
(Pick ups without dialogue)

SETS & SCENE NUMBERS: LOCATION:

1) TEST: SMOKE & FLAMES AGAINST THE SEA   ACAPULCO
   /*Prueba: Efecto de humo y flamas contra el mar.

ARTIST	CHARACTER	M-U/WARD	ON SET
A.N. OTHER	SEXY BOY	2:00 pm	4:00 pm

PRODUCTION REQUIREMENTS:

PRODUCTION: Check requirements with all Departments./*Checar detalles con todos los Departamentos.

CAMERA: Mitchell Mark II - Anamorphic Lenses - Moy Gearhead - dustbin liner (waterproof blimp).

SPFX: Flame-throwing equipment, smoke bombs, flippers and goggles.

GRIPS/ELECTRIC/ART: As per Director & Cinematographer's instructions. PROPS: large parasols, plastic bags for bathing suits.

CATERING: Breakfast for 30 served at airport 7:15 am. (Check with A.D. for gate number.) Luncheon by pool at Princess Hotel. Subsequent breakfasts to be coordinated with hotel's room service. Alcoholic refreshment on hand at all times, in all locations.

WARDROBE: Stand by with towels.

TRANSPORTATION:

```
6:45 am    FRED ELMES        SUITES AMBERES      7:15 at airport
           LESLIE WERNER     HOTEL CENTURY       (AM #303 at 8:00 am)

6:45 am    CREW and equipment from studio to airport.
```

ADVANCE SCHEDULE: The rest of the week: same test, same location.
Next week: Cancun.
Dates T.B.N.: Puerto Vallarta
              Mazatlan
              Zihuatanejo (No room service; all meals served at
                          Green Parrot.)

Jesus Marin
Assistant Director

Second unit call sheet, June 15, 1983.

Week 14: June 20-26, 1983

Monday, June 20: DAY NINETY-TWO (8 hrs)

Talk about strange coincidences – this time an unhappy one.

Last Wednesday, out of nowhere, I flashed on the idea of doing Lowry's *Under the Volcano* with Jack in the lead.

Today at lunch, Cyril (one of the people in wardrobe) mentioned that he'd been asked to do a bit of work on a film starting in July in Cuernavaca – something about a volcano, from a book written in the thirties – all taking place in one day – a diplomat drinking himself to death… It rather upset me. John Huston is making it, with Albert Finney, Jacqueline Bissett, and Anthony Andrews.

I guess that's the trouble with good ideas – they occur to other people as well…

Tuesday, June 21: DAY NINETY-THREE (9 1/2 hrs)

After an incredible thunderstorm yesterday evening I went out wandering in search of Jack. I found him in the restaurant of his hotel. We had supper, then took off in pursuit of a bar. We wound up at Lombard's – which, from the decor, must once have been a bordello. A friendly waitress who was just like a younger, Spanish-speaking Lila Kedrova. When that place closed down, we made our way to another – the very noisy one across Amberes which often wakes me up at night. From there, in search of coffee. We had a three o'clock breakfast at Vips on Niza (where Anatol and I landed that first morning in the city). And all the time, Jack was going back over the Herbert Noble story (the Texas gangster he told us about that Saturday at the Galeria Plaza). He wants me to write it into a script. Read the material he's gathered, then go to Texas to do some research – archives, talking to people who were connected with it… It really sounds like a viable story.

Wednesday, June 22: DAY NINETY-FOUR

Anatol obviously realizes that things have gone wrong between us. At the end of last week he said that despite our difficulties, we have to stick together on this project as protection against being screwed altogether (by the way, we discovered that the two of us together are being paid only a bit more than one stills photographer – George is getting about $300 a day). And I don't know how many times now he has said that once I've got my screenplay I'll take off and make it myself, leaving him behind. Yesterday morning he came out and asked how much I want to be paid for it – again saying I'll probably go off and do it myself, not even giving him a "story by" credit.

The thing is, although he knows it's gone sour, I really think he believes it's all on my side – he's constantly talking about my temper, saying I should start taking tranquilizers. Yet I've never yet exploded the way he does, become absolutely impossible to talk to (I'm not saying I'm not moody and difficult). The difference between us is, I think, that I realize when I'm being awkward, but he doesn't.

On top of it all I've grown to hate so many of his mannerisms...

I think my little "joke" a while back stopped David short because the comment was actually true – and maybe he knows it. His penchant for – *unpleasant* things has been completely cut loose because of the huge budget (yesterday he had Paul Smith tear the tongue out of a dead cow and eat it – I had to leave before they did the shot). Without a strong producer to keep the lid on, all the bogies are coming out of David's mind – and he *doesn't* have a sense of proportion.

Between the ham-handed De Laurentiis production technique and David's obsessions I'm beginning to lose faith in the viability of this project. I think *Dune* may turn out to be an awful mess, much of it alienating the audience. I really hope I'm wrong, that this feeling is just a projection of my current negative state of mind – but I'm not the only one who's feeling this way; quite a few people around the set have become a bit disgusted with the proceedings.

Sunday, June 26: DAY NINETY-EIGHT (10 1/2 hrs, 8 hrs, 10 1/2 hrs, 4 hrs)

Feel exhausted...

The big news this week is, of course, that Apogee is off the picture. Dykstra finally told them he can't possibly work under these conditions – and since he still doesn't have a contract ... it's in the hands of the lawyers, as Greg put it.

A practical move, of course. Halfway through the shoot, with no other major effects house available, and what's rumoured to be a very good worm test just delivered – if De Laurentiis doesn't back down and act reasonable about the budget, the project is in serious trouble – it'll be crippled by cut-rate effects. The next couple of weeks will tell – they'll *have* to get Dykstra back, and on his own terms.

I heard from Maggie something which goes further to confirm David's lack of a sense of reality – I'm beginning to find him a little horrifying beneath that gee-whiz facade. Before that business with the effect which burnt Jurgen, it was David's plan to have a plastic surgeon (specifically the awful young woman doctor who's on set during the day) actually cut a hole in Jurgen's cheek for

The Atreides ship lands at the Arrakeen spaceport. Photograph copyright Universal/De Laurentiis.

the smoke. Maggie was present when Raffaella went to David and said "you're not going to cut any of my actors" – and he was, Maggie said, furious about it. He told Raffaella he'd do it himself. She said he could cut himself up, but only *after* the film was done.

I got a letter from Fred Clarke. The book rights are automatically mine – no problem. He wonders why I haven't been in touch about covering *Dune*. Mike Kaplan, the managing editor is coming down this week, so I'll have some direct contact.

Paul Sammon arrived Wednesday evening. Brought me down some stuff – the recorder next to useless, because it's too big to carry around (the whole point in having it).

We spent Thursday pulling out the shots he wanted for his promo film – I set up all the cassettes so they were ready to go at the right spot. Friday we took the player over to Pronarte and they plugged it into their system (it took a long time), transferred the material to one-inch. By then it was lunch time – I left him, taking the cassettes.

In a way, we were far too generous. Sammon took writer, producer and director credits, and we didn't argue – but he neither produced nor directed, merely wrote, narrated, and edited. Neither Anatol nor Pablo can stand him, and I have to admit he's more than a nuisance, pushy. And it *was* his outline that Armstrong sent down to us (Sammon was a bit nonplussed that we'd seen it).

And speaking of Armstrong – he was down for the Universal "convention" (a visit of over a hundred exhibitors on Friday). The same old thing: quick talk, little substance. He took back the first thirty cassettes (illegal – the Mexican censor is supposed to see them first), told us that sure we'd be editing (though they haven't decided on the actual form yet – got a dozen ideas including Sammon's – but he hasn't asked *me*, has he?). And he'll "take care" of us on the matter of the promo thing.

Pyramid on the mountain above Tepoztlan.

Jack's in a bad way. Pains in the gut. On antibiotics, pain killers – but still drinking.

Thursday evening there was a thunderstorm. We went up on top of the Royal to watch it. Had some drinks, talked. (We got into a rhapsody on the french fries there – very good.) The bar closed around midnight. We were up there alone. He stood in the light rain by the lawn and declaimed a passage of Shakespeare – beautifully. It was very moving.

We went on down to the basement bar, where we met John Stirber. He'd had a lot to drink – talked about how this job is ruining his family but he can't help it, it's what he wants to do. His plans for an invention he hasn't been able to get off the ground. A rather depressing encounter.

From there we went to the sleazy joint on Insurgentes, where Jack became obnoxious – a loud drunk. The problem was that Maria, the woman we met there last time, didn't want to strip in front of him, wanted him to leave – he ordered more and more drinks. With her help, I finally managed to get him out. We were going for a coffee when one of the many touts in the area handed him a card – a bar where there are girls, etc. Jack went on to the place. I came back to the hotel.

I wish there was something I could do for the guy, but what? He's become self-destructive (says he's going to die in Mexico). He seems to like me – wants me to work on that script for him, calls me up a lot. That night he told me that

I was the only one who had the guts to face the way he really is – no one else will stick with him on these night journeys.

He finally read the outline of "Café Universal". Nasty, vicious, sordid – but he likes it a lot.

Today, I went to Tepoztlan with Helen Bickham and her stepson Danny. We climbed a mountain to a small pyramid, had lunch on the town square, looking out on the market. Seems like a fairly nice place, nestled at the foot of steep mountains at the end of a huge valley.

A very positive response from her about my article.

Week Fourteen Documents

```
                        CALL  SHEET
PRODUCTION TITLE: "DUNE"              DATE: MONDAY June 20th, 1983.
PRODUCER: RAFFAELLA DE LAURENTIIS           *LUNES
DIRECTOR: DAVID LYNCH                 CREW CALL: 10.00am
                                      LEAVE HOTEL: 9.30am
                                      CAMERA/ELECT/GRIP: 9.00am

                        RED  &  BLUE  CAMERA
                       (PICKUPS WITHOUT DIALOGUE)
```

SETS AND SCENE NUMBERS	D/N	STAGE/LOCATION
INT. GREEN PORCELAIN ROOM-GEIDE PRIME Sc: 48A	D	STAGE #3
INT. BARON'S ROOM-GEIDE PRIME INSERTS TO COMPLETE) Sc: 52pt	D	STAGE #3
INT. PASSAGEWAY-ARRAKEEN PALACE (CU of Jessica on stretcher, tied and gagged) Sc: 128 pt.	N	STAGE #6

ARTIST	CHARACTER	D/R	P/U	M-UP	ON SET
FRANCESCA ANNIS	JESSICA	When available or finished with 1st Camera.			

STAND INS:
                FOR JESSICA   When available or finished with 1st Camera.

CROWD:
2 HARKONNEN GUARDS (The tallest available)   9.00am   10.00am
          *(Los más altos disponibles)

REQUIREMENTS:

PRODUCTION: Security Guards on Stages # 3 & 6- Coffee Service on Stages
       3 & 6 and actress' dress room- doctor on set- KEEP CLEAR the front
       access and corners of Stages for generators and prod. cars.
       *Vigilancia en Foros 3 & 6- Servicio de café en Foros 3 & 6 y ca-
       merino de actriz- doctor en set- DEJAR LIBRE el frente y las es-
       quinas de los foros para generadores y coches de prod.

CAMERA: As per J. Devis' instructions. *Según instrucciones de J. Devis.

PROPERTY: Sc. 48A: Pieces of hair, meat and blood.
          *Pedazos de pelo, carne y sangre.
      Sc. 52pt: Cylinder with Duke Leto's message- "Squoods" (Living food)-
          Cilindro con mensaje del Duque Leto- "Squoods" (Comida
                                                       viviente)
      Sc. 128pt.: Gag and binds for Jessica- Stretcher.
          *Mordaza y ataduras para Jessica- camilla.

SP/FX: Sc. 52pt: Gloglobe lit. *Globobrillo. Water bubbling. *Agua hirviendo.
      Sc. 128pt.: Smoke. *Humo.

ELECT: Sc. 128pt: Lights dimming. *Luces apagándose.

SET DRESS: Check mentioned sets as per comtinuity.
       *Checar sets mencionados según continuidad.

CATERING: DUNE Restaurant open from 7.ooam. Lunch ready from 12.00noon.
       *Restaurant DUNE abierto desde las 7.00am. Comida lista desde las
       12.00pm.

TRANSPORT:
ARTIST CAR #1   Pick up FRANCESCA ANNIS as per 1st camera's call. ?

First unit call sheet, June 20, 1983.

Lab bill for tape transfers for promo piece.

Weeks 15 & 16: June 27-July 10, 1983

Monday, June 27: DAY NINETY-NINE (9 hrs)

The impressive full-size third stage Navigator. Photograph copyright Universal/De Laurentiis.

Just spoke to Tim - he's coming down here next month.

Friday, July 1: DAY ONE-HUNDRED-THREE (11 hrs, 12 hrs, 9 hrs)

My desire to keep this journal has all but fizzled.

Armstrong is obviously going to fuck us - no intention of talking - just take our material and do what he wants with it - no guarantees. I feel no sense of obligation to him or to Universal.

Big party Wednesday night at Dykstra's - very good time. I lingered on into the early hours.

I stayed home Thursday - slept until one, then wrote. Going quite well.

Supper with Jack - heard from him of a party - a farewell thrown by Sting on the roof of the Royal. A real bash with endless quantities of champagne. Sting's actually a nice guy, intelligent and friendly - if moody. I'll be able to read his *Gormenghast* script (Steerpike's story, of course) after a couple of other people are through with it here.

Jack got very drunk - went on to the club on Insurgentes. He got so loud and obnoxious, seeming to threaten violence, that I finally got up and left him there (with Malcolm, from props). It's too hard to watch – he seems hell-bent on destroying himself. And of course there's nothing I can do about it.

Anatol is getting thoroughly nauseating about Marie – it's embarrassing to watch (and I see Marie not being terribly pleased with some of his more effusive expressions of affection). He almost got into a drunken fight at the end of Sting's party with one of the stuntmen who was pursuing her.

I find his mannerisms – vocal and physical – almost impossible to bear these days.

Wednesday, July 6: DAY ONE-HUNDRED-EIGHT (6 hrs, 8 1/2 hrs, 11 hrs, 7 1/2 hrs)

Saturday, didn't do anything. Anatol decided to go visit Marie and simply never showed up at the studio.

That evening there was the big party – Raffaella's birthday do at the San Angel Inn – a beautiful old hacienda, huge. Ate supper with Jose Ferrer and his wife, Patrick Stewart, and Jack. Then after the meal, went on to another party – another birthday (Ellie, from special effects). A good one. Met some production people from *Sadat* (including Andrew McLaglen's son). Jack got obnoxiously drunk again.

Jack is really bad now. Saturday, at the studio, he was talking about "taking the cure" – going to a place in Texas which uses aversion therapy (sick-making drugs). Saturday evening, he got vile again.

I ran into him at the studio early Monday afternoon – he looked shaky, on his way to the Mexican restaurant to drink (he constantly "needs" a drink now). Yesterday, Cuauhtemoc [Blanco] was talking to me about how worried he is about Jack – but neither of us could think of anything to do – Jack gets hostile if you start talking about his drinking. I'm afraid I'm at the stage where I'm avoiding him – I don't want to go out and watch him get drunk – particularly now that he's blacking out and bordering on violence.

Maybe I should have a word with David – it's quite possible that he's not aware of the situation, that the "favour" of keeping Jack down here indefinitely is wrecking the guy.

Monday, I went for a lonely supper at La Pergola. Ran into Patrick [Stewart] there. A while later, Kyle came in with Sian Phillips, Linda Hunt, and Everett. Kyle asked me to join them – I did, after I'd finished eating. Ken McMillan came in a bit later, then Molly [Wryn] and Virginia [Madsen], and finally Ed George. We were there till about midnight. Except for poor service and Ken's loud New York manner, it was fun.

We walked back in the rain.

Thursday, July 7: DAY ONE-HUNDRED-NINE (8 hrs)

Spent quite a bit of time with Jack yesterday. We didn't shoot anything, and I left the studio at four with Jack (we'd all had lunch together). He seems quite serious still about the Herbert Noble story.

I helped him move from the Geneve to the Krystal, had a couple of drinks in the bar there with him and Anatol. Then the two of us had supper in the restaurant there. He was drinking quite a lot, but not getting unpleasantly drunk (apparently he hit Ellie's husband at the party Saturday night - or so he says).

Friday, July 8: DAY ONE-HUNDRED-TEN (10 hrs)

Flying off to Zihuatanejo this evening for the weekend - a crew charter, forty or more *Dune* people. It'll be a problem keeping away from them all for two days, but I'll give it a try. I need a complete break.

First unit shut down yesterday for the rest of the week - Kyle walked off, as he said he would if he didn't have a signed contract by Wednesday. Jack puts it down to his being a spoiled brat - apparently it's not that unusual for someone to go through a whole movie without anything being signed; what's unusual here, of course, is that no one trusts De Laurentiis - he's exhibited no signs of good faith (omitting important clauses when the terms get written down, as with Patrick Stewart; simply forgetting important parts of the original agreement, as with Dykstra); why should anyone trust him? But it's true that the ones who are complaining most are the ones who have never made a movie before and have no experience of the way the business is conducted.

The Fremen Great Hall from behind.

Weeks Fifteen and Sixteen Documents

Raffaella

will be delighted to have
the pleasure of your company
at her birthday party
to be held
on Saturday 2nd. July, 1983,
from 8:30 pm.
at the San Angel Inn
– palmas 50, esq. altavista –
Col. San Angel Inn.

Raffaella's party invitation.

```
                    CALL  SHEET.              Production N° 79.

PRODUCTION TITLE : DUNE        30 Min.Later       DATE : Wednesday July 6th, 1983.
PRODUCER : RAFFAELLA DE LAURENTIIS                CREW CALL :   8.30am at Studio.
DIRECTOR : DAVID LYNCH         30 Min.Más Tarde   LEAVE HOTEL : 8.00am.

SET & SCENE NUMBERS :                             LOCATION :

EXT.HARKONNEN THOPTER - DESERT -  Sc.:137d (N)                        STAGE #8
EXT.ROCK - DESERT .               Sc.:138pt,140,142b,148a,151a pt (N) STAGE #8

ARTISTS              CHARACTERS          D/R         P/U         M/U         ON SET

FRANCESCA ANNIS      JESSICA             218         6:30am      7:00am      10:00am
KYLE MacLACHLAN      PAUL                217         8:30am      9:00am      10:00am


STAND-INS :

JOSEPHINE LOVELL     FOR JESSICA                                 8:00am      8:30am
GONZALO IRIGOYEN     FOR PAUL                                    8:00am      8:30am


CROWD:

2 Harkonnen Guards (with wigs)                                   7:00am      8:30am


REQUIREMENTS:
PRODUCTION:          Security Guards in Stage #8 - AD's desk rigged to Stage lights,bell
                     and telephone - coffee service on Stage & dressrooms - mobile dress-
                     rooms for actors on Stage - KEEP CLEAR front, access and corner of
                     Stage for production and actor's cars.
                   * Guardias de seguridad en Foro #8 - Mesa de Asst. Dir. conectada a lu-
                     ces, campana y telefono de Foro - servicio de cafe en Foro y camerinos
                     - Camerinos mobiles para actores en Foro - DEJAR LIBRE frente, acceso
                     y esquinas de Foros para carros de producción y actores.
CATERING:            Dune Restaurant open from 7:00am - Lunch ready from 12:30 noon
                   * Restaurante Dune abierto desde las 7:00am - Comida lista desde las
                     12:30 hrs.
ART DEPT.:           Harkonnen ornithopter - Yueh's sign on it.
                     Ornithopter Harkonnen - signo de Yueh en él
PROPERTY:            Leto's signet ring - Yueh's satchel (fremkit) glowing green letter
                     words, litter jons, stilltent, energy caps, makerhooks, thumpers,etc.
                   * Anillo de Leto con signo - mochila de Yueh (Fremkit), letras verde
                     fosforescente, litter jons, stilltent, capsulas energeticas, ganchos de
                     hacedor, golpeadores etc.
WARDROBE:            For Sc. 137d, thru 142b, gown for Jessica and sand uniform for Paul
                     (continuity from Sc. 135)
                     For Scs. 148a and 151a, stillsuits for both.
                   * Sc. 137d hasta 142b, camison para Jessica y uniforme de arena para
                     Paul (continuidad de Sc. 135)
                     Sc. 148a y 151a, destiltraje para ambos.
SP/FX:               Wind - steam from thopter - dust /* Aire - vapor de thopter - polvo.
TRANSPORTATION:      Stand by combis for actors in front of dressingrooms /* Combis pen-
                     dientes para actores en frente de camerinos
ADVANCE SCHEDULE:                                                J.López Rodero
TO COMPLETE      For Wednesday July 7th, 1983.                   Assistant Director
EXT. HARKONNEN THOPTER - DESERT   Sc. 137d (N)                        STAGE #8
EXT. ROCK - DESERT                Sc. 138pt,140,142b,148a,151a pt (N) STAGE #8
```

First unit call sheet, July 6, 1983.

Weeks 17 & 18: July 11-24, 1983

Monday, July 11: DAY ONE-HUNDRED-THIRTEEN (9 1/2 hrs)

The Fremen Great Hall at Sietch Tabr over Paul's shoulder, the backlot set enhanced with a matte painting. Photograph copyright Universal/De Laurentiis.

Thursday, July 14: DAY ONE-HUNDRED-SIXTEEN (7 1/2 hrs, 9 hrs, 2 hrs)

The flight to Zihua was quite an experience – an old twin-engine Convair which seemed to crawl rather than fly. It took two hours to make the usually fifty-minute flight. The airport at Zihua was closed – no transport. We wound up hiring two airport maintenance pick-ups into town – like a hayride – we had seventeen squeezed into ours. A hot, humid night, clear sky.

After checking in (to a filthy room) a bunch of us grabbed a cab into town – to a bar called Coconuts. In the end, only five of us remained; myself, Gordon, John Stirber, Ros and Anne. We wound up at a little café.

Saturday, I was on the beach with Fred and Nancy. Anne joined us. We wound up at the bar at the Villa del Sol.

After a lot of swimming and sun, everyone went to crash later in the afternoon. I slept 'til almost eight. Went down the hall to Ron Downing's room to see if he was going along to Los Tortugas, a restaurant in town.

Everyone gathered in the hotel bar, then we headed off for supper. No cabs. We started walking down the hill. Somehow, a pickup was appropriated. The others were still waiting for a table. It was pretty crowded. Very pleasant. A big meal of fresh crayfish.

Zihuatanejo.

Me on the beach at Zihua, John Stirber in background.

From there we walked over to Coconuts. We headed for the disco (a tiny place, thatched, open to the sea, music not too loud). I danced a lot with Karla – a very likeable redhead down here with the effects people (she's an old biker's girl, complete with tattoos), staying on long after most of the others had left.

On the plane out on Friday, a joke got started at Ian Woolf's expense. He was told (by Len Barnard and Mary, the accountants, backed up by Golda) that we

Zihua street.

weren't planning to return from Zihua until Raffaella agreed to meet our terms about improving work conditions. He swallowed it whole. On Saturday Mary spent some time trying to convince him that it was a joke. He wouldn't believe it. Seeing his job on *Conan II* in jeopardy, he bought a ticket and flew back to the city Saturday evening – much to everyone's merriment when we learned of it on Sunday.

Zihua was a gorgeous break. Far too humid – but the sea was warm and clean and the location beautiful. I swam a lot, drank quite a bit. And despite my intentions, hung out with *Dune* people all weekend (the only ones I actually avoided were Anatol and Marie).

Hotel Sotovento, Zihua.

Anatol has become a pain in a new way. He's now treating me like a hired writer. He's gone beyond that annoying "how much do you want for the script?" Yesterday he had the gall to say he must read what I've written so far because he has no idea what I'm cooking up and he has to check it.

He further pissed me off by giving Marie "permission" to keep the copy of the article I lent her – completely oblivious of the fact that it's not his to give. I only want people who count to have a personal copy (David has one, and Jack, and Catherine) – Marie isn't special to me, she has no connection to David, or to *Eraserhead* – there's no reason for her to keep one (everyone else who's borrowed it has given it back when they're through).

He also keeps on about letting her read my outline – and type out the script as I produce it. I don't want her all over it – but he seems to think it's another way to impress her – as if it was his work. I'm fed up with it.

I learned yesterday that Maggie is only coming back for a day – arriving tomorrow evening, leaving Sunday morning. I probably won't get to see her because we fly to Juarez at seven Saturday morning.

Dune crew members waiting for return flight at Zihua airport.

Saturday, July 16-Saturday, July 23: DAYS ONE-HUNDRED-EIGHTEEN to ONE-HUNDRED-TWENTY-FIVE: Samalayuca Desert, Chihuahua

An intense week just south of the U.S. border, shooting in the desert and drinking pina coladas in the hotel pool. Although the battles are faked, the extras are dropping like flies from the heat.

On the dunes at Samalayuca, where temperatures reached 120+ degrees by noon. Photograph by George Whitear, copyright Universal/De Laurentiis.

Extras in very hot, uncomfortable costumes running through a battle scene. Photograph by George Whitear, copyright Universal/De Laurentiis.

Paul (Kyle MacLachlan) prepares to summon Shai-Hulud, the giant sandworm, on the dunes at Samalayuca. Photograph copyright Universal/De Laurentiis.

Sunday, July 24: DAY ONE-HUNDRED-TWENTY-SIX

Back from Juarez last night. A hot, but surprisingly humid place – it clouded up almost every afternoon, rained a couple of times. The town itself is a scruffy border town with El Paso just across the way. Not terribly prepossessing. But the location – Samalayuca Dunes – was gorgeous (if an awful place to work) – beautiful smooth rolling white dunes, very fine sand, mountains in the distance.

The Friday before we left was wonderful. After packing, I had supper with Jack at the Bellinghausen. I then went over to the Century where Maggie had just got in. We chatted briefly and I left her with a copy of the "Café Universal" outline. I went across to the Krystal to meet Jack again. He was watching a thing about Elvis on TV. After a while, we went down to the lobby.

A bit later we headed across to the bar in the basement of the Royal ("the bunker") – myself, Jack, a couple of the English effects people brought in to replace Dykstra. We met Jack's Scottish friend there and it became quite a party – much drinking and singing. It was very pleasant.

We finally left – turned out.

I got hit by Montezuma's on Sunday, lay exhausted in my hotel room most of the day, slipping in and out of consciousness –

The location was hard and poorly organized (insufficient drinks, local extras treated badly – just a bag lunch) and very slow work. The shooting was awfully slow in the desert – scenes taking a long time to set up because of the numbers of extras and effects. We didn't stick around very much, even took Wednesday off and went to El Paso, caught a couple of movies (*Return of the Jedi*, an awful mess, technically uneven, with some good moments; and *Twilight Zone*, which I liked except for the Spielberg segment).

There are times now when I literally can't stand Anatol – I hate to be anywhere near him.

I bought a bunch of tapes in El Paso and a book (William Burroughs' *Cities of the Red Night*).

Tried to track Tim down – no joy. When I got back here last night there was a message slip in my box – no date, no time, no name, no message, just Tim's Vancouver number. I called again this morning – they still say it's out of order. Don't know what the hell's going on.

Tim just called (six o'clock) – he'll be coming down as soon as he gets his passport.

Weeks Seventeen and Eighteen Documents

```
                          C A L L   S H E E T .            Production N° 82.

PRODUCTION TITLE :   DUNE                        DATE : Monday July 11th, 1983.
PRODUCER : RAFAELLA DE LAURENTIIS                CREW CALL :   8.30am at Studio.
DIRECTOR : DAVID LYNCH                           LEAVE HOTEL : 8.00am


SET & SCENE NUMBERS :                     LOCATION :

1) EXT.ROCK - DESERT .   Sc.:        ,148a,151a pt.   (N)      STAGE #8
   (ON COMPLETION, UNIT MOVES TO STAGE #4  TO LINE UP & REHEARSAL FOR:
2) INT.ROCK LEDGE - HALL OF RITES - SIETCH TABR.
              Sc.:188.190.192,194,196,198
                   200,202,    (N)                             STAGE #4
```

ARTISTS	CHARACTERS	D/R	P/U	M/U	ON SET
FRANCESCA ANNIS	JESSICA	217	6.00 am	6.30am	9.30am
KYLE MacLACHLAN	PAUL	218	8.00am	8.30am	9.30am
SYLVANA MANGANO	R.M.RAMALLO	203	Stand by at home from 12.00 noon		
EVERETT McGILL	STILGAR	204	12.30 noon		T.B.N
SEAN YOUNG	CHANI	208	"		T.B.N
MOLLY WRYN	HARAH	205	"		T.B.N
PATRICK WELSH	MONK #1	209		2.30pm	T.B.N
SALVADOR GODINES	WATERMASTER #1	211		2.30pm	T.B.N
DANNY CORKILL	ORLOP	212	12.30 noon		T.B.N
DIEGO GONZALEZ	KALEFF	212	"		T.B.N

```
STAND -INS :
JOSEPHINE LOVELL      FOR JESSICA                            8.00am    8.30am
GONZALO IRIGOYEN      FOR PAUL                                 "         "


CROWD :

  6 Watermasters                                           12.00 noon
 23 Virgins                                                    "
 11 Monks                                                  12.00 noon


REQUIREMENTS
PRODUCTION :      Security on Stages #8 & #4- A.D's desk rigged to Stage #8 lights,bell &
                  telephone- coffee service on Stage #8 & #4 & dress.rooms- mobiles dress.
                  rooms in Stage #8 for actors- KEEP CLEAR front, corners & access of
                  Stages for Prod. & actors cars./* Vigilancia en Fors #8,#4- cafe en
                  Foros #8,#4 y camerinos- mesa de Asst.Dir.conectada a luces,campana y
                  telefono de Foro #8-camerinos moviles para actores en Foro #8- DEJAR
                  LIBRE entrada, accesos y esquinas de Foros para carros de Pro.y actores.
CATERING :        Dune 's Rest.open from 7.00am- lunch ready from 12.30 noon /* Rest. de
                  Dune abierto desde las 7.00am - comida lista desde las 12.30 hrs.
PROPERTY :        Leto's signet ring - Yueh's satchel (fremkit) with " litter jons,
                  stilltent,energy caps, maker hooks, thumpers, etc..."
                  For sc.: 188,190 etc...:  horns for monks,musical dispticks,pots for
                  burning spice,cleansing bags, water sacks & spouts,straps for Jessica ,
                  blue water
         *        Anillo de Leto- mochilla de Yueh (fremkit) con " litter jons,stilltent,
                  capsulas energeticas,ganchos de hacedor,golpeadores etc..."
                  Para Esc.: 188,190 etc... : cuernos para monjes,varillas musicales,
                  recipientes para incienso, bolsas de limpieza,bolsas de agua y escupide-
                  ras, ataduras para Jessica, agua azul.
SET DRESSING :    Litter for  R.M.Ramallo & throne chair for Jessica /* litera para R.M.
                  Ramallo y silla  del trono para Jessica.
WARDROBE :

                  For sc.: 148a & 151a pt.:stillsuits for both.
                                                                            .../...
```

First unit call sheet, July 11, 1983.

```
                         CALL  SHEET

PRODUCTION TITLE: "DUNE"                    DATE: Monday July 11th, 1983.
PRODUCER:  RAFFAELLA DE LAURENTIIS           CREW CALL: 8:30am
DIRECTOR:  DAVID LYNCH                       LEAVE HOTEL: 8:00am
2ND. U. DIR: JIM DEVIS                       CAMERA/ELECT/GRIP: 8:00am

                    * RED & BLUE CAMERA *
```

SETS & SCENES NUMBERS:		LOCATION:
1) BLUE BACKING TEST If test is satisfactory:		
2) INT. TUNNEL - STAIR CASE - GEIDI PRIME	Sc. 169 pt.	STAGE #2 Blue Backing
3) INT. STEEL TENT - EMPEROR SPACE SHIP (Baron spinning)	Sc. 272 pt.	

ARTISTS	CHARACTERS	D/R	P/U	M/U	ON SET
KENNETH McMILLAN	BARON	206	8:00am		9:00am for rehearsal.

STAND INS:
A.N.OTHER   FOR BARON (Floating rigging)   9:30am   10:00am

REQUIREMENTS:
PRODUCTION: Security guards in Stage #2 - coffee service in stage and dressing-
                   rooms - red light and bell rigged to Stage #2 - KEEP CLEAR stage
                   front, access and corners of stages for generator, production and
                   artists' cars.
                * Guardias de seguridad en Foro #2 - servicio de cafe en foro y came-
                   rinos - luz roja y campana conectadas en Foro #2 - DEJAR LIBRE
                   acceso, esquinas y frente de foro para generadora y coches de
                   producción y artistas.
CATERING: Dune Restaurant open from 7:00am - Lunch ready from 12:30pm.
                * Restaurante Dune abierto desde las 7:00am - Comida lista desde las
                   12:30pm.
CAMERA: As per J.Devis instructions - Revolving mount required
                * Según instrucciones de J.Devis - Montura revolvente requerida.
SP/FX: Rig mechanism for Baron floating and spinning Rehearsal at 9:00am
                * Conectar mecanismo para flotar y girar al Baron.Ensayo a las 9:00am.
OPT.FX: Blue backing required
                * Fondo Azul requerido.

TRANSPORTATION:

1 PRODUCTION CAR   (own instructions)   J. DEVIS

1 PRODUCTION CAR   (own instructions)   V. ALBARRAN

ARTIST CAR   8:00am   KENNETH McMILLAN   HTL. KRYSTAL   8:30am

                                             Victor Albarran
                                             Assistant Director

Second unit call sheet, July 11, 1983.

```
                                CALL SHEET              Production No. 91
    PRODUCTION TITLE: DUNE                              Thursday 21th, 1983.
    PRODUCER:  RAFFAELLA DE LAURENTIIS    #352          CREW CALL:   6:00AM
    DIRECTOR:  DAVID LYNCH                              LEAVE HOTEL: 5:00AM
                                                        TRAVEL TIME: 1hr.
```

SETS & SCENES NUMBERS:

1) EXT. DESERT   Sc. 226b to complete   LOCATION:
2) EXT. DESERT   Sc. 215,217,219,219b,219d Samalayuca Dunes
                                             Chihuahua

ARTISTES	CHARACTER	M/U	P/U	ON SET
KYLE MacLACHLAN	PAUL	5:30am	6:30am	7:30am
EVERET McGILL	STILGAR	6:00am	6:30am	7:30am
PATRICK STEWART	GURNEY	5:15am	6:30am	7:30am
DANNY CORKILL	ORLOP	T.B.N.		
DIEGO GONZALEZ	KALEFF	T.B.N.		
HONORATO MAGALONE	FEDAYKIN # 1	7:00am	6:00am	7:30am
RICHARD HUMPHREYS	Stunt coordinator + Stuntmen		5:00am	6:00am

STAND - INS

Gonzalo Irigoyen	for Paul		5:00am	6:00am
a.n.other	for Stilgar		5:00am	6:00am
a.n.other	for Gurney		5:00am	6:00am

CROWD

14 Fedaykins	(Mexicans)		5:00am	7:30am
12 Fremen drumers	(10 mex + 2 locals)		5:00am	7:30am
26 Fremen	(El Paso - Locals)		5:00am	7:30am

Red Camera:

35 Smugglers	(locals)		5:00am	7:30am
12 fremen	(Locals)		5:00am	7:30am
40 Harkonnen/Miners	(army)		5:00am	7:30am

REQUIREMENTS

Production: Security guards on location for camp and set - radio communication from camp to set ready for call time - loud speakers system rigged on set. Water and coffee service uninterrupted on set and camp - motorhomes for actors ready on set at 6:00am - camp facilities ready from 5:00 am./*Guardias de seguridad en locación para campamento y set - comunicación de radio de campamento a set lista para la hora del llamado - sistema de altavoces conectado en set - aqua y café ininterrumpido en set y campamento - motorhomes para actores listos en set desde las 6:00am - facilidades en campamento listas desde las 5:00am.

First Aid: Ready on camp from 5:00am - ready on set from 6:00am - ambulance standing by on camp from 5:00am/*Listo en campamento desde las 5:00am listo en set desde las 6:00am - ambulancia pendiente en campamento desde las 5:00am.

Catering: Lunch at location ready from 12:00 noon - Breakfast to be arranged at Hotels ready from 4:00am/*Comida en locación lista desde las 12:00 hrs. - desayuno debe ser arreglado en el hotel listo desde las 4:00am.

Property: Weapons for smugglers - weapons for fremens & fedayking - weapons for harkonnen - maula pistol - weirding modules - Gurney's knife - Big thumper - fremen drums & other rythm instruments - ceremonial maker hooks - Paul's thumper/* Armas smugglers - armas fremen y fedaykins - armas harkonnen - pistola maula - módulos misteriosos - cuchillo Gurney - golpeador grande - tambores fremen y otros instrumentos de ritmo - ganchos ceremoniales - golpeador de Paul/ Ropes, hooks, thumpers & accesories for fremen/* Cuerdas, ganchos, golpeadores y accesorios fremen.

First unit call sheet, July 21, 1983.

```
                              CALL SHEET              Production No. 92
                                                      Friday 22nd, 1983
PRODUCTION TITLE:   "DUNE"          #352              CREW CALL:    6:00am
PRODUCER:    RAFFAELLA DE LAURENTIIS                  LEAVE HOTEL:  5:00am
DIRECTOR:    DAVID LYNCH                              TRAVEL TIME:  1hr.
```

SETS & SCENES NUMBERS:

1)   EXT. DESERT   Sc. 215, 217, 219, 219b, 219e.   Location:

                                                            Samalayuca Dunes
                                                            Chihuahua

ARTISTES	CHARACTER	M/U	P/U	ON SET
KYLE MacLACHLAN	PAUL	5:30am	6:30am	7:30am
EVERET McGILL	STILGAR	6:00am	6:30am	7:30am
DANNY CORKILL	ORLOP		7:00am	8:00am
DIEGO GONZALEZ	KALEFF		7:00am	8:00am
HONORATO MAGALONE	FEDAYKIN # 1	7:00am	6:00am	7:30am

STUNTS

Richard Humphreys	Stunt coordinator + stuntmen (6)		5:00am	6:00am

STAND-INS

Gonzalo Irigoyen	for Paul		5:00am	6:00am
a.n.other	for Stilgar		5:00am	6:00am

CROWD

14 Fedaykins	(mexicans)		5:00am	7:30am
12 Fremen drumers	(10mex + 2 locals)		5:00am	7:30am
26 Fremen	(El Paso - locals)		5:00am	7:30am

Red Camera

12 Fremen	(locals)		5:00am	7:30am
40 Harkonnen/Miners	(army)		5:00am	7:30am

REQUIREMENTS :

Production: Security guards on location for camp and set - radio communication from camp to set ready for call time - loud speakers system rigged on set. Water and coffee service uninterrupted on set and camp - motorhomes for actors ready on set at 6:00am - camp facilities ready from 5:00am/*Guardias de seguridad en locación para campamento y set - comunicación de radio de campamento a set lista para la hora del llamado - servicio de agua y café ininterrumpido en set y campamento - motorhoems para actores listos en set desde las 6:00am - facilidades en campamento listas desde las 5:00am.

First Aid: Ready on camp from 5:00am - ready on set from 6:00am - ambulance standing by on camp from 5:00am/*Listo en campamento desde las 5:00am - listo en set desde las 6:00am - ambulancia pendiente en campamento desde las 6:00am.

Catering: Lunch at location ready from 12:00 noon - Breakfast to be arranged at Hotels ready from 4:00am/* Comida en locación lista desde las 12:00hrs - desayuno en Hoteles listo desde las 4:00am.

Property: Weapons for smugglers, fremens, fedaykins & harkonnen - maula pistol - weirding modules - big thumper - fremen drums & other rythm instruments -

First unit call sheet, July 22, 1983, page 1.

Property: (continues)	ceremonial maker hooks - Paul's thumper - ropes, hooks, thumpers & accesories for fremen/* Armas smuggler - armas fremen y fedaykin - armas harkonnen - pistola Maula - módulos misteriosas - golpeador grande - tambores fremen y otros instrumentos rítmicos - ganchos ceremoniales - golpeador de Paul - cuerdas, ganchos golpeadores y accesorios fremen.
Electric:	Rig generator for Camera Lightflex and sound (P.A.)/*Conectar generador para cámara Lightflex y sonido (altavoces).
Sp/Fx:	Heat waves/* Ondas de calor.
Wardrobe:	Globes for fremen implanting thumper/*Guantes para fremen enterrando golpeador.
Transportation:	Vehicles for production and artistes movement from camp to set ready on location from 5:30am/Vehículos para movimiento de producción y artistas del campamento al set listo en locación desde las 5:30am.

ADVANCE SCHEDULE:

Saturday July 23rd, 1983.

EXT. DEEP DESERT   Sc. 215, 217, 219, 219b, 219e
                            to complete

                                        J. LOPEZ RODERO
                                        Assistant Director

First unit call sheet, July 22, 1983, page 2.

Weeks 19 & 20: July 25–August 7, 1983

Monday, July 25: DAY ONE-HUNDRED-TWENTY-SEVEN (9 hrs)

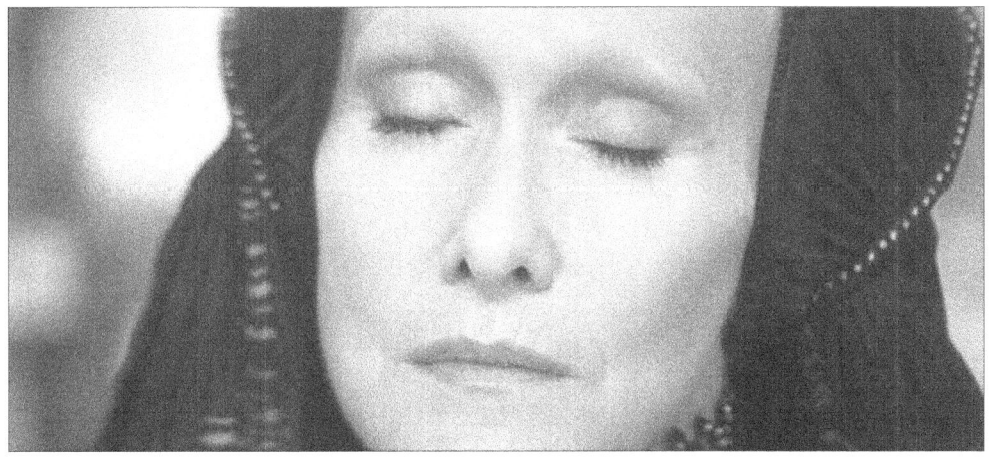

Sian Phillips as the Bene Gesserit Reverend Mother Mohiam.
Photograph copyright Universal/De Laurentiis.

It's possible we'll be staying on here longer than expected.

We spoke with Raffaella this afternoon. The idea is to cover the model and effects work on *Dune* after principal photography has been completed – and periodically cover the production of *Conan* at the same time (much of it on location) – occasionally hitting L.A. to check on the assembly of the *Dune* material.

We'll call Armstrong tomorrow to put it to him (Raffaella said she'd also call him). She seemed to accept the idea without a moment of doubt, as if it were the most natural thing. With her, it seems, we're firmly established.

Tuesday, July 26: DAY ONE-HUNDRED-TWENTY-EIGHT (5 1/2 hrs)

Just finished the first draft of "Café Universal" – the last thirteen pages this afternoon (handwritten, it's 72 pages long).

I don't want Anatol to know yet.

An awful evening. No one to share the moment with. It became very lonely and depressing.

Friday, July 29: DAY ONE-HUNDRED-THIRTY-ONE

Just finished William Burroughs' *Cities of the Red Night*. Couldn't make head or tail of it.

Sunday, July 31: DAY ONE-HUNDRED-THIRTY-THREE

I heard from Tony Masters that Raffaella wants Peter Weir to direct *Tai-Pan*. With another producer, great – but with her, I hope he has other plans.

Tuesday, August 2: DAY ONE-HUNDRED-THIRTY-FIVE (9 1/2 hrs, 3 hrs)

Bunuel died last weekend and David Niven sometime last week.

I finally had to tell Anatol the script is finished. Yesterday evening he was pushing so hard I either had to tell an outright lie or admit it. Actually, he was pushing so hard, I have a feeling word had already gotten to him – I'd told a couple of people (Pablo, Molly, Greg Gubi ...). He won't read it until it's typed, though.

Thursday, August 4: DAY ONE-HUNDRED-THIRTY-SEVEN (7 hrs, 9 hrs)

Emilio Ruiz del Rio making last-minute adjustments to the Arrakeen foreground miniature.

A good day, surprisingly. Two interviews. The second with Emilio Ruiz del Rio, who's in charge of the live-action miniatures. A fascinating, energetic, enthusiastic man whose work in itself is extremely interesting. We'll be doing more on him. It was the first time we'd all been interested in ages – in fact, we'd all been feeling at the end of our tolerance for the job. I've been depressed all week, Pablo's having marital problems, and Anatol was ready to quit.

Met the guy [Barry Nolan] who's taken Dykstra's place, doing the opticals. Claims he does better work, of course. Then proudly announces that he did "most of the De Laurentiis pictures of the last fifteen years" – such effects classics as *Conan*, *King Kong* and *Flash Gordon*. Also did *Logan's Run*. Now I'm really worried about the way *Dune* will turn out.

Apparently there's about three hours of the film assembled so far. With an expected first cut of five hours. Universal wants a two-and-a-half hour maximum, Dino – I think – two hours. It could become incoherent by the time it's released.

Meanwhile, a number of people have voiced the fear that the film will be, quite simply, dull.

Friday, August 5: DAY ONE-HUNDRED-THIRTY-EIGHT (3 hrs)

So – shortly after eight yesterday, I took a walk over to the Krystal. No one there. Around the block and back. Still no one. I called Anatol. He and Marie were planning to go later – they'd pick me up. I dozed off. Phone woke me at nine-forty-five – Marie: They were on their way. I went downstairs to wait.

About ten-fifteen, John Baker walked in – to call up to John Stirber's suite and tell him that Anne would like his presence. A group had met at the Krystal after all. I waited until about ten-twenty-five, then walked over. Had a quick drink – then five of us piled into a taxi and headed for the party – me, John Stirber, Andrew Kelley, Anne, and Anita.

The party – in a really obscure part of town, reached through winding little lanes barely more than alleys – turned out to be quite small and pleasant. Drank quite a bit, talked to various people. I had a little chat with a woman called Valerie who's in love with Malcolm – then went to sleep on a wooden bench in the living room.

I got a ride back here shortly after seven with Trevor.

The reason Anatol and Marie didn't show up yesterday evening was that at ten o'clock Anatol's jeep was totalled. They were lucky not to be killed. A car barrelled through a red light, hit the jeep dead centre and sent it spinning three times, into another car, then into a fence.

No one was seriously hurt – shaken up, whiplash. Damned good thing they hadn't picked me up yet – I'd've been rattling around loose in the back.

Didn't stay long at the studio. Got some releases signed – I'm embarrassed to present the fucking things to people. Some are a little hostile about them.

Then picked up the IBM typewriter I've just rented, came back here, started on the script, took a nap, went out for supper, typed some more. Got a third of the script done already. Unbelievably wonderful feeling having a typewriter again – a very good one too.

Saturday, August 6: DAY ONE-HUNDRED-THIRTY-NINE (1 hr)

Rainy day, Mexico City.

The studio was shut down today – shooting had been completed on two stages, so they decided to let people go for the weekend. I found that out after I got there.

A long, arduous day, nonetheless. I typed out the whole script – it comes to a total of ninety-eight pages – and looks vastly better for being typed. It is without question the best script I've written (but is that saying very much, really?).

Pablo tells me Anatol is dying to read it. Suppose I can't really delay. I'll run off some copies on Monday – send one to Jack Leustig in L.A. – see if anything happens. Certainly, for all his talk Anatol hasn't got the faintest idea where to look for money.

Sunday, August 7: DAY ONE-HUNDRED-FORTY

Just spoke to Tim – still in Vancouver – still waiting for his passport. Ready to come down at a moment's notice.

Proofed the script this morning, retyped where necessary. I'll run off a few copies tomorrow.

The glow I felt yesterday has worn off, of course – that feeling you get looking at a freshly completed manuscript – a sort of loving warmth, like a mother with a new baby. The inevitable detachment is already setting in – once the thing is finished and sent on its way, I seldom feel any sense of personal connection – the process of writing becomes forgotten and the end product is just an object somewhere outside.

I'm approaching the stage where I think it's a complete piece of rubbish which would be embarrassing to show anyone.

Weeks Nineteen and Twenty Document

```
                              CALL SHEET              Production No. 92
                                                      Monday July 25, 1983
PRODUCTION TITLE:    "DUNE"                           CREW CALL:    8:30am
PRODUCER:     RAFFAELLA DE LAURENTIIS                 LV. HOTELS:   8:00am
DIRECTOR:     DAVID LYNCH

SETS & SCENES NUMBERS:

1)   INT. ROCK LEDGE HALL OF RITES      Sc. 251pt              STAGE # 4
2)   INT. ROCK LEDGE HALL OF RITES      Sc. 200pt, 202pt
                                        (pick ups)

ARTISTES                 CHARACTER           D/R      P/U        M/U        ON SET

FRANCESCA ANNIS          JESSICA             217      5:45am     6:15am     9:30am
KYLE MacLACHLAN          PAUL                218      8:00am     8:30am     9:30am
EVERETT McGILL           STILGAR             204      8:15am     8:45am     9:30am
PATRICK STEWART          GURNEY              206      7:30am     8:15am     9:30am
SEAN YOUNG               CHANI               208      6:15am     6:45am     9:30am
MOLLY WRYN               HARAH               205      6:15am     6:45am     9:30am
DANNY CORKILL            ORLOP               212      7:30am     9:00am     9:30am
DIEGO GONZALEZ           KALEFF              211      8:30am     9:00am     9:30am
HONORATO MAGALONE        FEDAYKIN # 1        215                 8:30am     9:30am
PATRICK WELCH            MONJE # 1           209                 8:30am     9:30am

STANDINGS

A.N.OTHER                FOR JESSICA                             8:00am     8:30am
A.N.OTHER                FOR PAUL                                8:00am     8:30am
A.N.OTHER                FOR STILGAR                             8:00am     8:30am
A.N.OTHER                FOR GURNEY                              8:00am     8:30am
A.N.OTHER                FOR CHANI                               8:00am     8:30am
A.N.OTHER                FOR HARAH                               8:00am     8:30am
A.N.OTHER                DOUBLE FOR MONK # 1                     8:00am     8:30am

CROWD

13 Fedaykins (stillsuit)                                         7:00am     9:00am
 6 Fremen women (stillsuit -sietch cloth)                        7:00am     9:00am
24 Fremen men (stillsuit - sietch cloth)                         7:00am     9:00am
10 Monks                                                         7:00am     9:00am
 4 Water masters                                                 9:30am    11:00am
22 Virgins                                                       9:00am    12:00pm

REQUIREMENTS

Production       Security guards in stage # 4 - AD's desk rigged to stage light, bell and
                 telephone - Coffee service on stage and in dress rooms - Mobile dress
                 rooms for artistes on stage - Keep clear stage front access and corners
                 for production and artistes' vehicles - Mobile dress rooms for crowd on
                 stage/* Guardias de seguridad en foro 4 - Mesa de AD's conectada a luces
                 del foro, telefono y timbre - Servicio de café en foro y vestidores -
                 Camerinos móviles en foro para actores - Mantener libre el acceso al foro
                 para vehiculos de actores y producción - Camerinos móviles en foro para
                 figuración.
Catering         Dune restaurant open from 7:00am - Lunch ready from 12:30 noon /* Restaurante
                 Dune abierto desde las 7:00am - Comida lista desde las 12:30 hrs.
Property         For sc. 251pt : Weapons for fremen, monk amplifying horn - war drums.
                 For sc.     200pt, 202pt: Pots for burning spice (incense) - dipsticks
                 (musical) - smoke cleansing bags - water sacks and spouts - blue water./*
                 Para sc. 251pt: Armas fremen - corno amplificado para monjes - tambores de
                 guerra. - Para sc.     200pt, 202pt: Recipiente para especie (incienso) -
                 dipsticks musicales - bolsas para limpiar humo - odres y recipientes para
                 agua - agua azul.
Wardrobe         For sc. 200, 202pt: sietch clothes for fremen - For sc. 251 - Stillsuits
                 for fremen STILLSUITS MUST BE CLEAN./* Para sc. 200, 202pt: ropas de sietch
                 para fremen - Para sc. 251: Stillsuits para fremen STILLSUITS DEBEN ESTAR
                 LIMPIOS.

SP/FX            Incense smoke - soft wind stand by/* Humo de incienso - suave viento pendiente.
Transportation   Stand by combies for actors in front of dressing rooms./* Combies pendientes
                 para actores frente a camerinos - actores.


ADVANCE SCHEDULE:

Tuesday July 26, 1983.

1)   EXT. ROCK LEDGE              Sc. 251pt              Stage # 4
                                  (if not completed)

2)   INT. MAKER ROOM              Sc. 187a, 237, 241 (N) Stage # 3


                                                 J.LOPEZ ROMERO
                                                 Assistant Director
```

First unit call sheet, July 25, 1983.

Week 21: August 8-14, 1983

Monday, August 8: DAY ONE-HUNDRED-FORTY-ONE (7 1/2 hrs)

Well, I couldn't make the copies today – I got up to page twenty-seven and the copier broke down. Nothing personal, I hope.

I actually took the plunge this evening and went to a movie (theatres here are awful). By myself. Peter Yates' *Krull*. Awful. Dumb script, leaden direction, horrendous costume and set design.

Six people involved whom I now know personally – two actors: Freddie Jones and Francesca Annis – and four on the crew: Andrew Kelly (now on Kit West's crew here), Ken Warrington (now doing the plates for opticals on *Dune* – taking over from Apogee's people), our very own Kuki Lopez Rodero (David's A.D.) and Vicente Escriva who has just left us without warning because of some argument with Raffaella.

Although the effects are generally pretty poor, there is one sequence – David Allen's crystal spider animation – which is really very good.

A truly horrible wall-to-wall James (*Star Trek II*) Horner score.

On the whole, for all its twenty-five-or-whatever million dollars, it looks remarkably like a cheap Italian sun-and-sweat epic (an impression much aided by the dismally handled monster-villain, "the Beast").

I'm glad going to movies here is so cheap (about 60¢ US).

Tuesday, August 9: DAY ONE-HUNDRED-FORTY-TWO (8 hrs)

Witnessed an incredibly stupid decision at the studio yesterday. Second unit was doing a major effects shot – the wall of the Emperor's ship being blown out on Stage 5. Sections were pulled away by cable, followed by air cannons firing debris and gas jets sending up a wall of flame. (Later, the Baron is to be composited in, flying out through the hole as he dies.)

The set was constructed a couple of months ago with this effect in mind. It took all morning to rig it. They got one take before lunch – it had to be cut short because it almost started a fire. They set about rigging for a second take. Almost three o'clock, rigged to go – and in rushes Tony Masters – "we want it changed; a bigger hole, the pillars have to go too…" Now, all of this would essentially require rebuilding the set. A lot of money. Raffaella is away until Wednesday – so the decision to throw all that extra money in can't be made yet. So, the logical thing to do would be to do the second take as is, have it in the can just in case, since it's all paid for already (it was ready to shoot). But instead, Pepe Lopez said, no, scrap it. So if Raffaella when she gets back says she's not spending all that extra money, they've still got to waste money setting up the shot again they were ready to shoot yesterday. I can't understand the way these people think.

Did fuck all today. We went out this morning to do some shopping. Got back in time for lunch. After lunch, lingered a bit – then Anatol and I went to a movie.

Called *Possession*, it was made a few years ago in Berlin by a Polish director called Zulawsky, in English, starring Isabelle Adjani and Sam Neill. It's one of the wildest films I've ever seen, brilliantly directed, superbly acted (Neill is incredible; Adjani has never been better). The camerawork had me squirming in my seat in ecstasy – I don't think there was a dull shot in the film, very few conventional shots – Zulawsky keeps the camera moving almost constantly – but it's never annoying or gratuitous – generates a perpetual tension as the film gets more and more insane. It's the closest experience to *Eraserhead* I've come across – but far different – instead of David's careful, stately elegance, Zulawsky is wildly energetic, almost crude – but for all his explosiveness, he's as controlled as David, obsessed with details, tiny mannerisms, quirks of character. I haven't been so thrilled by a film in ages – despite the scratchy, broken print, the intermittently disappearing sound, often inaudible dialogue. I *have* to see it in a good print.

Carlo Rambaldi is here for a few days, doing something with the sandworm. We'll interview him possibly tomorrow. Actually, we could almost justify going to *Possession* because Rambaldi built the creature Adjani gives birth to which eventually becomes Neill's doppelganger. A nice piece of work it is too, though little seen in the film.

Wednesday, August 10: DAY ONE-HUNDRED-FORTY-THREE (4 1/2 hrs)

A good day today.

Anatol didn't show up with the car, so I wound up riding in with Rambaldi and his assistant. Talked a bit about *Possession*, and some of his other work.

We took the camera out to the backlot this morning where Rambaldi was detailing the large worm segment (using a whole lot of condoms to create tissues and tendons). He gave us a little impromptu interview, part English, part Italian, with his assistant (Bruno) acting as interpreter. We had quite a chat with him – he's articulate, communicative about his work, very friendly. We'll continue to cover him; next week the third-stage navigator is due to arrive from L.A. – sixteen feet long, requiring twenty-five people to operate it.

Carlo Rambaldi applying last-minute details to the full-size worm segment on the backlot, Estudios Churubusco.

John Schlesinger, in Mexico to shoot a movie called *The Falcon & the Snowman*, stopped by to see what was going on and chatted with David Lynch.

My script has now gone to four people – Anatol, Fred (with Leslie to read it after him), Pablo – and Bob Kocourek of Patsa – though I gave it (a mistake) to Marie to deliver to him and apparently she'll pass it on to him after *she's* finished with it (which at her speed could be weeks). I was really pissed off when I heard that (from Bob) because he's a production connection – in other words, business. She's just a spoilt brat.

We took off for lunch in Coyoacan sometime after one. Anatol and Marie in her car; Pablo and me in his. We lost them when she made an illegal turn. For which we were both grateful. Pablo and I wound up at a restaurant where we proceeded to have a seven-thousand peso lunch. (Including *two* bottles of wine.) After which we went on to catch the afternoon show of *Possession*.

This time I followed much more of the dialogue, caught most of the surface action. I was surprised at just how fast it sweeps along (it seemed very long yesterday). I absolutely love it.

Adjani is strange – sometimes in a film she seems beautiful (*Adele H.*); other times I find her rather unattractive (*The Tenant*) – in *Possession* she's simply gorgeous.

David Lynch talks to John Schlesinger on the backlot "worm" set.

Well, Anatol just called. Says he likes the script – though he thinks it would be hard to sell to an American producer. My response is: so what? I'd prefer to make a European film anyway.

Friday, August 12: DAY ONE-HUNDRED-FORTY-FIVE (11 hrs, 7 hrs)

We've done very little all week – and now the three of us are planning to get away next Friday morning for three days in Acapulco, if possible (reservations may be a problem).

Meanwhile, Anatol has had enough of Marie – the constant bitching and complaining have finally gotten to him – maybe. He vacillates a lot.

Pablo likes the script – read it through twice yesterday evening.

Fred's reading it. I gave a copy to Kyle this morning (I'll get one to Jack Leustig through him in a few weeks). And Bob Kocourek seems interested in reading it (if Marie ever lets go of the copy she took). Greg Gubi also wants to read it.

I may run off a few more copies – give one to David.

It looks as if Fred has just been pushed out of the film. – he seems resigned to it. After all the shabby treatment, the constant taking of his equipment, making it impossible to shoot, it seems he'll be leaving in September and whoever remains will take over all the elements he was to shoot.

There are also rumblings of problems between David and Raffaella, that she's starting to put responsibility for all the delays and problems onto him – nothing, of course, to do with her ineptitude as a producer.

Heard why Vicente has left: apparently his brother, married to Raffaella's sister, broke with the company in New York and left with his wife – so the whole Escriva family (including a sister also employed by Dino, and Vicente himself) have simply ceased to exist for De Laurentiis.

Just called Tim: he should have his passport next week. So, barring unforeseen problems, he'll come down the Monday of the week after next (the day I get back from Acapulco – if I go).

Week 22: August 15-21, 1983

Monday, August 15: DAY ONE-HUNDRED-FORTY-EIGHT (3 1/2 hrs, 8 hrs)

Saturday we got a very good interview with Kit West. I'm finally beginning to see a few things which actually can be cut together.

Effects supervisor Kit West [centre left] with one of his crew.

Apparently Kit told Raffaella he was quitting last week. He didn't leave – but he's not happy with the way things are. His crew is stretched very thin – and now he's apparently having to do things Rambaldi contracted for (Rambaldi's baby worm for the water ceremony is just a dead lump of rubber – Kit's people had to hollow it out and install mechanisms to give it life) – apparently Rambaldi's known for this kind of problem.

Today, we went to Azteca Stadium where Jimmy Devis' unit was doing a shot with a foreground miniature. Devis is very cooperative – in fact, invites us in and makes suggestions.

On returning to the studio, we went to the backlot where David was preparing to film the full-size worm segment. We covered that from all angles, then wrapped.

David has selected thirty-seven *Eraserhead* production stills to send to *CFQ*, plus contact sheets of three hundred frame blowups.

Anatol shooting over the wall of the Arrakeen foreground miniature at Azteca Stadium.

Fred likes the script - as a first draft. He spoke to Anatol - I haven't talked to him yet - and what I got second hand was very positive - but he thinks it's very sketchy - characters have to be filled in (Pablo said the same). For me, the characters have to be filled in by the way they're portrayed, defined by the action. I don't want to load them with expository dialogue.

Kyle read the script Friday evening (like Pablo, twice in one sitting) - liked it, but was baffled by the politics. A response which baffles me - the politics are generalized, abstract - not referring to any particular real situations, but to various attitudes which should be clear from the characters' words and actions.

He passed the script on to a friend who's staying with him.

I took another copy to Bob Kocourek - Marie still hasn't finished the one I sent originally - she reads a few lines here and there in between doing tasks in the office. It's no wonder she has trouble following it; she doesn't know how to read.

Just finished Lorenzo Semple's adaptation of Bester's *The Stars My Destination*. A passable script with some very clumsy bits - but the tone isn't right. It's too soft, jokey at times - as if Semple were trying to get a Vonnegut feel into it. It should be harder, grittier, yet more poetic. Considering what Semple did to *King Kong* in the remake, I'm surprised at how seriously he treats this material - but it's still not enough.

Wednesday, August 17: DAY ONE-HUNDRED-FIFTY (9 hrs, 8 1/2 hrs)

Yesterday was a bust. We were ordered to follow yet another tour of the studio – foreign press – and got awful footage – no light, bad sound ... and Strick treating us like lackeys.

To our surprise, Francesca popped up in the afternoon and asked if we still wanted an interview, had we changed our minds ... she seemed quite eager to do it.

Had dinner with Fred Monday evening – good long chat. He really likes the script. Would like the artist clarified a bit – and other characters identified more securely (just for reading – he doesn't think much extra dialogue should be put in). He's already thinking in terms of how to realize it visually. A very favourable response.

Bob Kocourek knows people at Handmade Films (they do the Python movies and others, such as *The Long Good Friday*). If we can get the script to them through him, even if they aren't interested, it might reach others through them who would like this kind of thing.

Anatol spoke to Armstrong yesterday. We're to pack up and ship out the moment principal photography finishes (around the second week in September supposedly). Then, meetings in L.A. to decide what's next.

David seemed a little shocked when we told him today. Strick was surprised.

Thursday, August 18: DAY ONE-HUNDRED-FIFTY-ONE (6 1/2 hrs)

Another dead day – we didn't do a thing.

Two interviews lined up for tomorrow – Bob Ringwood (who's reluctant) and the obnoxious Alicia Witt (child genius) and her bizarre family. Then both Pablo and I are splitting early – he with his family to Cocoyoc, me to Acapulco.

Meanwhile, Anatol has broken with Marie (at last) after interminable squabbles and her constant bitching. She finally brought back the little stories she borrowed at the same time as the *Eraserhead* article (that came back a few days ago) – but only after photocopying them. She's so bloody possessive – didn't even ask first.

We split early today and went to see Wenders' *Der Amerikanische Freund*. Superb film.

I'm not looking forward to tomorrow, the interview with the Witts. I just finished reading a bunch of clippings about the kid – who supposedly spoke at one month, read at nine months, memorized and quoted Shakespeare before she was two, read college textbooks before she was three, plays piano, writes stories and articles (and, her mother says, types a hundred words a minute) ...

and is in telepathic communication with her mother ... a real-life Alia, a monster born with total consciousness...

How the fuck can I talk to her – or rather to the family? We have to "discuss" the whole thing first with the parents – to make sure we won't be "negative".

Saturday, August 20: DAY ONE-HUNDRED-FIFTY-THREE (8 1/2 hrs)

Well, here I am, sprawled on the floor of a hotel room in Acapulco half-drunk after the two-for-one happy hour.

Bob Kocourek read the script – and flipped. He reads a lot of scripts for his job – ones already slated for production – but still, he loved "Café Universal". Looked at me, rather surprised, and said, "You're a *great*

Diane Witt displaying her Guinness record hair. Photo courtesy Dianne Witt.

View from my hotel room in Acapulco.

writer." Also said I should definitely peddle the script around. Though it needs a special producer. In his estimate (and that's his job), it's fairly expensive – over five million. The cheapest way would be with a French director and crew. Which brings me back to Anatol. I really don't think he can do it – he's already coming up with "ideas" I don't like (Eric read it, liked it, told Anatol it has everything but religion – so Anatol wants to stick in a group of nuns crossing a street, the light changes, they have to pick up their habits and run – like a can-can chorus – which has nothing to do with anything, won't fit anywhere, would be a cheap laugh (?) which, Anatol says, "says it all about religion" – with judgement like that, his involvement would be the kiss of death). I have to get a copy to Jack Leustig – and hope he really does have contacts in France.

Meanwhile, Bob is going to think about who best to get in touch with. (He passed a copy on to Moira, production manager on *Conan II* – I'm not sure why – except perhaps to expand the possible circle of contacts.)

Just had a very brief chat with Tim – he won't be coming Monday – probably late next week or the week after.

Weeks 23 & 24: August 22-30, 1983

Monday, August 22: DAY ONE-HUNDRED-FIFTY-FIVE (6 hrs)

Anatol has backed off considerably about the script – I don't know why. Seems to accept that if I can sell it, it'll be up to the producer who directs.

Greg Gubi likes it (with a few reservations about specific points); Eric really likes it. I gave a copy to Everett McGill today (there's a part in it for him).

Somehow – I don't know how – I seem to have written something good. The responses are not just a matter of politeness – they're very positive. It doesn't seem to be a run-of-the-mill script. I'm amazed.

Eric threw out an excellent suggestion at lunch – David Bowie for the drug dealer in the script.

The "fantasy cast" is quite an expensive lot – David, Sissy Spacek, Bowie, Max von Sydow, Jack, Lino Ventura, Everett, Gerard Depardieu, Simone Signoret…

They hooked up a U.S. pay channel here at the hotel last week. So now I find myself watching the tube a lot – last week, *Brimstone and Treacle* and a few bad films; just now *Dragonslayer* – I still love it. Coming up next month, both *Mad Max* and *Road Warrior*.

Tuesday, August 23: DAY ONE-HUNDRED-FIFTY-SIX (6 hrs)

I have to retype the script.

It's not completely "in format" and Leslie Werner told me today that a lot of people won't even read such a script – take a look then put it aside because their poor little eyes can't follow a slightly different form. A dreary job.

An interesting indication: Leslie offered to type it on her word processor in return for a part of it.

Of course I'm not giving any of it away – but that someone who's been in the business for years is interested in getting a piece of the script is perhaps a promising sign.

Wednesday, August 24: DAY ONE-HUNDRED-FIFTY-SEVEN (12 hrs)

Everett gave back the script yesterday. He was most effusive about it – praising my skills – suddenly very friendly. I'm amazed at the respect this thing is gaining me.

He wants to get together to talk about it.

Anatol, for some reason, has become very resigned about it – I wasn't that obvious, was I? He's talking openly in terms of other people directing it.

Friday, August 26: DAY ONE-HUNDRED-FIFTY-NINE (12 hrs)

We were back at Aguilas Rojas, the garbage dump, for night shooting again yesterday (tonight as well) – I actually felt a kind of fondness for it. And for all the waiting yesterday, it wasn't as uninteresting as those nights back in April – there was a spectacular battle scene with huge naphtha explosions.

Patrick Stewart wants to read my script – I left a copy at his hotel this afternoon.

Sunday, August 28: DAY ONE-HUNDRED-SIXTY-ONE (11 1/2 hrs)

Another good night at Aguilas on Friday.

For some reason, a lot of people have been getting a bit nasty with us – saying we're never around, implying that we haven't been working here. Even David has made a few comments about hardly ever seeing us.

Sammon showed up Friday evening – with a re-cut convention piece. Edited out of all the tapes Armstrong took back. Despite his assurances, they're running and working with the masters, not duping the material.

Finished retyping the script.

Just sat through Cimino's *Heaven's Gate* – the uncut version. Beautifully produced – but the script was dreadful, completely unfocused. If it's supposed to

War on Arrakis: Aguilas Rojas, Mexico City.

be about class struggle, the capitalist establishment crushing the poor immigrant proletariat, why is two thirds of it concerned with the passionless love triangle involving Chris Walken, Kris Kristofferson, and Isabelle Huppert? And for all the length, the characters are never given any depth. The elaborate prologue becomes meaningless because it's completely detached from what follows – after dominating it, John Hurt becomes totally extraneous throughout the rest of the film. As for the epilogue, it's even less connected with what went before.

Penny Shaw, by the way, was one of the assistant editors.

Monday, August 29: DAY ONE-HUNDRED-SIXTY-TWO (9 hrs)

Tim is arriving Wednesday evening.
Moira likes the script. And I've given a copy to Molly.
I spoke to Armstrong this afternoon. We can forget about remaining to cover the model work. And I suspect – though it's hard to decipher his evasive manner – that we can forget the editing too.
I'm sending a copy of "Café Universal" to the WGA West to get it registered – a necessary precautionary measure.

Tuesday, August 30: DAY ONE-HUNDRED-SIXTY-THREE (9 hrs)

The wrap will probably be sometime next week.

Our video camera overlooking Arrakis, the planet known as "Dune."

We got an interview with Kyle this morning.

We're all a bit down. I'm afraid Anatol and I have pretty well accepted that next month will be the end for us. If it becomes apparent that we're not going to edit, that Armstrong just wants us temporarily to show him around the material, I'll tell him to find his own way and leave. I've got to find a place to go and live – neither the States nor Canada.

Weeks Twenty-Three and Twenty-Four Documents

Draft of first unit call sheet, August 23, 1983.

```
                            C A L L   S H E E T .        Production N° 121.

PRODUCTION TITLE:  DUNE                          DATE : Monday August 29th,1983.
PRODUCER : RAFFAELLA DE LAURENTIIS               CREW CALL :   8.30 am at Studio
DIRECTOR : DAVID LYNCH                           LEAVE HOTEL:  8.00am
```

SET & SCENE NUMBERS: LOCATION:

INT.THRONE ROOM-EMPEROR'S PALACE . Sc.:9,12,15,17 (N)   STAGE #1
                  MENTAL IMAGES :   Sc.: 11,14
                                    (to start)

ARTIST	CHARACTER	D/R	P/U	M/U	ON SET
JOSE FERRER	EMPEROR	206	8.45am	after rehears.	9.30am
STAND-IN: A.N.OTHER	FOR EMPEROR			8.00am	8.30am

CROWD :

1 Regular Stage Navigator (A.Garciarubio)(S/by 2nd Stage Navigator)		7.30am	9.30am
5 Regular Guildsmen		6.00am	9.00am
10 Regular Guildsmen		7.00am	9.00am
10 Tanked Guildsmen		8.00am	9.00am

REQUIREMENTS:
PRODUCTION :   Security guards on Stage #1- special security for NO SMOKING - A.D's des
                  rigged to Stage bell, lights and telephone- coffee service on stage &
                  dress.rooms,also for crowd - mobile dress.room for actor on stage-
                  covered place & benches for crowd- KEEP CLEAR stages front, access &
                  corners for Prod. & actors cars.
         *   Vigilancia en Foro #1 y especial vigilancia PROHIBIENDO FUMAR - Mesa de
                  Asst. Dir. conectada a luces , campana y telefono de Foro #1- cafe en
                  Foro #1, camerinos y tambien para figuracion- camerino movil para actor
                  en foro #1- sitio cubierto con bancas para figuracion- DEJAR LIBRE
                  entrada, accesos y esquinas de Foros para carros de Prod.y actores-
CATERING: Dune's Rest.open from 7.00am-lunch ready from 12.30 noon- 30 box lunche
                  ready from 12.30 hrs.- breakfast box lunches for 7 people ready from
                  6.30am-
         *   Rest. de Dune abierto desde las 7.00am- comida lista desde las 12.30hrs.
                  30 box lunches listos desde las 12.30hrs.- 7 box lunches de desayuno
                  listos desde las 6.30am.
NAVIGATOR: Carlo Rambaldi & crew ready at 8.30am- Navigator on action.
PROPERTY: Vacuum cleaners /* aspiradoras.
SP/FX :   Box finish opening- please all wind machines for ventilation available-
                  Orange spice gas- mike already in position-
         *   Caja terminandose de abrirse- todos ventiladores disponibles para ventil
                  cion- gas de especie naranja- microfono ya en posicion.

TRANSPORTATION   Artist combis stand by in front of dress.rooms /* combis para actores
                  estar en espera en frente de camerinos.

ADVANCE SCHEDULE: Tuesday August 30th, 1983
                  INT.THRONE ROOM- EMPEROR'S PALACE .

                  Sc.:9,12,15,17,11,14 (N) to be continued   STAGE #1

                                                      J.Lopez Rodero
                                                      Assistant Director.

First unit call sheet, August 29, 1983.

```
                              CALL SHEET
PRODUCTION TITLE: DUNE                    DATE: August Monday 29th, 1983.
PRODUCER:  RAFFAELLA DE LAURENTIIS        CREW CALL:    11:00am
DIRECTOR:  DAVID LYNCH                    LEAVE HOTEL: 10:30am
                                          CAM/ELEC/GRIP:   10:30am leave for
                                                                   Stadium
                         RED & BLUE CAMERA


SETS & SCENES NUMBERS:                    LOCATION:

1) EXT. ARRAKEEN PALACE (Retake)  Sc. 65c   (D)      AZTEC STADIUM
   (Emilio's Shot)

   THEN MOVE TO STUDIOS:

2) INT. GREAT HALL - ARRAKEEN PAL.  Sc. 281pt.       STAGE # 7
   (Insert-Bull Head)

3) INT. JESSICA'S ROOM-CALADAN      Sc. 35pt.        STAGE # 7
   (Insert-Int. Box-Paul's hand
   burning-1st.&2nd.stage)


ARTISTES             CHARACTERS      D/R       P/U      M/U       ON SET


DOUBLES:

LUIGI ROCHETTI       PAUL (hand)                                  5:00pm.


CROWD:

20 Atreides soldiers (with short hair and banners)    10:00am   12:00noon
40 Atreides soldiers (with short hair)                10:00am   12:00noon


REQUIREMENTS:

Production:    Security guards at Aztec Stadium & Stage 7 - Communication from Stadium
               to Production Office - Coffee service at Stadium & Stage 7 - AP system
               rigged at Stadium - Red light & bell rigged on Set # 7 - Doctor on set and
               at Stadium - KEEP CLEAR front, access & corners of stage 7 for generator
               and production cars - 4 radios for electricians and 4 radios for production
               & Ad's.
          *    Vigilancia en Estadio Azteca y foro 7 - comunicación entre Estadio y oficina
               de producción - servicio de café en Estadio y foro 7 - Altavoces conectados
               en el Estadio - Luz roja y campana conectadas al foro 7 - Doctor en Estadio
               y foro - DEJAR LIBRE el frente, acceso y esquinas del foro 7 -para autos
               de producción y generador - 4 radios para electricistas y 4 radios para
               producción y asistentes de dirección.
               AMBULANCE AT STADIUM READY FROM 10:30am/AMBULANCIA EN ESTADIO DESDE LAS
               10:30am.
Camera:        35mm - 40mm lenses for Emilio's shot at Aztec Stadium.
          *    Lentes 35mm - 40mm para toma de Emilio en el Estadio Azteca.
Sound:         As per Ing. Carles' instructions - Ready at Aztec Stadium at 11:00am.
          *    De acuerdo a las instrucciones del Ing. Carles - listos en Estadio Azteca
               a las 11:00am.
Sp/Fx:         Heat waves, wind & dust effect (one big wind machine & one small fan).
          *    Efectos de ondas de calor, viento y polvo (una máquina de viento grande y
               un ventilador).
Property:      Weapons for Atreides - 20 banners for atreides-for sc. 35 green box.
          *    Armas atreides - 20 banderas para atreides - caja verde para sc. 35.
Wardrobe:      60 atreides soldiers to get dressed at 10:00am at Studios.
          *    60 soldados atreides para vestirse en los Estudios a las 10:00am.
Casting:       60 atreides soldiers with hair already cut at Studios at 10:00am.
          *    60 soldados atreides con el pelo ya cortado a las 10:00am en los Estudios.
Catering:      Dune Restaurant open from 7:30am - lunch ready from 12:30 noon - 135 box
               lunches for crowd and crew, ready at Stadium at 12:30 noon.
          *    Restaurante Dune abierto desde las 7:30 am - comida lista desde las 12:30
               hrs. - 135 box lunches para figuración y personal listos en Estadio desde
               las 12:30 del día.
```

First unit call sheet, August 29, 1983 (Red & Blue camera units.)

```
                                                    Production No. 127
                         C A L L   S H E E T
PRODUCTION TITLE: DUNE                      DATE: Monday, September 5th, 1983.
PRODUCER:  RAFFAELLA DE LAURENTIIS          CREW CALL:    8:30am
DIRECTOR:  DAVID LYNCH                      LEAVE HOTEL:  8:00am
```

SET & SCENE NUMBERS:					LOCATION:	
1) INT. HALLWAY, EMPEROR'S PALACE		Sc. 229	(N)		Stage #4	
2) " " " "		Sc. 8,10,13,16, 19.			Stage #4	

ARTISTES	CHARACTER	D/R	P/U	M/U	ON SET
SIAN PHILLIPS	R. M. MOHIAM	208		8:00am	9:30am

STAND-INS:

A.N.OTHER	FOR R.M. MOHIAM			9:00am	9:30am

CROWD:

1 SECOND STAGE NAVIGATOR (A. Garciarrubio)		7:00am	9:00am
5 REGULAR GUILDSMEN		6:00am	9:00am
6 BENNE GESSERIT WOMEN		7:00am	12:00noon
4 SARDAUKAR GUARDS		9:00am	10:00am

REQUIREMENTS

PRODUCTION: Security guards on Stage #4 - A.D's. desk rigged to stage's lights, bell and and telephone - Coffee service on set and dress'rooms - Mobile dress'rooms for Actors on stage - Benches for Crowd - KEEP CLEAR stage front, access and corners for Production and Artistes' vehicles.
* Vigilancia en Foro #4 - Mesa de Asist. de Direc. conectada a luces, campana y teléfono del foro - Café en foro y camerinos - Camerino móvil para Actores en foro - Bancas para la Figuración - DEJAR LIBRE acceso, esquinas y frente del foro para carros de Producción y Artistas.

CATERING: Dune Restaurant open from 7:00am - Lunch ready from 12:30noon - Box lunches for 25 people ready from 12:30noon.
* Restaurante "DUNE" abierto desde las 7:00am - Comida lista desde las 12:30 del día - "Box lunches" para 25 personas listos desde las 12:30 del día.

PROPERTY: Weapons for Sardaukars - Guidsmen microphone.
* Armas para Sardaukars - Micrófono para Guildsmen.

SET DECORATION: Chair for R.M. Mohiam (and three more if necessary).
* Silla para R.M. Mohiam (y tres más si es necesario).

TRANSPORT: Artistes' combi S/By in front of dress'rooms.
* Combi de Artistas lista y esperando frente a camerinos.

REMINDER: CONMEMORATIVE PICTURE WILL BE TAKEN ON TUESDAY, SEPTEMBER 6, DURING FIRST UNIT BREAK FOR LUNCH (1:30pm APPROX.) AT STAGE #1. ALL PERSONNEL TO ATTEND.
CORDATORIO: LA FOTO CONMEMORATIVA SE TOMARA ESTE MARTES 6 DE SEPTIEMBRE DURANTE EL RECESO A COMER DE LA PRIMERA UNIDAD. SE REQUIERE EL PERSONAL DE TODOS LOS DEPARTAMENTOS.

ADVANCED SHEDULE:

Tuesday, September 6th., 1983.

INT. THRONE ROOM - EMPEROR'S PALACE	Sc. 7pt.	STAGE #1

J. López Rodero,
Assistant Director.

First unit call sheet, September 5, 1983.

Epilogue

When my friend Tim arrived from Canada, I stopped writing the journal and spent much of the final two weeks of the production showing him around the studio and introducing him to people. We spent the last week in Mexico touring the Yucatan in a rented car, then returned to Canada with a one-day stopover in Chicago, where I handed the photos for the *Eraserhead* article to publisher Fred Clarke.

Two months later, I made a quick trip to visit Jack Leustig in Los Angeles, before flying to England where I lived for the next year, with a three-month break travelling in Europe during the summer. Jack represented my script for a while, but needless to say it remained unsold and unproduced. I first saw my article in print when I bought a copy of *Cinefantastique* in Munich; it looked quite impressive, though some of the text had been cut, and occasionally my wording had been altered in irritating ways. It ended up taking almost two years to get paid the small fee I earned for the effort.

I briefly connected with David Lynch again in London, where he was using a studio to do some ADR for *Dune*, and also met up with John Dykstra while he was supervising effects work for Tobe Hooper's under-rated *Lifeforce*. But on the whole, what connections I had made on *Dune* all eventually lapsed. The most enduring was with Jack Nance, for whom I wrote a script while in Europe. We got as far as meeting with a representative of Oklahoma oil money – a truly bizarre twenty-four hours in Las Vegas, which turned out to be a dead end.

Muad'dib (Kyle MacLachlan) enters the Great Hall to assume control of Arrakis, flanked by Stilgar (Everett McGill) and Gurney Halleck (Patrick Stewart).
Photograph copyright Universal/De Laurentiis.

Jack was on and off the wagon over the next few years, moving from one place to another, and I eventually lost touch with him as well ... it was a shock to read in the papers of his strange, sad death in December 1996.

And finally, what about the movie *Dune*? Is it a "good" movie? A "bad" movie? I'm probably incapable of making a truly objective judgement because even three decades later I still see it through the filter of my experiences in Mexico during the summer of 1983. But I nonetheless do have an opinion – or opinions – about it.

When I first saw *Dune* at the magnificent Metropolitan Theatre in Winnipeg in December of 1984, I was so wound up that it passed in a kind of dream. I had to go again a few days later before I could see it clearly. And my feelings were very mixed. I felt then as I do now that the film is a magnificent folly, in many ways ill-conceived, yet awe-inspiring in its ambition. It remains one of the most impressively designed movies ever made, with a look quite unlike anything else; this visual richness alone raises it far above the category of "bad movie". And yet it was almost fatally crippled by decisions forced on Lynch by his producer and distributor.

David Lynch's script, in trying to encompass all the major points of the book, was huge, dense and ultimately unwieldy; it was more concerned with interior states than action and the mechanics of plot. It was obvious even on my initial reading of it during the first week in Los Angeles, before heading for Mexico and getting a look at the scale of the production, that the film would be much longer than two hours. And then on set, it was quickly apparent that Lynch was directing scenes at an *Eraserhead* pace, drawing everything out even longer. Part way through production, Universal sent down people to start cutting pages out, to save time and money, while Lynch was just as quickly adding in new scenes. Even at three hours it would have been hard to do the material justice.

So in order to crush it down to two-and-a-quarter hours, its guts had to be torn out. For better or worse, Frank Herbert's novel was written in the early days of a public awakening to the importance of ecological issues. There are layers of politics and religion in the book, and much of that survived into Lynch's script – but the heart of the story was the idea that we as a species must live in harmony with our environment, a lesson embodied in Herbert's conception of the Fremen and their relationship with the desert. This, although much of it was actually filmed, was what got stripped out of the theatrical cut.

What remained was a story about two warring noble families trampling violently over the little people – only to have the son of one of those families assume the leadership of those little people in order to win the war. The idea that those little people actually held the key to all the power of *Dune*'s universe (they alone understood the source and nature of the spice) was lost. The emphasis on noble families and a single "great man", combined with the slow heaviness of the storytelling, ended up making *Dune* ponderous and obscure for those who weren't familiar with the book, while all that was cut out infuriated those who already knew the story well.

I didn't see the "extended cut" shown on television until it appeared on DVD. Even then I naively hoped that the added running time might have restored some of the balance which I knew was there in what had been shot, but David Lynch's non-involvement and his opting to remove his name and assign that version to the legendary Alan Smithee should have been enough to warn me away. Whoever re-edited the film for television didn't have a clue what they were doing.

The ridiculously drawn out prologue, packed with pre-production art and buried under turgid narration, was no more helpful than Irulan's much briefer introduction to the theatrical version; but its clumsiness did manage to telegraph that even this version was going to be hopelessly obscure. And later, when some of the excised material was reinserted, it was done without understanding. When Paul fights and kills Jamis, the entire point of the scene is that he cries after killing a man for the first time, this shedding of water for the dead marking him as something strange and different from the extremely pragmatic Fremen; this is the beginning of his power over them. That moment was completely lost in the theatrical version when the fight was cut almost to nothing. The TV editors restored most of the fight sequence – but then cut off the crucial final moment of Paul's weeping, turning the reinserted footage into mere padding which adds nothing to the narrative.

And so on...

I've seen *Dune* many times in the years since I haunted those sets in Mexico and I've long since come to terms with its mutilated form. What I see now is the scale and power of its visual imagination. What Lynch and his crew managed to put on screen in those pre-CGI days is remarkable; its many pleasures have very little to do with Frank Herbert's story and everything to do with the power of cinema to create visions which can inhabit our memories.

It's a shame that we will never get to see the film David Lynch originally intended – the experience of making it was obviously painful for him (he has essentially expunged it from his filmography) and he has long-since moved on to many better, more fully realized films. Looking back, it seems such a strange thing that David Lynch, with only two small art features behind him, should have found himself in the position of writing and directing such a monstrously large feature; the temptation of such a project so early in his career must have been overwhelming. But the pains it inflicted sent him back in the direction on which he had originally embarked. Every film he has made since *Dune* has been unquestionably a "David Lynch film", indelibly stamped with his personality. That personality can still be glimpsed in the nooks and crannies of this baroque epic, but in the end he was never able to bend the monster to his own will.

DUNE GALLERIES

It was forbidden to take unauthorized photographs on the sets of *Dune*, a ban which I initially adhered to. But later on I did start taking my Nikon with me to the studio and the Aguilas Rojas location on the edge of Mexico City. I didn't take a lot of pictures, but I include here a selection from the shooting of five particular sequences.

Dune was made in the pre-CG era so shots which today would easily be created in a computer had to be pieced together through a combination of full-scale live-action elements and practical effects shot on set with miniatures which were composited optically in post-production.

Riding the Worm: Estudios Churubusco backlot

One component of Paul Atreides' initiation into the Fremen culture involved him having to harness and ride one of the giant sandworms of Arrakis. This sequence consisted of a number of elements, which included some shots from the location shoot in the actual desert outside Juarez; some bluescreen work shot on one of the stages at Estudios Churubusco; some miniatures shot in post-production — and some live action with a section of full-scale worm built on the backlot.

The "worm" consisted of two segments mounted on a frame which ran on rails, hitched by cables to a pickup truck which would speed away from the set. The camera ran on parallel dolly tracks while Kyle MacLachlan as Paul would run beside the "worm", through clouds of dust blown by big wind machines, and jam his Maker Hook into the folds between the segments.

Production designer Tony Masters [centre] watches David Lynch consult with crew on the backlot sandworm set.

The sandworm section and parallel camera track.

The camera crew on the dolly, ready to shoot.

Lining up the shot with Kyle MacLachlan's stand-in, Gonzalo Irigoyen.

Kyle MacLachlan as Paul rehearsing his run beside the speeding sandworm.

Catching a worm is not so easy.

Paul walks away unscathed.

Arrival at Arrakeen: Azteca Stadium

The arrival of the Atreides family at Arrakeen was accomplished using a beautifully detailed foreground miniature constructed by one of the masters of the technique, Emilio Ruiz del Rio. The process uses a model placed close to the camera (in this case on a high tower in the parking lot of the Azteca Stadium in Mexico City) which is strategically placed so that background action in the distance can be photographed through gaps in the model, creating the seamless illusion of live action in a set which would be too difficult and expensive to build full-size.

This tower, built in the Azteca Stadium parking lot, supports a foreground miniature of the entrance to Arrakeen

Anatol and Pablo shooting over the miniature Arrakeen wall on top of the tower.

The miniature rock wall.

Miniatures expert Emilio Ruiz del Rio, assistant director Pepe Lopez Rodero, and second unit director Jimmy Devis discuss the shot.

Jimmy Devis lining up the foreground miniature shot.

The crowd of on-lookers on either side of the steps is concealed from the camera by the foreground miniature.

The full-size wall with honour guard waiting for the arrival of the Atreides family.

The Attack on Arrakeen: Aguilas Rojas

A climactic moment during the battle at Arrakeen, representing a series of bomb strikes outside the city wall as the Harkonnens crush Atreides resistance, involved an army of stuntmen and extras running among a series of explosions. The charges were placed in canisters set into the rocky ground, designed to shoot their naphtha fireballs straight up and away from the extras running between them. Anatol and I stood on a rock outcrop at the end of the set and both received singed eyebrows and a touch of instant sunburn at the end of the sequence, from the nearest explosion which was located just below us. Thanks to the auto-wind on my Nikon, I managed to photograph almost all of the explosions in the few seconds that the "attack" lasted.

Small signs mark the location of the charges in front of the Arrakeen wall.

The crew and extras preparing for the battle.

The first of a series of explosions.

Although difficult to see, a group of stuntmen and extras are running just behind the explosions.

As the explosions got closer to our camera position, we could feel the heat.

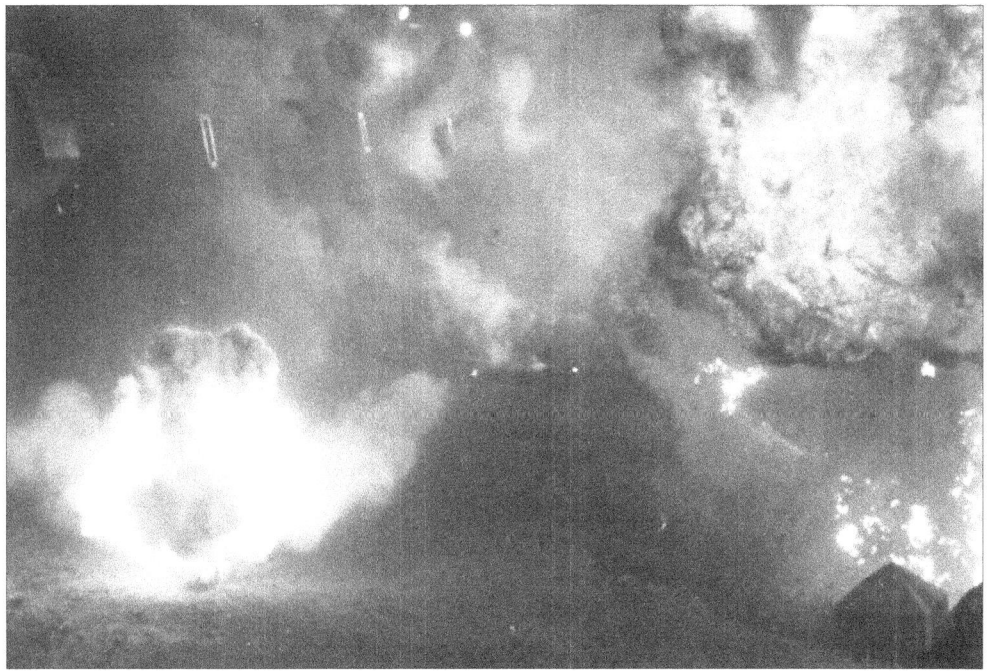

We were beginning to get worried.

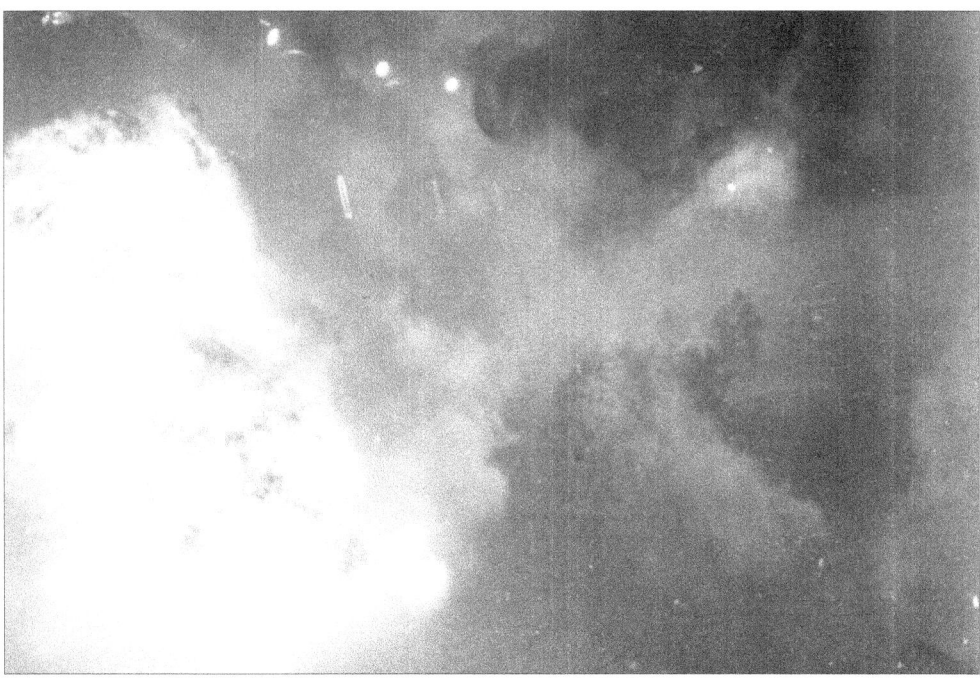

This last one, just below us, literally singed our eyebrows.

Rabban at the Arrakeen bridge: Aguilas Rojas

After the Harkonnen attack on Arrakeen and the defeat of the Atreides forces, the Baron's nephew Rabban amuses himself by throwing captured soldiers off a bridge outside the city wall. Here, Paul Smith (Rabban) rehearses for the night shoot at the Aguilas Rojas location just outside Mexico City. The location was a former garbage dump, more or less cleaned up for the shoot, although its rough terrain still concealed some unpleasant surprises. It was nicknamed the "dead dog dump" by the crew for self-explanatory reasons. The natural dust was a very fine, sharp grit which would sting when the big wind machines stirred it up during takes.

The start of another long night of shooting at Aguilas Rojas.

The crew gathering at Aguilas Rojas.

Paul L. Smith with stunt coordinator Richard Humphreys on the Arrakeen bridge.

Paul L. Smith practices throwing Richard Humphreys off the bridge.

Throwing an Atreides soldier to his death.

Rehearsal with sandstorm courtesy of Kit West's effects department.

David Lynch going over final details with Paul L. Smith, now in Rabban costume.

After the Final Battle: Estudios Churubusco backlot

The aftermath of the final battle between the Fremen, led by Paul, and the Harkonnen and Imperial troops, led by the Emperor himself, was shot at night on the backlot at Estudios Churubusco. Here David Lynch prepares a key element of the sequence, coaching seven-year-old Alicia Witt for her gruesome moment of ecstasy, wandering around the field of battle dispatching wounded soldiers with a knife.

Preparations for shooting the aftermath of the battle for Arrakeen, on the Churubusco backlot.

Freddie Francis [right] adjusting lights by walkie-talkie.

Anatol and Pablo [left] shooting video on the field of battle.

David Lynch talking to Alicia Witt about her bloody role in the battle's aftermath; Diane Witt watches at the far left.

Anatol gets up close as David Lynch talks to Alicia Witt.

As always, there's a lot of waiting on set.

David Lynch and Freddie Francis surveying the backlot battlefield.

Interviews

Anatol Pacanowski and I shot about seventy-five hours of videotape during the six months we spent on the set of *Dune* and behind the scenes at Estudios Churubusco in Mexico City. At the end of production, we were ordered to pack all those tapes up and ship them back to Universal Studios in Los Angeles; at that point we were unceremoniously kicked off the payroll, the verbal agreement we had had with Gordon Armstrong in the Universal publicity department not worth the paper it was never written on.

Although a number of times in the ensuing years I tried to track down all that material (my rather unrealistic fantasy was that it could be used to put together a kind of *Hearts of Darkness* documentary about David Lynch's experience on the movie), I could never seem to penetrate the corporate swamp. It was only in November of 2010 that I finally learned that all the tapes had been destroyed shortly after *Dune* was released and turned out not to be the blockbuster Universal and De Laurentiis were hoping for.

However, not long before our time in Mexico ended, for some reason I dubbed a handful of our interviews onto audio cassettes. I no longer know why I did it – whether it was to have the interviews handy for transcribing, or whether I had some half-conscious suspicion that we would never actually get to put together the making-of documentary – but I brought those cassettes away with me, and they've been packed away with a lot of other bric-a-brac for the past three decades. Coming across them recently, I've finally transcribed them ... although I have to admit that, as interviews, they don't amount to a lot. Most of them were shot on the fly and I wasn't really prepared at the time to dig very deeply.

Many of the interviews we did are now lost. Just a few of those "missing in action" are Kyle MacLachlan, Freddie Francis, Tony Masters, Ron Miller, Paul L. Smith, and the parents of Alicia Witt among others. These recordings are in fairly poor shape, but they're all that remain of six months of sometimes exhausting work. Listening to myself chatting with David Lynch and Max von Sydow, Jurgen Prochnow and Patrick Stewart, the whole thing seems very unreal to me now. Here is the proof that I was there, but I feel little connection with the person I can hear on the tapes (the person who wrote the diary reprinted in this book). These are traces of another life, one which it would be nice to live over again knowing what I know now.

David Lynch

David Lynch's cameo as a spice miner. Photograph copyright Universal/De Laurentiis.

Sunday, May 8, 1983. In David Lynch's hotel room in Mexico City.

Anatol Pacanowski: So what's the situation on the music, David? I've heard that the Polish composer Penderecki may be involved.

David Lynch: Penderecki? No. Well, I don't know, 'cause I never talked to Penderecki. He's still living, but I always felt that *Dune* is this, you know, this … it's a film that's got this power and this other world, right? And it's got a big, big feeling. And it has to capture, you know, tremendous power. And so to me it needs a huge orchestra, and a huge, you know, choir. And maybe even added, you know, basses, you know, stuff like this. Not brass. Huge strengths and, I mean, power. And every time I think about this, I think Eastern Europe or Russia. And, not that, you know … one thing I think, like Russian films, Russian art has got some sort of power, and it's … they seem to understand that. And that flavour is not a dark, you know, thing. They understand, you know, it's almost … sometimes, you know, it's like the spiritual power of the whole universe. And so Gilbert Marouani is the guy who's come from Paris and he's been contacting many many people, and telling me about other people that could be to my liking, you know, for music. And he says he's come with very bad news that no one wants to work on the project, right, and then he gives me a list of about twenty groups that, you know, are really keen on working on *Dune*. And the possibility may be that, right now I can't say for sure, but maybe of a Russian orchestra and there's a Polish composer and a Czech composer, they're apparently not real well known, but one of them has done quite a few film scores and the other one hasn't. But I haven't heard their work yet. He's going to get me some of their stuff, but that could be something. And then if some of these rock groups become involved, their music may be transferred to orchestra, and it could be very wild. Plus, you know, we could maybe blend, like the group Toto was here yesterday, right, and we were talking about blending synthesizers and orchestra both, which would be pretty cool.

Kenneth George Godwin: Have you ever heard of Brian Eno?

DL: I've heard of Brian Eno.

KGG: I was going to suggest to you …

DL: He apparently wants to, you know, work on *Dune*.

KGG: He's always said he wants to work on movies, but no one ever offers him decent projects.

DL: Well, I know we're probably going to talk to Brian.

AP: There's also Jean-Michel Jarre … it's the best synthesized stuff possibly so far. There's a German group called Kraftwerk, but that's all towards disco. Some of their stuff is very good, but it's too much dance kind of stuff. Tangerine Dream as well. Jarre has this … well, he was the first one to open China.

KGG: He was the first modern Western musician to give concerts in China. Although actually after seeing what's going on here, I began to wonder whether synthesized stuff might not be …

DL: No, synthesizers I don't like. It has to be … I don't even like now a studio recording, it's too clean and there's too much, it's too plastic. And what I'd like to do is have an orchestra play in, like, a giant hall, like you know in performance, but no people. And get the sound of, you know, the hall and get a more organic sound.

AP: That's like why Pendericki would have been … he's not synthesized …

DL: No, no, no … Penderecki is one of the greats. That guy is incredible, and I … but I would like to use maybe several different people and blend, you know, find a way to blend them all together.

KGG: Did you ever see *Altered States*? Do you remember the music in *Altered States*? John Corigliano's score ... it's extremely distinctive. It's all done with a live orchestra, but it sounds sort of distorted, synthesized, but he did it all live with an orchestra. Very bizarre effects. Even the musicians didn't want to use their instruments that way. It's an amazing sound.

DL: That's probably the best part of the film.

KGG: It's one of my favourite film scores.

DL: Ah-ha. What did you think of the film, though?

KGG: I really liked it.

DL: You did, huh?

KGG: I'm a Ken Russell freak.

DL: You are, huh? Get out of here! Get out of here, George!

AP: I'm not ...

KGG: Yeah, he's a specialized taste.

DL: No, that's ... ah ... super cool.

KGG: You know, I was saying, seeing what's going on here, how did the design evolve? There are all these elements, you know, Maya. Aztec, a lot of Jules Verne and H.G. Wells, a sort of Edwardian feel to it, where did ...

DL: Where did it all come from?

KGG: Yeah, where did it start?

DL: Well, right from the beginning ... you know, like, *Dune*'s a film about, *Dune* has got to be real, number one. And it can't be ... I don't like, you know, a slick modern science fiction feel. And I love, you know, textures and I love organic things. And we have four different worlds there, and so it was like when Tony came on the picture, we started working, you know, sort of against traditional science fiction. But we didn't have a feel for these places, it evolved over many many months. And the thing that really changed everything, kind of opened up a door, was one day Dino called and said he wanted me to come to Aveno, northern Italy, and he was there with, for the mud baths. And so we went over there and he was bored out of his, you know, mind. You know, he works twenty-four hours a day, and he'd had plenty of mud baths so he went over for a script conference. And we had about an hour's worth of script conference, but then one night we took off and we went into Venice. And Dino and Raffaella and Raffaella's ex-husband G.P. and I went in and it was about an hour, maybe an hour drive from Aveno, and we got a gondola and, you know, headed out and we stopped at a certain place and Dino says "we've gotta get out right here," you know, 'cause he wanted me to see Saint Mark's Square in the most perfect way. So we went down this little teeny street, we went right through here and all of a sudden it just opened up, whammo! You know, there we were. And right there in Saint Mark's Square was where it all kind of came together. We went into this, you know, cathedral there and we were looking around and these things just drove me crazy. And then Dino bought me this book on Venice, you know, right outside the place there, and we got a cappuccino, got our picture taken. Then we went out to Torchello for this meal that was just incredible. So the whole thing … and then we went at night back in this boat and Venice at night was a whole 'nother thing. Venice in the day inspired Caladan and inspired, you know, some of the Emperor's court. And it kind of gave a feel for this, you know, idea that in *Dune* there might have been a renaissance or something five thousand years ago. All the ships, you know, were built then, all the technology, everything was built, done so well and it was done so richly and it just lasted. It was just done so well that it lasted. And so the highliner, for instance, you know, is at least five thousand years old and, but it's just built, you know, so beautifully. And Venice at night inspired Geidi Prime. We were passing this building, it was like just black, it was a very cold light deep within, and it was just, it was one of these buildings where it didn't seem like there were doors and that's the same way with Geidi Prime, there's no real doors, there's just many many holes and they go through a sort of a labyrinth, you know, to go to the inside. And so that cracked it, and from then on things just started, kept evolving from that.

KGG: How do you feel about doing … I mean, it's one of the most complex effects projects ever done? The effects are all combined with live action rather than being done separately …

DL: The more we can get in the camera, you know, the better. But it's still, there's many many effects that will be done optically in post-production with John [Dykstra]. But it's, first off all, like I said, a real, it's gotta be a real feeling. And you know it's like you've gotta make a whole world seem real. And it is real, you know, it's just as real as can be. And the people are so important. And science fiction, that's one thing about *Dune*, Frank has got people that you really care about and even though they are strange, underneath they're normal, like everybody, and they have, you know, feelings and all this stuff is super important. If those feelings among the people and the audience for the people come through, like hit number ten, then it'll be, I think … I don't know, but maybe like a first where you really are into a people story and the rest of it, all these strange worlds and all this kind of stuff, if that's a ten too, then you've got the whole thing. But it's also, there's another element, it's like science fiction a lot of times you have strange worlds, but they're on the outside and in *Dune* you have strange worlds that you go inside, right. So you've got people and you've got strange worlds on the outside and you've got mental worlds, and you've got those three kind of different textures, you know, all swimming and if they swim and they blend and they, you know, you can go into so many nifty areas. You can go way out in space or you can go way inside, right, and ... so there's little portholes, you know, little ways to go in, and little ways to go here and little ways to go there and just, it's gonna have a great feeling.

KGG: The script is very dialogue-heavy. I understand you're trimming as you go, but is it difficult to keep it going when you have so much dialogue?

DL: Well, in a way, see I've always been real ... well, I never knew about dialogue, right, 'cause I came from, you know, painting. But dialogue is real neat in a way if it's, if it's ... it can be a great texture, you know, dialogue. It can be like music, and it gives you so much information and it can be good. In *Dune*, we've got different types of dialogue, as you know, and maybe there's too much and maybe some of it will have to go, but it's such a complicated story that no one ever knew how much, you know, you have to explain and how much you could get away without explaining, so it's one of those things where in post-production I'm a sure a lot of it's going to go out the window, and then the stuff that will remain will be there as a music.

KGG: There's a strong Islamic thing that goes through the book and it's also in the script. Did you think you might have a problem with that considering the recent, the political thing in the Middle East, that people might be put off ...

DL: No. I'm sure Frank ... Frank is, he's a collector of, you know, millions of bits of information, and *Dune* is ideas from space and ideas from different parts of the world and it's not really Middle East or anywhere, I mean, it's more Middle East maybe than Alaska 'cause it's desert, right, but it's not really from one place.

KGG: You have the concept of jihad and so on ...

DL: Yeah, but you have, you know, holy wars are like, they're everywhere.

AP: There's a lot of Eastern Europe ... the seitch, and Cossacks ... I don't know where Frank has got it from ...

KGG: There's a lot of dead languages ...

AP: Gypsies ...

[Break to change videocassette: resumes in the middle of discussion of Werner Herzog]

DL ... is a very emotional fellow.

KGG: If you ever get a chance to see *Burden of Dreams*, he's incredibly obsessive. After seeing *Werner Herzog Eats His Shoe* and *Burden of Dreams*, I got a much clearer idea of what Herzog is doing in his movies, because he has to get mentally totally into what he's doing ... sometimes if it's a little off target, the film turns out badly, but when he's on target you get something like *Aguirre, Wrath of God*, it's incredible.

DL: I've never seen that, but I saw the one where the couple come over with their father to America ... I was in England and I turned on the TV one night and I didn't see the beginning of that, just turned it on. I didn't know if I was watching a documentary, a real thing, or if I was watching a movie and I couldn't believe it, you know, I just loved that movie. And when that guy is sitting in that garage and he pulls his tooth out, you know, with a pair of pliers ... you remember that? He had a toothache or something like this and he's sitting in there, he pulls this, you know, tooth out ... what was the guy trying to do with that little machine he had, the father? And the wife's over whoring at the truck stop and then they went ... and it finally ends up with those chickens pecking at that, little drops of corn would come down, they'd peck more and more would come down, you remember that?

KGG: No, I can't remember ...

DL: They'd peck on this little thing and a bell, it would light a little thing, they were ... it was a funhouse sort of thing. The chickens would, by pecking for corn, would light these lights and make this, you know, thing work. And so it was like very, a very nifty idea. I love the idea that, I love mechanical things, you know ...

KGG: Yeah.

DL: And I love the idea of a series of events ... it's like music, you know, you plan out. Did I tell you about my ball-bearing thing? Did I ever tell you about that, George?

KGG: I'm not sure ...

DL: In art school, my ball-bearing ...

KGG: Oh right, yeah ...

[Interrupted by phone]

KGG: We should get back to that first question, why you're doing *Dune*?

DL: Ah, George ... well, because of those things I was telling you. It's a film that, it's got ... since I love textures, right, and I love dreams and strange worlds and, still, I like real scenes ... *Dune* is tailor-made. I mean, it's got everything and it's, like I said before, it's a film that goes way way out and it goes way way in. And it's an evolution in the film, and it's ... ah ... it's a mystery, you know, and it's ... it has the possibility of existing on different levels, so it's a great adventure story and it's also a film of ideas and mysteries and it maybe can capture tremendous power, and just be the most fantastic feeling, you know, to watch it ... it has the possibilities of things coming together, like they say, the whole is greater than the sum of the parts. There can be some magic with sound and picture in *Dune*, with this building of the inner and the outer that could be very powerful.

KGG: Have you got any concrete concepts now of what you're going to do with the sound?

DL: No, you see, I'm ... Alan ... this is the first time, anyway, that Raffaella says she's ever brought someone on this early and, but really, like, on *Eraserhead* and *Elephant Man* Alan [Splet] and I talked, you know, long before we started shooting about sound and this and this, and generated on *Eraserhead* lots and lots of sounds, and did experiments and things like that. But now Alan's working on his own in San Francisco, so I don't know what he's got, but he's, he's decided that instead of trying to second guess me or anything like that, he's just collecting tons of raw sounds, and he's not really putting them through any machines really. And so when we get together, we'll just have, like, a feast of listening to different things, and if something pops then we can, you know, put it through the business and start, you know, developing it. And like I told you, you know, about *Eraserhead*, most of the time the picture dictates the sound, so we've got to get more and more picture before Alan and I can start going on the sound. But there's a lot of machines and a lot of maybe different presences and different moods that'll, you know, and a lot of little machines and little sounds that will be in there. And there's a lot of different sounds for the voices and there's these dreams and visions and things, so it will be a big sound ... Alan already had a list of a hundred-and-twenty-five sound projects for *Dune*, and that was just in the beginning. I mean, I'm sure there'll be more. So there's some real, you know, nifty stuff for sound.

KGG: Are you going to have to rethink the dream sequences now that John Dykstra's effects budget is being cut back?

DL: Yes, but it's ... here's the thing: instead of a compromise, which you can't, you shouldn't ever, you know, compromise ... I mean it's a nice idea to say, but you always end up ... what you have to do, if you get up into a corner, instead of just two possibilities, one is do it and, you know, one is throw it out, there's never just two possibilities. And that's one thing that's been the hugest lesson on this film, because there are so many restrictions. So instead of just, you know, going along and selling out to these restrictions, you can ... it can force you to think of new things. And the new things are much better than the original way. And these dreams, I think, are going to be much better and much more interesting and, than if they'd been optical things, so much optical ... some things still have to be, but so much of them are mood and the images can be gotten here in Mexico and put together in the right way and it'll be fine.

[After a short break]
DL: So what's next?

KGG: It's kind of early to start thinking about it ... after you finish *Dune*, which is going to be a long time, are you going to try to get back to some small, more personal thing, or are you going to be involved in *Dune 2*?

DL: I'm going to be involved with probably other *Dunes*, but I'm also gonna do other things too. But I don't have another project. You know, I like *Ronnie Rocket*, but I don't know if I'm going to do *Ronnie Rocket* right now. I want to do a film in the '50s, you know.

KGG: *Blue Velvet*?

DL: I don't know if I want to do ... see, *Blue Velvet*, the first two thirds, you know, something's happening. But the ending is, is terrible and it needs a lot of work. Did you ever read *Blue Velvet*?

KGG: No.

DL: I'll have to let you read it. I love the idea of *Blue Velvet*, but it's got a lousy ending. And it, but it could be fixed. I mean it just needs, you know, a lot more work. But it's a total mood piece, and it would be a lot of fun to do it. But I don't know what's going to happen. I don't ... I have a feeling that there's something out there, you know, but I don't know ... and I can't really think about it because I've got to think about this.

KGG: This has got more narrative than anything you've done before. Is that a big shift, harder to do?

DL: Well, see the thing is, I like slipping off this track, you know, and going into ... it's like suddenly just falling into a hole somewhere and floating off into, you know, some strange different place. But this has got those places, you know, so it's a narrative film, but like I said it can easily slip away and all of a sudden another mood can come out, and it can be, you know, it's really got all the stuff.

AP: We haven't covered much about your painting, and I know you don't have much time to paint now, which is painful ...

DL: Yes. Are you painting now, Anatol?

AP: I'm not. I haven't painted in a couple of years. Just on the way down here, I didn't even know that they're getting upset with me because I don't want to do the show because of the film.

DL: You have to do them.

AP: Well, they'll have to wait on me, but it was confirmed they want me to do it and I hope that maybe I'll become a Sunday painter on the production.

DL: Yeah, I hope I will ... see this table, now Giles designed this – Tony's son – and it's gonna, I'm going to do drawings here right now. It looks awfully pretty, but it's meant to be a work table, and so I'm going to go to work.

AP: It's hard though, to be interrupted by the production, but again it's almost indispensable, it's the only therapy that we know of.

DL: Yeah, it's unbelievable, you have to do it, you have to do it. But see now, did you ever see *The Angriest Dog in the World* cartoons? Did you, George?

KGG: No.

DL: They're running every week in the L.A. Reader. So I've got my *Angriest Dog in the World* cartoons and I've got other ideas for these other, you know, projects that are not so much film related. And I've got, you know, these ideas for these books, and I want to do these photographs of Mexico City and all this. I mean, it's like there's not enough time to do all the stuff we want to do.

KGG: We keep seeing these flashes of really sort of vignette type things around. We want to do this thing which will be like "welcome to Mexico City", and there'll be this long collection of shots of the buses here with the black smoke, with little electronic noises like spaceships … with the smashed windows and the doors hanging off and pouring out that black smoke.

DL: They've sure got the buses … no, that's fantastic.

AP: Have you noticed the building that's down …

KGG: It's way down [*inaudible*] … it's off to the left when you're heading towards [*inaudible*], it looks like a spaceship sitting on top of this building in concrete. You expect it to take off.

AP: John Dykstra, you know, we have to point that out … it's like a penthouse and yet it's not a penthouse because it's an office building.

KGG: It looks like some kind of a blockhouse sitting on top of this building. You expect it to have lasers sticking out … it's very bizarre.

DL: Very strange.

AP: Architecture, old architecture is fantastic here, you walk at night and see these pieces of facades, little details that I've never seen anywhere in the world. It's really strange, it's eerie …

DL: No, Mexico City is one of the strangest cities in the world.

KGG: There are these huge devastated areas down nearer the location. It looks like photographs of Hiroshima.

DL: Yeah.

KGG: … like it's been levelled by a huge blast. It's a very bizarre place.

DL: No, I love Mexico City.

KGG: Really?

DL: Oh yeah, because, you know, it's like, it's a city of ideas. It's just like a Bob's shake, you know, there's an idea in every shake, there's an idea right around every corner in Mexico City. And it's … especially at night in Mexico City, these little tiny lit places, your mind just goes out, you know, you see them, it's just incredible.

KGG: Have you got any ideas for projects specifically …

DL: I like the idea of … I was in this town Caborca, and it's, you know, it's like cowboy hats and pick-up trucks and cactus and these little lights on a string, and the strangest neon. And heat. And then these two lovers walking down this road, the road is practically not a road, and the gravel on the side, and they go into this little, it was like a, it wasn't really a dance hall or a coffee shop or a restaurant, it was just a sort of vacant cantina. It had a counter, but it had strange chairs and a huge open kind of strange linoleum and little booths. No one was there and these lovers in this heat, you know, in this … now it's cool in there, right, having a water or something and just, you know, kissing in this booth. It's just an inspiration. There's some sort of stories for these places that could be really something. And Mexico is a country that's been so far out of everyone's thoughts that there's lots of things here that I think people will discover and it could be the new sort of thing. It's gonna be an influence, I think.

KGG: When we were driving down, which was like Hell, it's just like a Bunuel movie, these very bizarre sights. Dead horses by the road where they'd been hit and all swelled up in the sun …

DL: Yes, and you know, dead dogs just between here and the trash dump is … you just cannot believe the amount of dead dogs you see.

AP: And trucks just burned …

KGG: We saw at least four buses lying in ditches, all overgrown with weeds and everything, just rusted …

AP: Cars just abandoned …

KGG: Rusted … god knows how many people dying in these accidents, but they were just sort of left there …

AP: Or the classic stuff … a guy on a mule and a woman …

KGG: … walking three paces behind.

AP: Things that don't exist anywhere … amazing.

DL: It's amazing.

AP: Everything's a little too much in this country, everything's gone to the edge.

KGG: Yeah, it's all pushed to the extreme.

DL: We're living here, George, we're living here.

KGG: Do you have all the bits you cut out of *Eraserhead* stored somewhere?
DL: You bet.
KGG: You didn't pull any frames from those sequences for …
DL: No, but maybe for the book.
KGG: I would love to see some of those.
DL: Yeah, I want you to see the telephone call sometime, Henry gets a telephone …

KGG: Digging for dimes …

DL: Digging for dimes, yeah, and the landlady. You've never seen her, no. She's really something, she's a good one.

KGG: I saw *Eraserhead* again at the beginning of last December, which was the first time in it must be a year.

DL: How did it hold up?

KGG: Oh, it was great. It was totally different because I finally got all of this stuff out, you know, I'd written the article and it was way in the past, and it was like going to it entirely new … and it was so funny. I couldn't believe it. 'Cause I'd always been annoyed when people laughed before when I was watching, because it was so intense, you, what was wrong with these people … and I was laughing all the way … it's an hilarious movie.

DL: Oh, it is hilarious, yeah.

KGG: I'd always seen these bits of humour in it, but they'd never struck me that forcefully before.

DL: That's what I want to do, is I want to go to Poland or, Poland I think, and do Kafka's *Metamorphosis* in an apartment in Poland.

AP: Or Czechoslovakia, those are perfect choices. East Germany maybe …

DL: Yeah, too much.

KGG: Somebody actually made a film of that.

DL: I know, I don't care. I don't care if anyone ever sees this thing. I've got to do it. It's not … I don't know, I think the problem with it is that it'd be hard to stretch that to a feature. It's a good solid hour picture and so it probably wouldn't have a market, at least in the theatres. I like the idea of doing subtitles on it, and totally black-and-white with subtitles. Don't tell anybody, and scratch this off the tape.

DL: Let's go ten more minutes, and then I'll throw you guys out and I've gotta call home …

KGG: So, Mr. David Lynch, what is your name and what do you do?

DL: I've got to think of a good answer, George. You want this on the tape now?

KGG: We do need something you say to the [convention] fans, and we need a little bit that we can give to Anne [Strick].

AP: From this cassette.

KGG: We just changed cassettes, so all this other good stuff is sitting over there. This is a new …

DL: This is the part that I don't like because I don't know these people out there in that convention …

AP: You're not exactly a science fiction fan.

DL: No.

AP: So, well we get into this long and complicated question of what is science fiction, is it literature or just like a detective story …

DL: Well, I love detective stories.

KGG: Some of those are literature.

AP: Right.

DL: And science fiction doesn't … I don't dislike science fiction. I just don't like a one-thing thing.

KGG: Like *Star Wars*.

DL: Well, I don't want … I say that I think … I don't even want to get into it, you know. You know, it did change the whole cinema world, *Star Wars*, and it was a … the timing and what it did was incredible. George has got a great kind of like calling, you know, he's so important to billions of people, and you can't argue with that, it's incredible what he just fell to do, and it was, like, a blockbuster. And it just changed everything.

AP: Also it would be very hard to change the science fiction fans ideas about what science fiction should be.

KGG: What you're doing is, at least visually from what we've seen, is vastly different from what people have come to expect from science fiction, so that the general audience out there is going to …

DL: Well, the thing is, see, I've tried to be true to the book and everybody working on this film is, you know, we've been kind of tuning into the original, which is *Dune* the book, and also Frank is to me an idea man, and I like to be an idea man, you know, ideas are the neatest things in the world and, like, ideas are better than food and better than money. I mean, it's magic to be sitting in a chair and get an idea. I mean it's incredible, and where do they come from and they're floating about and they're, you can get these things. And then a whole thing can explode in your head, you know, and Frank has put out these little seeds in these sentences that you can pass over or you could screech to a halt and let them, you know, grow. And so some of the things in *Dune* are – the movie – have been inspired by just one or two little words, you know, in the book, and they've been chosen to grow more than they were in the book. Other things, you know, have kind of fallen away and … so science fiction for *Dune* is not a problem, it's just doing the book and letting the book be interpreted through film, you know.

AP: It's like decoding, in a sense. The codes are there, you just need the key to unlock it.

KGG: Has working on this increased your interest in science fiction?

DL: Well, I don't know. Every project is different. I could read a science fiction book tomorrow and freak out, you know, or I could read a detective story and flip, or I could get an idea for something different, so I'm open to anything.

[Later. A brief conversation with David Lynch in an unspecified location.]
KGG: I saw you playing the drums at the party Saturday night. It's an old hobby, playing the drums?
DL: Oh yeah, I love ...
KGG: So what about the trumpet yesterday?
DL: I almost bought a trumpet yesterday afternoon, but it was $235 and I should play it before I spend that kind of money.
KGG: I was expecting you to play something out on the lawn.
DL: They couldn't find a trumpet.
KGG: Those ones you were looking at ...
DL: They were no good. One of them was a bugle, one of them was a trumpet. The trumpet was, it was a joke, you couldn't get a squeak out of it. And the bugle, you can't play what I wanted to play. I want to play "America the Beautiful". And what I would like to do, well sometime ... I might buy a trumpet, I will play the snare drum and the trumpet while Alicia [Witt] recites the Declaration of Independence.
KGG: Would you do that down here or back home?
DL: I want to do it right here. Would you like to record that?
KGG: Sure.
DL: I mean it would be unbelievable. She recited the entire Declaration of Independence for Dino – he stopped her half way through, and then Ian recited *The Night Before Christmas*, which is a long poem, a long poem. Ian is three, he's known it since he was two or something.
KGG: How old is she?
DL: Alicia's seven, going on forty.
KGG: Is there a problem directing a child?
DL: No, she's fantastic. She knows, there's no problem about memorizing a line, zero. And she takes direction fantastically, all the little subtleties, all the little things, there's no problem. Sometimes she gets tired and a little bit goofy, but when the camera starts rolling she settles in and she's professional. She taps her feet when she acts and so they have to put a little blanket under her.
KGG: So, we're well over half way now?
DL: We're well over half way, George, yeah.
KGG: I've lost track of what's been shot.

DL: Yeah, you and me both. Now today is a special day, because Tony Gibbs and Raffaella have taken some film up to show some Universal people, and see how it goes.

KGG: They've seen some before though.

DL: Yes.

KGG: But not cut?

DL: Bob Rehme has seen some cut stuff.

KGG: What are they showing them?

DL: They're showing them, one thing they're showing them is a sequence starting with the death of Dr. Kynes, then Rabban carries him about, tears the stillsuit, goes inside the ship and pulls the tongue out of the cow, goes in, the Baron's flying around the shower, Jack Nance is playing music with a dwarf, right, then the Baron and Rabban talk and Rabban's mouth is filled with this tongue, and then Rabban leaves and Sting comes out of the shower. So it's pretty cool.

KGG: I was wondering how all that was going together. With the shots all spread out, it's hard to see the sequence.

DL: Yeah, it's a pretty good sequence.

KGG: You've got the sound on that now?

DL: No, there's no sound. We put a sound in for the hunter-seeker and it was not good, it's just barely better than no sound at all.

KGG: How did the robot fight look once Alan had …

DL: No, Alan didn't … there again, it's not …

KGG: It's not finished.

DL: It's not finished sound, and so he grabbed what he could here … it's much better, he put together eight tracks, you know, and did a little mix, but it's … it's good, but it's not right. It served a purpose.

KGG: Have you settled on the music yet?

DL: No.

KGG: It's still up in the air.

DL: No, it's still up in the air. Gilbert's coming on the 12th or 14th and I hope to talk to him about some, he's going to bring some Eastern European composers' work and I can hardly wait to hear some of this stuff.

KGG: It's hard to picture any particular music with what's going on.

DL: Yeah well, it's going to be fantastic.

AP: The editing's going to be done here?

DL: The editing? Possibly. I was told that I wouldn't be leaving until Christmas, if then.

KGG: I'm sure you're looking forward to that.

DL: Well, you know, I'm pretty happy here in Mexico City. I mean, I kind of miss my family.

KGG: Yeah, it's been a long time down here.

DL: Yeah. But now I think once post-production's coming around, I'll be able to fly home more often.

KGG: Are you going to finish shooting by the beginning of September, going a couple of weeks over ...

DL: I think we're five days behind now. But that's awful good for fourteen weeks. And I think I can catch up. I'm hoping.

KGG: Are you cutting more bits out of the script.

DL: No. With the second unit barrelling along, we're moving pretty good. We get tons of stuff done each day with two units.

KGG: Well, thanks a lot, David.

DL: Yeah, I'm going to go back over now to the set.

Jack Nance (Nefud)

Jack Nance as the Baron's court jester, Nefud. Photograph copyright Universal/De Laurentiis.

Documentary crew's office, 2nd floor of Admin building, Estudios Churubusco.

Jack Nance, Anatol Pacanowski, Pablo Ocampo Pinan (our sound recordist) and myself retreated to our office after a rather long lunch one afternoon. It was a slow day and with nothing significant to go and shoot, we settled down to tape an interview with Jack. He sat on a couch. Anatol set the camera up, pointed it at him, and then drowsily lay down on the floor. I sat beside the tripod and Pablo operated while Jack and I began our conversation. There had been much sangria at lunch and Jack had a bottle, a plastic cup, and some ice. He drank and smoked steadily as we talked over the next couple of hours and, as will be apparent from the following transcript, things became a bit fuzzy ... but this messy, at times rambling and incoherent session provided some sense of who Jack was. Listening to it again as I transcribed the tape, the whole afternoon came back to me vividly although it happened thirty-two years ago.

Kenneth George Godwin: Okay, Jack. Where do you want to start?

Jack Nance: [*laughs*] I could start with "Annie Laurie".

KGG: Well, first of all, tell us about Nefud.

JN: Nefud, the doorstop. Yeah, who is Nefud? That, I hope, is what all the nation will be asking themselves once they see this epic. "Who is Nefud?" and "Why is he still alive?" [*laughs*] Nefud is the last living redhead on the planet. He somehow makes it through, either by his own – what? Stumbling through? I don't know. I think it's because maybe, maybe Nefud likes … no, no, wait a minute … how do you describe Nefud? Wait a minute, I know … Nefud, I think, genuinely likes the Baron, if it's possible for somebody to like the Baron. And I think that perhaps, if it's possible for the Baron to have any kind of feeling, human feeling for anyone, he might have that kind of thing for Nefud. Nefud and the Baron might have some kind of genuine sort of human emotion going back and forth there that is lacking in any of the slaughter that goes on in this blood bath epic. Perhaps that's why Nefud lives. He sort of senses that, that there's bad business happening and doesn't like it, feels sort of maybe sad about it.

KGG: What does he do for the Baron?

JN: He is a doorstop for the Baron, primarily a doorstop. About all I know about Nefud. And that he once had red hair.

KGG: How's it working with David again after all these years?

JN: Who?

KGG: David, all these years after *Eraserhead*. Has he changed a lot?

JN: David Lynch. David Lynch. Tow-headed kid, where's he from? Nebraska?

KGG: Missoula, Montana.

JN: Missoula, Montana. Montana boy, yes, that's right. His grandfather's wheat farm was wiped out by Mount Saint Helen's, did you know that? Ash from Mount Saint Helen's wiped out Lynch's grandfather's wheat farm in Montana. Hundreds of miles to the East. I asked him, you know, "Did your old grandpa ever say anything to you, David, when you were a kid, you know, 'my God someday, you know, a volcano …'" [*chuckles*] … never would've thunk it. Otherwise … what did you say?

KGG: I asked if he'd changed a lot since *Eraserhead*, now he's working on a big film.

JN: Oh, has he changed …

KGG: With big producers and big studios.

JN: No. You know what? We had talked about this a lot of times … you're talking about when we were working, we were carrying hundred pound bags of plaster, we would talk about, you know, when something like this would come about, you know, the biggest movie in the world [*laughs*] and there would be guys who were built like refrigerators, who would be happy to lift hundreds of pounds of equipment, tons of … And so it's just, it's nothing new really, it's something that's been in the works for years. I mean, I sort of recognized everything that's going on, yes, yes. And?

KGG: Compared to the other directors you've worked with, what makes him different?

JN: Other directors I've worked with … what makes him different? That's good, George. To respond to this seriously, you know, I'd really like to respond to this … [*speaks very slowly, feeling his way*] compared to other directors I've worked with, what makes him different? That's good, 'cause there's … I like that. All right, compared to other directors I've worked with, Lynch is different because Lynch has a kind of a vision of his own that he imprints on the project. You know what I mean? Whereas … which is, it's different than a director who is … who has an image of … try it again. That's real neat. Lynch … wait a minute … Lynch has a vision of what the project, what the project is, rather than a joker who is directing a project … try again. What is the difference between working with a director … Lynch will never be a hired hand. All right? That good? Lynch's images are his own and they're not dictated by what you might think ought to be up there on the screen. Does *that* make any sense?

KGG: Yeah. But what about Wenders? Was *Hammett* dictated by what he thought ought to be up there rather than what he wanted to do because he was doing a film for Zoetrope?

JN: Oh, is that what you, oh, that's what you were talking about, yeah. Yeah, well that was, you know, he had his idea of what American kind of gangster movies were about, but he was, he had much the same kind of imagery or vision, whatever, as far as that goes. It was his own, his own image or idea of what he thought … great director as far as the work, everything very meticulous, say the words, make the funny faces, turn this way and that … great stuff. I love it. I don't know what he put down on film, how it worked out. Were you … you were trying to determine some kind of …

KGG: Something very special …

JN: … some kind of dichotomy there …

KGG: No, just what … 'cause David's films are very very individual. I just wondered what, if you had the key.

JN: Well, I don't know. I can relate to Lynch person to person as, you know, pals or whatever. And then just have to stand back and, I mean, love to see him, love to see him work out. And I particularly liked other actors' reactions to his direction, you know, because he's, he gets like this, you know, big bug-eyed, blue-eyed, and other actors ... "yes, yes", you know, and then, but understand exactly how it works. It's real neat to see because they go "ah, yes, right" [*Jack's expression of awed comprehension can't be conveyed properly in words*]. He's just remarkably intense, up close and very very personal and, you know, you understand the guy when he's saying something. When we came into that big room, what is it? the Great Hall? ... I hadn't been inside the room until, you know, we'd lined up outside and we're supposed to be marching into this room, or being marched into this room, I guess. We were on our way to the slammer or whatever, and "quiet, rehearsal" and, you know, "go!" We're marching in and I stepped into the room and looked around and there's this, there are nine-thousand of these Fremens, there are five-thousand more of them on this side of the room, and it was, I mean, it was vast. I was over-awed by it, right. I'm supposed to walk down here, I'm following ... and so I started cracking up, right. I couldn't help it. Look at that! Oh God! [*laughs*]

KGG: We're having video technical difficulties.
[break]
KGG: Here we are back again, chatting with Jack Nance in Mexico City.
JN: Oh, we are?
KGG: A commercial break there, Jack. ... You were talking about walking into the Great Hall.
JN: Yeah, walking onto this *vast* set for the first time, where there are, you know, a hundred-and-eighty some odd people in costume and all of these ... and I was over-awed by walking in with this group, and I was just taken in by the spectacle, I'd never seen the room lit before, I'd never seen [*laughs*], you know, so many people in one place, like a Super Bowl game or something. It was huge and I started cracking up, "Oh God, look at that!" [*laughs*] Okay, walk through, in place, the camera fifty yards away, I saw David step out from behind the camera, the eyes glaring right at me, you know. He came stalking across, I'm going, "Oh God, okay, straighten up, Jack." And he came up to me and he says, "Jack, just ..." "Okay, David." [*laughs*] "Yes, I know." And it was like, there was no need for dialogue, you know what I mean? There was no need to say anything. "Jack, just ..." "I know." Not really that much conversation or cerebralizing or analyzing. My whole school of acting is to say the words and make the funny faces, you know, as juxtaposed to some kind of intense, real soul-searching emotional sort of ... I mean, I can be intense, emotional, and very bored. [*laughs*] Or I can sit very placidly and just be excited as hell. What next ... He deals in real simple terms when he's describing what's going on in a scene. He expresses it in very simple sort of language, you know?

KGG: Like with Jorge in the torture scene. "A walk in the park."

JN: Like when I'm being tortured by this gorilla and he says, you know, this makes him real happy, you know, this is just a walk in the park for him, he says, it makes him real happy but no big deal, you know. But you understand those simplistics somehow much much better, much more clearly than trying to delve into the cerebrals, you know, trying to connect the little synapses and motivate everything. That's, I think, one of, maybe one of his real unique characteristics, is he's, all of this homespun country boy kind of stuff, but you know there's so much of that … but it's the fact that he can, he can take difficult and very involved kinds of events and, you know, present them very simplistically to an actor who's basically simple [*laughs*] and I think, you know, actors respond to that with kind of a sense of relief actually, I think, you know [*sighs*] "Is that all there is to it?" Yeah, you know, it's as simple as that. "You mean I don't have to intellectualize?", you know. Actors don't have big brains, you know, they're not … most of them, I know I'm not, I prefer to just, you know, go along on a basic kind of fairly primitive hedonistic kind of level, and not have to think about any kind of higher levels of consciousness, you know. But actors somehow are compelled to be well versed in philosophy or theology, you know, politics, whatever the hell. Hey, say the words, make the funny faces. And Lynch can present an acting problem to an actor in such a simplistic and uncomplicated way that it seems like a piece of cake, and it makes it just kind of … I mean it's a real challenge to do something that simple and make it something great, which you know it is going to be. He's wonderful. He can, you know, instill a kind of a … it's good for confidence, you know, which actors have none. I think that's neat stuff, George, don't you? It's … I like that. Here's something … I'll light a cigarette butt. This is an old habit of mine I developed before I went on the De Laurentiis payroll. [*strikes a light*] When down here in Mexico I usually manage to stay in cigarettes, but [*long satisfying draw on cigarette butt*] … man, that's coffee [*chuckles*] … you know that blurb? Joker did that … "man, that's coffee."

KGG: [*referring to cup in his hand*] Is that coffee?

JN: [*rattling ice cubes*] So is this [*drinks*], hmm. Well, I've tried to analyze the shit out of Lynch [*laughs*].

KGG: We can get away from him if you like.

JN: [*laughs*] Let's see … I don't know. Wenders was great, though, I really liked him a lot. What next? What can we do?

KGG: You said David wanted you for *The Elephant Man* …

JN: No, no.

KGG: Can we go back to the beginning?

JN: I don't know, what do you want …?

KGG: How did you get into movies?

JN: Hmm?

KGG: How did you get into movies?

JN: I became an ac-TOR. [*laughs*] Oh, hell, I could talk about that. I could talk about that. All right. There's a phenomenon that occurs of jokers who come to Hollywood to get in the movies, you know, or they come to Hollywood to become actors, whatever, which is a sad thing to see a lot of times. You don't come to Hollywood to become an actor or to, you know, learn to be an actor. It's the worst place to try to learn to become an actor, you know. I mean, I never did that and I don't know anybody who's ever done that, you know, Hollywood to become an actor. If you're an actor, then, you know, go to Hollywood and take a shot at getting in the movies, but, I mean … if you're an actor going to Hollywood and trying to get in the movies can kill you, you know, and yet there are people who come to Hollywood to try and be actors. And it's bass-ackwards, you know. When you become an actor … go to Cincinnati to become … or Milwaukee or Seattle or … I was kind of lucky growing up in Dallas, in my hometown, the Dallas Theater Center, a great company, and there are, you know, theatres, regional companies, Louisville, Minneapolis, anywhere but Hollywood. New York even, hit the streets and try and be an actor. And if you make it, then take a shot at Hollywood. Anybody can try it, you know. Either that or, you know, I really missed my best shot at getting in the movies when I turned down a football scholarship to Notre Dame, man, you know, gone from there to the Green Bay Packers and gone from there straight into the movies [*laughs*], you know, wouldn't even have had to be an actor. Or flunked out of the Olympic swimming team.

KGG: Who was your first film with?

JN: A thing with Candy Bar in Juarez [*laughs*] … no. You guys can see that film. I've got a print at Irma's [*laughs*]. Sorry [*rattles ice in cup*], shit. No, I came out to California to go to the Pasadena Playhouse, and I'd been touring around the country doing shows for little kids, one night stands in little towns around Kansas.

KGG: What kind of shows?

JN: Oh, they were great shows. [*laughs*] The little lame prince … But I came to California to do, to go to the Pasadena Playhouse. I took a bus from Oklahoma City, I think, or Tulsa … Oklahoma City, and went into the Playhouse sort of unannounced. I mean, I didn't call and make an appointment. I had the name of the dean, you know, "I wanna go to the Pasadena Playhouse" [*laughs*] … and that was, you know, "Great, Jack, but you know the Playhouse is shutting down at the end of this summer." And the guy, I can't remember his name, the dean of the school, but was very kind to me and taught me a couple of things, and, you know, one was, it was a sad thing the Playhouse …

[end of tape]

KGG: These are twenty-minute reels.

JN: Twenty-minute reels.

KGG: Okay, back to the Pasadena Playhouse.

JN: Yeah, well, the Pasadena Playhouse was, you know, a prestigious kind of institution. I went in unannounced and was told, you know, the Playhouse was shutting down, which was kind of a sad event, whatever the problems were. Anyway the Pasadena Playhouse passed into history. But I was told a couple of things by this man, who was the dean of the school, and I can't remember his name and I'm sorry, and one was whatever I was going to try and do, whatever I did, get training and train hard and work hard. And one of the things that was a rule there for anyone who was going to the school was that while you were at the Playhouse you didn't go running into Hollywood chasing after agents, and you didn't go running into Hollywood trying to make the connections, that you weren't going to be there with stars in your eyes. You were going to be there to work your ass off and that that's what training was all about. And that wherever I went from there, that that's what I should try and pursue without any kind of pie-in-the-sky, stars-in-the-eye kind of thing, and don't go running into Hollywood. Which is I guess what I was just trying to say a while ago, you don't go running into Hollywood … hell, I don't know, I tried to approach it seriously, art, you know, I mean I was kind of brought along with that school of thought, that it's somehow an art. And I worked hard. I did that, you know, I mean I tried to find good training, serious work and whatnot. For what it's worth. Maybe that's why I'm not so intense about it. It's really simple kind of stuff. It's what's neat about the way David, you know, lays out the task. Yeah, right, easy … easy. It's what made Henry easy, you know, put on the suit and the tie and there he is. Or Tony Robozo.

KGG: So when did you finally actually make it to Hollywood? And why?

JN: And why? Let's see … well, I finally went to Hollywood long after I'd made my bones as an actor, you know, when I had all the SAG cards and the Equity cards and all of that business. And … what? I went to … after San Francisco … how'd I get to San Francisco? Sounds like an epic. After the Playhouse closed, I went to San Francisco. Middle and late '60s. The best time, the best place … it was serendipitous. San Francisco, I had some friends there, broke, and it was the greatest place to be at the best possible time and I spent all the middle and late '60s in San Francisco during all the business that went on there. Was … let me see, let me try … I can't remember how … yeah, there was a lot, a lot going on politically, socially, sociopolitically. There was, umm, a great kind of resurgence at that time in American theatre, a lot of stuff coming out of Cafe La MaMa, a lot of new playwrights. There was a lot of politically, socially-oriented kind of radical theatre, kind of … the theatre took on a kind of a voice, at the time, like social values and mores and whatever were changing and the hippies hit town and, you know, stock brokers started wearing their hair over their ears and, you know, the country was undergoing a big turnover in thinking, attitudes … racial, political, social kind of things and of course upheavals of major events and whatnot. The theatre at that time really started to sort of take on a role or develop a form, the way … sort of, began to mesh with music and poster art and fashion, and theatre became kind of a mainstream sort of medium, you know, because what was going on on television was something that was too hideous to be seen, and what was happening in the movies was too phantasmagorical to be believed, but, you know, on the streets was theatre and it was vibrant … what was the word? Relevant, relevant, yeah. Gotta be relevant … doesn't matter what we do as long as we're together, you know, if just enough people would get together [*laughs*], you know, and it was, it was a force, an influence. And to be on the stage doing some of the kinds of things that we were doing was, it was an intense sensation of, of … I don't want to say power, but hell, it was power [*laughs*], it really was. I mean, you could influence people's thinking, maybe because … I mean, the hippies were really pretty dumb, you know, and spaced out and very gullible and, and very malleable. And it was, it was not all that difficult at that time to start a parade, you know. All you had to have was, you know, a clown suit and a drum and, you know, somebody would follow you down the street throwing flowers. So it was, it was like ripe kind of territory for any kind of movement, agitation, whatever, and to me, I mean, you know, we're just doing a play here, right. And I mean I was a Dallas boy, you know, and I'd seen all of that business that was, you know, pretty recent [*laughs*], pretty recent history, and knew the FBI and the Commies over here and the pinkoes and the John Birchers and I felt like I had some kind of objective, objective sort of attitude about all that. It was something to watch and it was something to participate in, and it was a hell of a time and place to be an actor, you know. I don't know, I don't know that I miss all that stuff, you know, but a lot of things about life have seemed pretty dull ever since, you know. I don't know what all the fuss about Watergate was. [*laughs*] I don't have any politics of my own. It wasn't political at the time. Tried to be a voice of reason, for crying out loud! … you know [*laughs again*], but I was Tom Paine and I guess they sort of expect things out of radical firebrands, I don't know. [*laughs*] Now I'm nobody's advocate. Things are better, things are quieter. Things *are* better. Course we could get into this about … I mean, we're in Mexico City right now, you know, and I do find some things here kind of raising my blood. I don't know if the balloon'll go up down here or not, but something makes me wish I was here if it does, you know. [*laughs*] I don't know about that. I mean, I don't want to throw rocks … I'm trying to get back …

KGG: How you got to Hollywood …

JN: I just left Pasadena. Yeah, why I didn't go straight from Pasadena … [*lights cigarette*] I go down to Hollywood … go from Hollywood … *Eraserhead* and *Dune* … okay, I want to talk about this, *Bushman*, okay? 'Cause this is part of … In San Francisco at the time, a guy came to the theatre, named David Schickele, making a movie called *Bushman*, which was the story of a Nigerian student who'd come to the United States to attend school, he was at San Francisco State College. It was a sort of a *cinema verite*, semi-documentary thing about a Black African student's experiences in America at the time when all of the racial kinds of things were going on, to which the Nigerian guy had no relation whatsoever except for the colour of his skin, you know, he was not … he had absolutely nothing, no experience whatsoever in common with what the American Black man was going through on the streets at that time. And yet was caught up in it simply because he was black and because it was demanded of him, I suppose. And we made that movie under some difficult circumstances because reality, events, sort of caught up with, with the picture. I mean we were trying to keep up with what was happening to the guy and events got way ahead and it turned into a remarkable picture called *The Bushman*. Never widely seen or never widely released, it went around the festival circuits and whatever, but it's a little slice of life from the era that's … when I saw it years after the fact, it was a startling, shocking kind of thing. It premiered at the very first FilmEx in L.A. and was, you know … and there I was, in a movie [*laughs*].

KGG: That was your first…

JN: It was the first feature film, yeah. Felix the Queen, Felix was a nice guy, but had a little bent … had some kind of Jamaican evil eye put on him or something, I don't know. Don't know Felix's story really, but … but years after the fact, I think it's still around somewhere and is a good piece of stuff. Umm, Francis Coppola came to town and started Zoetrope Studios and all of a sudden movies became kind of a thing in San Francisco. You know, there's a lot of movie stuff in San Francisco. About the same time we toured *Tom Paine* to L.A. and it was a phenomenal kind of a theme, "up the revolution", but to the wrong audience. You know, somehow L.A. knew it was a great production, but they weren't ready to take to the streets, like, it didn't have the same kind of real organic sort of … But was a dynamite kind of production, attracted a lot of attention and agents, producers, TV people and all of this, you know, all of the Hollywood stuff flocked to the show because it was a real, you know, it was a hit. And that was kind of new to us, you know, playing for half a dozen jokers from the William Morris Agency and [*laughs*] guys in suits and ties. Our audiences had consisted of the SDS and the Black Panthers and the John Birchers [*laughs*] … street people, you know. So I was young and a hotshot … and going to put me in a damned TV show. You know, great, a payroll [*laughs*]. Okay, fine, sign here, this releases you from the show. I said, "well, I don't want out of the show." They said, well, it's contractual conflicts, and the lawyers and all of this business. Well, sorry but when we're finished the show, then we'll … so I blew it in Hollywood [*laughs*]. And paid, what is it? … fifteen years, sixteen, seventeen years, and you pay and you pay and you pay … So, memories are short. Stumbled around Hollywood for a while, some hot rod movies, this and that, and one day was introduced to a character named David Lynch, who was making this short film in a few weeks, and would I like to talk to the guy about doing … *Eraserhead*, he told me was the name of it, right. And … at the AFI. I had done some AFI short films before and was kind of wary of short films. Lynch was kind of wary about myself as well, and didn't really hit it off when we first talked. Should I tell the story?

KGG: Sure.

JN: Yeah? So we met and talked in this little room and then went outside. We were out in the parking lot at the AFI and there was a Volkswagen with this wooden rack built on it that was an ingenious concept, a rack on a Volkswagen that had the capacity of a Mayflower moving van [*laughs*]. And I owned a Volkswagen at the time, I went "my god, look at that, it's absolutely ingenious, a rack on a Volkswagen with the capacity of a Mayflower moving van," I said, "you know, whoever came up with that must have some kind of smarts." And Lynch said, "well, thank you, Jack. I did that … and you're hired for *Eraserhead*." So, *Eraserhead*, I guess it's well-known, became a long term project and it was just fine with me [*laughs*] because that funny haircut dropped all of … you know what came to mind, it went, it went back to the Pasadena Playhouse, the guy said "don't go running into Hollywood, you know, don't go chasing after the …", you know, and that was exactly what I said to myself, you know … there was something … forgot all about the whole racket, you know, all about *Tom Paine*, hit show … all of it had something to do that was the right thing to do. And it took a long time, but it'll be around for a while. In fact, it's outlasted Columbia Studios [*laughs*]. Is it time for our *sandwich de pavos*, David? That's his latest, you know, *sandwich de pavos*.

KGG: You can't get Bob's shakes down here, so …

JN: That's his latest, god damn. [*lights cigarette*] Well, god damn, train of consciousness, George … steer me anywhere, man?

KGG: You want to take a rest for a while?

JN: [*rattles ice in cup*] I don't know, what are we doing? Guess what … up to date, *Dune*. Oh, okay, okay. *Dune*. *Duuunnne*. Ay, *Dune*, yeah. Well, I told David I thought General William Westmoreland should be directing this picture [*laughs*]. *Dune* is a big picture, certainly the biggest picture I've ever worked on, certainly the biggest picture …

Pablo Ocampo Pinan: Cut, end of the tape.

[*break*]

KGG: Get some mineral water down you, Jack, some liquid.

JN: Yeah, yeah, yeah, good.

POP: You have a cigarette?

JN: I hope to pee in your Post Toasties.

[*general laughter; rattle of ice in cup*]

KGG: That's on tape, Jack.

JN: Well …

Anatol Pacanowski: Well, actually the sound is, yes, the audio is …

KGG: Jack's gradually sliding to the left along the couch …

JN: All the tension's gone out of the waistband of my shorts, you know, sinking down … Mineral water, yeah.

AP: If you need a cassette, I'll open it for you, you know.

KGG: Well, we didn't want to wake you up.

AP: Thank you. That's really nice of you. This is very refreshing. I'm not really asleep. Other than snoring, I'm listening …

KGG: He snores while awake.

AP: This is bullshit propaganda, man. I'm not going to retire, no way.

KGG: Well, we're rolling, Jack.

JN: Bullshit propaganda. … What?

KGG: We're rolling. You were talking about *Dune*.

JN: *Dyooone*. Big movie, big movie, *Dune*. *Lawrence of Arabia* would fit in one little corner of the screen of *Dune*.

AP: Can you repeat that, Jack, because we didn't have the video.

JN: What? I said *Lawrence of Arabia* would fit in one little corner of the screen in *Dune*. *Dune* is the biggest picture I've ever worked on. I'm sure it's the biggest picture Jose Ferrer's ever worked on, too, actually [*laughs*]. I know it's the biggest picture … who's worked on this picture?

KGG: Everett McGill, Silvana Mangano …

JN: Who *hasn't* worked on this picture? My god … do you know that since this picture started, the rate of illegal aliens across the border has dropped by 35%? [*laughs*] Did you know that? It's like when, you know, Francis Coppola was doing *Hammett*, you know, it's set in Chinatown and he had the influx of boat people from Southeast Asia on the payroll as soon as they hit the docks … Jane Fonda was saying, you know, "What about these boat people?" Francis was saying, "Don't worry, Jane, I've got jobs for them in *Hammett*." … What is it called? *Dyooone*, *Dyooone*, *Dune*, yeah. Interesting simple little love story.

Costs, no ... god damn ... well, I don't know, what do you want to know about *Dune*? What can one say about *Dyoone*? [*laughs*] *Dune* ... we're going to summarize it? No. ... What's it about? I really shouldn't say too much about *Dune* because David's very secretive, well not secretive ... what do you call it? Protective. So *Dune* ... what the fuck ... my lips are sealed. The more you say, the more they'll want to know.

KGG: Is this the first time you've worked outside the States?

JN: Worked outside the States ...

AP: Besides Poland.

JN: Is this outside the States? [*laughs*]

KGG: Ask Pablo ...

JN: Outside the States ... *los estados unidos* of Mexico ... the difference ... same damn thing [*rattles ice in cup*].

AP: Mexican States ...

JN: Well, I don't know. For a boy who grew up in the shadow of the Alamo ... see, when I was a kid, my grandma took me through the Alamo, you know, she'd say, "Jackie", you know, she'd point out things, and it was a shrine, you know, it was, it was not a tourist attraction or a John Wayne movie set. It was a special place, you know, and my grandma was from San Antone, and she would point out all the places, you know, "here is where the bodies were stacked up, these were the stones where the blood ran, this is where the heroes died" and there was the portrait of Mrs. Dickinson, Didrickson, what was her name? Her and her little baby and a black slave were the only survivors of the Alamo, were given a burro and they rode out and the Mexican army let them pass ... but it was a special place where horrible things happened and, you know, my grandma's lesson to me was, you know, like, no more. It was never again. I was ... she showed me in the Bible a new commandment, love one another. It was what they say this side of the Rio Grande is simpatico. And I'm glad I'm here, you know. It's always been a remarkable place. You guys are going to Juarez. You can look across and that's Texas, you know, but I can't look across and say that's Mexico ... I'm just sorry as hell I've had to work every day. [*laughs*] This is a good place to be. I think somewhat the same way that maybe San Francisco might have been a good place to be at the time. This might be a good place to be at a good time. *Salud. Adios.*

Actors

One of the most rewarding things about working on *Dune* was having an opportunity to meet, and to observe the work of, a remarkable international cast.

Max von Sydow (Doctor Kynes)

Max Von Sydow as Dr. Kynes, the planetary ecologist and ally of the Fremen. Photograph copyright Universal/De Laurentiis.

In the actor's trailer, Estudios Churubusco.

Kenneth George Godwin: First of all, since you're sort of symbolic of Swedish film for so many years, how did you get your connection with Dino De Laurentiis?

Max von Sydow: How did I? I'm not sure, but I've worked in several films with Dino De Laurentiis now. The first one I think was already '74, in *Three Days of the Condor*, which was shot in New York and Washington, maybe. But after that [*interrupted by production assistant*] ... shall I rephrase that? Okay. I don't really know when I ... I think I met Dino De Laurentiis personally with my agent,

Paul Kohner in Hollywood in the early '70s or maybe even late '60s, I'm not sure. But the first film I was in that Dino De Laurentiis produced was *Three Days of the Condor*. And since then I have been in *Flash Gordon*, in *The Hurricane*, in *Conan* and now in this one, *Dune*.

KGG: Was *Three Days of the Condor* the first film you did in the States?

MVS: No no, no no, it wasn't. The first one I was in was already in 1962 and that was *The Greatest Story Ever Told*. And since then there have been several.

KGG: We'd really like to hear about the old days in Sweden ... you're probably fed up with talking about ...

MVS: Yes, well the old days in Sweden. I was brought up in a peaceful, idyllic country called Sweden, which in those days had a lot of theatre and quite a few quite good motion picture directors, among others Ingmar Bergman. But not only Bergman. There was another one by the name of Alf Sjoberg, who I think is most well-known for his film version of Strindberg's *Miss Julie*, which he did in 1950 I think. I was in that, that was my second film part. But I had no ambitions to leave that country in those days. I worked in municipal theatres, several, the first one in , not too far from Stockholm. It was a wonderful school for me because municipal theatre in Sweden in those days was a small theatre with a lot of opportunities for young actors. So I got immediately good, big, meaty parts in good plays, and played all kinds of things. Because of my features in those days, I was mainly cast as an old man. My career started out as a 90-year-old person and gradually I worked myself down through the ages, but it took a few years. But it was very good school and very constructive in the way Sweden worked in those days. Films were mainly made in the summer, so ... and of course Sweden being a small country, we couldn't afford having special theatre actors and special film actors and special – well, television didn't exist, but special, say, radio actors. So we had to do all, which also was a good school. So I played in the theatres in the winter and made a film or two in the summer, and every free time I had I worked in the radio, in plays, readings, poetry, novels, all kinds of things. But this went on until I met Bergman. That was, well I met him early in the '50s, but I didn't work with him until 1955 when I was hired to work at the municipal theatre of Malmo, where he was one of the directors. And I was in two stage productions with him that year, that season. And then the following summer he wanted to make a film based on a play he had written called something like "Wood Painting", which dealt with a knight and his squire who had returned from the Crusades and were in a bad mood and they had some pretty miserable friends travelling with them. And Bergman was also inspired in those days by, I think, Hofmannsthal's *Jedermann* and by – what's his name? -- the music by ... *Carmina Burana* by Carl Orff. And whatever came out in his notebooks was the script of *The Seventh Seal*, and he shot that against his producer's will for no money at all. But he had had a, quite a success the previous year with *Smiles of a Summer Night* and that, I think, convinced his producer that he should have his way and do this totally unnecessary project. All of us who were in it were very enthusiastic because we felt that this was a very special thing, and it was very artistic, and very profound in many ways, and we enjoyed it. And we shot it in eight weeks. I'm not going to mention the budget, it was ridiculous … and you can't really compare it to our standards. But that was the beginning of my work with Bergman. It went on for several years, we made I don't know how many stage productions at this theatre in Malmo. 1960, no '59, Bergman left for the National Theatre in Stockholm, and in '60 I joined him. I didn't work with him on the stage for a few years but continued on in several pictures with him. But through his films I came to the United States in 1962, and without his films I certainly wouldn't have done that. I never planned any form of international career, and I kind of fought it to begin with. But Sweden has changed, it's not the same today. I don't really know what it is like because I haven't worked there for several years, nine years, except for one film I made two years ago. But I think particularly for me the five years I spent in Malmo, at the municipal theatre there, was a very constructive and very productive time. Bergman was there for the four first of those years. I don't know what you know about Swedish films or Swedish theatre. Is there anything you would like me to …

KGG: More or less only what I've seen in Bergman films.

MVS: Oh dear. Alf Sjoberg was probably the most important director. He directed Bergman's first screenplay, called *Frenzy*, I think, or something like that, in 1943 or so. Which became a great success. And he also made several other films, which were all interesting, but never really … they weren't really successful financially. He was aesthetically very, very precise and a great perfectionist. I think Bergman learned a lot from him in many ways. But when Bergman then established himself as a film director and theatre director in his own right, I'm afraid there was a certain jealousy between the two. Unfortunately Sjoberg died prematurely through a traffic accident a few years ago, but he was, particularly for the Swedish theatre a wonderful power, wonderful strength and source of inspiration. He was, I don't know when he was born, I think he was in his seventies when he died, but he was a very very youthful person, and very interested in what was going on in the world, and totally self-educated, I think. He read tons and tons of books, and always worked our present day into the plays he directed, and always managed to find something which appealed to us in the audience, whatever classical play he produced. I miss him very much and I think there is a huge vacancy after him in Swedish theatre. And in a certain way also in Swedish film. Bergman is now returning to

Sweden, not to make films according to what he says, he has now made his last film, he says. I hope he's joking. But he's going to make, work in the theatre and also I think for television. I'm sure he will change his mind. I hope so.

KGG: Do you still do theatre work?

MVS: I haven't, since I left Sweden I've only made, been in two plays, both on Broadway. Unfortunately none of them very successful, although I enjoyed both productions very much. Next year I'm going to try to direct a film and after that I would like to maybe go back to the theatre again.

KGG: Where would you be making the film?

MVS: In Denmark. It's very exciting. It's a matter of money of course, but I think that we have the money for it. It's a story which is, it's a Danish classic novel by Herman Bang and the title of it is something like "Along the Roadside", a very bad title for a film and we cannot use that title, it will … it's totally misleading for what is in the story. But it's a wonderful novel which I've been in love with for about, I don't know, twenty-five years. And finally I've found a man who is willing to try to put up the money for it. I think we'll get it and it will be mainly a Danish production.

KGG: You haven't directed before?

MVS: No, I haven't, so I'm very much looking forward to it. But I have a screenplay now, it's almost totally completed. It's a very low key love story, but with wonderful undertones, and it's mainly a portrait of quite a fascinating woman and her … deals with her husband and her … I wouldn't call it lover, but … because nothing really happens, say would-be lover. But I'm very much looking forward to this.

KGG: Have you done much film work in recent years besides the few De Laurentiis films?

MVS: Oh yes, I've been working almost all the time.

KGG: Apart from those films, I can only recall *Death Watch*, Tavernier's film.

MVS: Oh *Death Watch*, yeah, that was one. *The Flight of the Eagle*, that was the Swedish film, Jan Troell directed a few years ago.

KGG: Who you worked with before.

MVS: Yes, many times, many times. And what else? I was in a French production last year, shot in Portugal, and in a Canadian production last year, shot in Toronto. And .. ah, I don't remember … no, I've been working in many films in between the De Laurentiis films.

KGG: Do you enjoy doing the sort of roles you've been getting in the De Laurentiis films?

MVS: Yes, I do. It's, it's a nice change, yes it is, because … well, *Conan*, *Flash Gordon* and also this one. Well, for me this one is not that, say, unusual, but the part in *Conan* and also the part in *Flash Gordon* were so theatrical in a way, and also based on fantasy so much. Dr. Kynes in this one is more realistic I feel. But it's a nice character. Of course, I miss a lot which is in the book, but there isn't room for it in the film though unfortunately. But Dr. Kynes in the novel was a very interesting character. I wish there could be ... I wish it could have been a television series.

KGG: Both Anatol and I were very impressed with your assassin in *Three Days of the Condor*.

MVS: Well, that's a very good part. It was a wonderful film, I think, a very good film, a very exciting film. It was fun to do that part because it was very well written, and it was a villain with surprises. He was certainly not a cliche. But somehow he, what was so good with him was that he played himself in a way, it ... the part established himself in the beginning by killing all these nice people and then he became a threat whenever he showed up, so I didn't have to do anything. I mean I could be as nice as any nice person and I would be a threat anyway. People ask me, or talk about him as a very evil person. I don't think he was. I think rather he is a bit unimaginative, say, emotionally. Emotionally not very intelligent, but intellectually extremely bright. But very professional in what he's doing, but not really evil. He doesn't hate his victims [*laughs*], he just does what he is paid to do and that's it. I'm not ... I'm not trying to excuse his actions, but playing a part, it's necessary to try to understand the part. You don't have to like the person, but you have to understand the person. I think I understand whatever his name was, I've forgotten.

KGG: If you do get to direct this film, do you plan to phase out of acting?
MVS: No, no, no.

KGG: It's still your first -
MVS: Oh yes, absolutely.

KGG: And you write as well?
MVS: I've written this screenplay, yes.

KGG: But you've not written too much over the years?
MVS: No, not really, no. Sometimes. It depends. I feel it's very difficult to get started. When I get started it's okay, but it's a matter of discipline I'm afraid.

Jurgen Prochnow (Duke Leto)

Jurgen Prochnow as Duke Leto, saying farewell to the watery world of Caladan before departing for Arrakis. Photograph copyright Universal/De Laurentiis.

Actor's trailer, Estudios Churubusco.
Kenneth George Godwin: Can we start with just some general background, where you came from ...?
Jurgen Prochnow: Whatever you want.
KGG: So, where are you from in Germany?
JP: I was born in Berlin and I was brought up there. Well, I was born during the war and at the end of the war we moved to Pommery because my grandparents were living there and our house was bombed in Berlin. So we moved to there, towards Pommery, and we stayed there. Then just in the end of the war we moved back towards Mecklenburg, which is another part of Germany, and there we stayed until the end of the war and one year more. Then we went back to Berlin to find my grandparents there, and they were living there, and my mother and my brother and me, we shared a flat.
KGG: That was in West Berlin?

JP: That was in West Berlin, yeah.

KGG: How did you get interested in acting? Was it early or ...?

JP: Probably at the age of thirteen, fourteen. I remember we went to a church, that was at Dusseldorf, later we moved from Berlin to Dusseldorf when I was twelve years old, and I went there to the church and there was a man at this church working and he always wanted to be a director, theatre director, and he founded a sort of amateur group there. And I was very interested to do that, to join this group, which I did, and my brother as well, and we started on plays, little tiny ones. For me it was great fun and something else, opposite the school and so on. So I liked it and began to get more and more involved in this sort of thing. At the same time, I started in the local theatre, I started to take jobs as an extra and so, because I was very interested in theatre and the whole atmosphere. And I did other jobs as well, lights and things like that in the theatre, and I watched the performances. Sometimes I saw a performance fifty times or more often, and every evening it was new for me and with open eyes I went to see it and I loved it. So I had quite a big, big experience, I would say, between fourteen and eighteen or so, and I saw a lot of plays and I saw the performances, I told you, sometimes I saw it fifty times or so. So I knew a lot about it and I think at that time it grew in myself, the wish to be an actor.

KGG: Did you study acting formally or did you just ...?

JP: No, afterwards then I started ... I left school, and my parents didn't want me to go to drama school directly. I had to go to a bank to go through an apprenticeship, a three years apprenticeship in a bank, because they wanted that I had a real profession. I came from a so-called little bourgeois family and they had no idea what it meant to be – I had no idea as well, but I had the wish myself and I wanted to be an actor always. And so I started in that bank [*interrupted by panting dog; laughs*] ... at the same time, I went in the evenings, I went to the theatre and did this job as an extra and lighting jobs as well, so that was ... and the same time I had the apprenticeship. Because I felt that that job was not right. It got in me, it became in me stronger and stronger the wish to become an actor. And I went to drama school and I was accepted in that drama school, and I did it secretly. I didn't tell my parents. And that was after one and a half years of bank and of course I wanted to leave, but in the end I finished it, I finished the three years of banking apprenticeship, and then I went to drama school when I was twenty, twenty-one, for three years, to a very good school in Germany at that time, a very famous school, and I finished it. And afterwards i got my first contract with a theatre.

KGG: We're getting a lot of panting ... as long as we see the dog ...

JP: [*Laughs*] Everything is collapsing.

KGG: So you were purely theatre to start with.

JP: Yeah, I started then and in the theatre I got a contract for two years as a beginner, in a small theatre in a town called Osnaburg, the north of Germany, a repertory theatre, and I started playing little parts and then bigger parts. And then I moved to another theatre after two years, for three years to another one, to a better company and bigger theatre, the town was called Aachen, and I stayed there for three years and afterwards I moved to another one, repertory theatre, to Heidelberg for a year, and then I began my first bigger contract, I would say, to a more or less famous theatre in Germany, tradition, and very good director, very good company, and I started there. And at the same time, at that time I would say after seven years of being in the theatre, being in the provinces or so, I started with movies and television as well.

KGG: How did you get into movies?

JP: Just by accident, I would say. I once went with my brother – he's an actor as well – [*calls his dog in German*] … he lived in Munich at that time and he said to me, once I visited him and he said to me let's go to the director of this company, he's a casting director for the Bavarian Studios, and let's go and say hello and so on and so on. And so we went and he saw me and I talked to him, had an interview with him and two weeks later had the first offer for television, a series, for a part in a series, and it went well. The first time I did it, I didn't like it at all, I thought it was awful in comparison to the theatre and so I'll never do it again. Then I got another offer and I did it and I liked it more. And so pretty soon I got a very good offer for a first movie, first big television movie and so on. So it started really without any, I didn't put any pressure on that, I never wanted it really for myself, or I never thought about it. I thought in terms of being a theatre actor always. And it was a complete new medium for me. And I was lucky, I was pretty soon successful in that medium. And later I started to realize what it is and that it's in a way for me, it was a completely new experience, in a way perhaps a new profession in comparison to the theatre work, I would say.

KGG: Do you still do theatre?

JP: Yeah, I … well, I never stopped doing it. But after *The Boat*, I did no theatre work after *The Boat*, because for me for the first time I got international offers and I thought of, because I wanted it, of having the chance, taking the chance for international offers and working on international movies. So that all happened after one movie, I mean, I'm a professional, I would say, almost twenty years, and one movie did it. [*laughs*]

KGG: *The Boat* has been your most successful film so far.

JP: Internationally, yeah. I would think so, yeah.

KGG: **That was a difficult project to get off the ground I understand.**

JP: Yes, very difficult.

KGG: Initially it was to have an American director and they just couldn't put it together.

JP: Yeah. I think the first idea, it was John Sturges, I think. He should be the director and they started already, and they started building *The Boat* already. I remember that because we were doing other movies at that time and they were talking about that huge project and so on and so on.

KGG: Robert Redford was considered ...

JP: Robert Redford was the star for one, that was I think the second ...

KGG: The Don Siegel one.

JP: Don Siegel, yeah. And they started already also preparing. But the first plan, I think, collapsed because they changed the script, they changed it in a way that the author said there's no way of doing it in that way. They put in additional scenes with Americans killed by the Germans and all that stuff, making really a sort of ...

KGG: Melodrama ...

JP: No, sort of, I would say ... these ... what is it? Typical American vision of Germans in the war, and they changed it in that way, as far as I know. And the second one became such an enormous project in terms of money, I think they wanted to construct it on platforms in the sea for the actors to be brought in on helicopters and such, and that's why it collapsed as well because all of a sudden they realized nobody could finance it. So in the end we did it and I think it was the best way, yeah. Yes, we were shooting one year on that one and there was the pre-production and a long post-production afterwards that was quite ... for me, it meant a lot, yeah.

KGG: It was done as a TV series as well.

JP: Yeah, we were shooting a six-hour version, that is the original in six books, the original stuff, the whole novel adapted or written into a script, and the movie is the extract of it.

KGG: What sort of things were missing from the film?

JP: Well the whole thing is more, it's dealing more with the characters, more with the characters on *The Boat*. You know them better than in the end, you know about every single individual on *The Boat*, you know more about every sailor and submariner.

KGG: It's a very intense movie. I can't really imagine it stretched to six hours.

JP: Yeah, yeah. No, of course it wouldn't work as a movie in a six hour version, of course not, but I think for a six ... they say, and I have the feeling as well, the six hour version is in a way our real work, what we did and what we shot and that materializes our work better I would say.

KGG: The film is a condensed version.

JP: Yeah.

KGG: Could you tell us a bit about working with Schlondorff, who's an interesting director. What is he like to work with.

JP: Well, he's very nice to work with. I worked with him on *Katerina Blum, The Lost Honour of Katarina Blum*, and I liked it very much at that time, and then he always said we'll do another movie together, but it never happened. I mean, that's always ... it's very often like that, there are not the right parts and so on. I did just only because I know him and I sympathized with that ... he did a movie, *War and Peace* it was called, and it's about the situation in Germany. It's not the novel. It is about the situation in Germany, about the peace movement, about the unemployed people and so on and so on. About all those things going on with Baader-Meinhof and so on, and afterwards. Well, about the country itself. And I worked with him only, that was only a day or so afterwards, after *The Lost Honour of Katarina Blum*. So I remember this and it's, what is it, it's almost ten years ago when we did that one and I liked it and I think it was a good movie. It was very successful in Germany as well. But with Petersen, I did five movies and we worked together again and again, we know each other very long and that's really, a friendship developed in that time, in these ten years, and we got on very, very well and we did better, I think, in every movie. And I think that is important, very very important. For me, it's important to have a partner like this to work with, to improve your work from movie to movie.

KGG: After *The Boat*, you got these international offers ... what sort of things ... I know you played the head of Russian intelligence in Thailand in *Comeback*, which seems like a rather strange thing ...

JP: Yeah, that was one of the first offers I got. He took me because he saw *The Boat* and he changed the character ... well, this character's there, he is still existing, and he changed the name of this character and he's a sort of mixture of Russian, German and Eurasian mixture, and therefore he thought ... he was looking for this character very long, I suppose, he told me and then he thought it's the best idea to take me for this character. In a way it's not that far away because a lot of Russian instructors are living there, and head of secret services and so on, so it could be. And therefore I thought there's ... and it's based on a real story, on reality. It happened to someone. So, he was there and he knew, a photographer from Australia, and he knew about the details and so on.

KGG: After that you got ...

JP: After that I did ...

KGG: *The Keep*.

JP: *The Keep*.

KGG: Was that the first fantasy film ...?

JP: Directed by Michael Mann. Yeah, I would say so, yeah.

KGG: How was it to work in a fantasy film for the first time?

JP: Well, I was in the more or less realistic part of it, and I was not so much involved in the science fiction stuff. I liked the character very much.

KGG: You played the Wehrmacht officer.

JP: I played Woermann, a German officer, and as far as I know it was a sort of realistic portrait, I think, in that script. It was both sides of the German character. On the one side Woermann, the good ... [*end of first tape*] I thought it's a very interesting character because, in that script, there were the two parts of the Germans perhaps at that time. And for me far more realistic than they are generally portrayed, only the bad guy, the bad Nazi, and there is the other one as well and they have the big arguments. All this is, I think, very interesting in that movie, for me it was very interesting. And perhaps to let a bigger audience know about this, for me a new aspect in an American movie.

KGG: So it's sort of extending what you did in *Das Boot*, it gave people a slightly different image ...

JP: Right, right, yeah.

KGG: Was the script good for *The Keep*? I read the novel and it's a good idea, which ...

JP: Yeah, I think it depends very much on how it's done, of course, and everything. It could be very interesting, I think.

KGG: How did you come to be offered *Dune*?

JP: I don't know really [*laughs*]. I think through my agency. I think they knew that they were looking for the part and ... I don't know, but I think I was recommended, and David hadn't seen *The Boat* at that time, so they told him to see *The Boat* ... first of all I think he didn't like the idea of [*laughs*] having a German for that part, but then he saw *The Boat* and I think he changed his mind and that's why I got the part.

KGG: What's your impression of *Dune* now that you're pretty well finished ...?

JP: Well, I can say I loved the work here on that movie very very much. I loved to work with David and it's a great experience for me. And it's absolutely marvellous when you have, when you meet people, new people, you became friends, you become friends. That is something really very extraordinary in our profession, I would say. It doesn't happen very often, but here I like the crew very much, very nice people, and all the colleagues, all the other actors. I think it's a beautiful cast as far as I can say that, I think it's really absolutely very very carefully cast and everything is going to work as far as I can see. I haven't seen any rushes, but I think it's, from my point of view, as far as it's possible to judge and to say that, I think it's going to work.

KGG: Do you find there's any problem with the mixture of nationalities?

JP: No, not at all. That's not the problem. If it's … I think if the other person, doesn't matter what nationality he is, if he's casted well, or if he is able to play the character, then it doesn't matter at all. It's only in private life that makes a difference, if you talk then and you talk about your life and he is talking about his background, then it makes a difference and you find out difference, which is interesting of course. But in the work it's not at all … well I didn't …

KGG: Mixture of accents doesn't …

JP: No, not at all. Perhaps for the others it does [*laughs*] working with me, but not for me.

Patrick Stewart (Gurney Halleck)

*Patrick Stewart as Gurney Halleck, the Duke's right-hand man.
Photograph copyright Universal/De Laurentiis.*

On set, Estudios Churubusco.
Kenneth George Godwin: You've had a lot of classical training with Shakespeare, so this is somewhat different from much of your earlier work.
Patrick Stewart: That's right.
KGG: So how do you approach a project like this?
PS: The major difference has been this ... my past experience, which has been mostly theatre, and classical theatre, where the whole performance and production is approached simultaneously as a unit, rehearsed as a unit, and finally performed as a unit. Here, over a period of four months, we're taking it in tiny sections, invariably out of sequence and ... The other day I was, for instance, shooting two fragments of scenes on two different sets simultaneously. And therefore taking things moment by moment in the action of the story rather than embracing the whole sweep of the story, which is what happens in the theatre.

KGG: Your part in the film is rather theatrical as well. Do you have a problem with maintaining realism or are you sort of playing it a little overdone?

PS: It is a theatrical story. The story is epic, the background of the story is epic, the themes both in terms of their morality as well as the narrative line of the story are epic, and I feel no unease in moving from the classical stage to some of the massive sets that we have here on this production. The role is a heroic role, he's one of the heroes of the film, a war-master, a troubadour, a poet, a musician, a soldier and a close friend, companion and teacher of Paul, the hero. So the role has a lot of size, a lot of scale to it. A big man. And I find that there's been little shift from the past work into all of this.

KGG: It's not your first film though.

PS: No, it's not my first film. In fact, my first major film ... my last major film was in a similar vein, it was *Excalibur* for John Boorman, which was equally an heroic and epic film. I played Leondegrance, who was one of the old warlords, Guinevere's father. [*a dog wanders by*] Hi, dog. One of our Mexican friends. *Cave canem*.

KGG: Is this the first time you've worked in Mexico?

PS: It's not. I worked here in the theatre twenty-one years ago. I appeared at the Bellas Artes as a spear-carrier with the Old Vic company, a company led by Vivien Leigh and Robert Helpmann in 1962. And we passed through here, I think we spent two weeks in Mexico. It was an exciting time. So it's not my first time here, though I find the city very changed.

KGG: Do you like working in film, as opposed to on stage? Is it not as serious work as stage work?

PS: It's been said that one of the problems with the English stage actor is that he doesn't take his job seriously enough. Certainly my experience in films is that people take the work very, very seriously. I find it fascinating and ... as a child, I was brought up with movies as my background, not theatre. It's always been my main passion and relaxation, and in terms of performance I can't get enough of it. It's a fascinating, wonderful medium for the actor.

KGG: It's not a problem that everything is split up and spread out over months?

PS: It's not a problem because the focus, the concentration is so intense on each one of those sections, and demands that actor, director and technician give everything for that moment. I think the danger is perhaps that one can be too relaxed, too at ease in filming. The work seems to go in periods of intense concentrated activity for, maybe only for a few moments or minutes, followed by long periods of relaxation. If there is a difficulty, I think my difficulty has been in sustaining concentration over long periods when perhaps you're only working maybe for in all an hour out of a ten-hour working day. That's difficult, being ready to work.

KGG: How is David to work with as a director?

PS: Delightful. I spoke just now of concentration; he seems to have formidable concentration. And that's encouraging and supportive. If you know that somebody you're working for is not going to miss anything that you do, it's encouraging. He has that quality, as well as being very imaginative. He establishes the atmosphere of each working day on the set, it's his responsibility, and the atmosphere here is first class. It's hard working and intense and yet very humorous and very relaxed, and very respectful too. I like it very much.

KGG: You're working with a very good cast as well, Max von Sydow and so on. How is it working with someone like that?

PS: It is a ... it is a quality cast, and I think this is, this is one of the pleasant areas in which the sense of ensemble work has been so good. It was a thrill for me to work with Max von Sydow recently. He had been a hero of mine for a good many years. It seems that images of Max von Sydow have been following me around for twenty years. A fine performer, great authority, strength. And there are other English actors here that I've worked with in the theatre in England. Francesca Annis, who is also, has been a member of the Royal Shakespeare Company, and Freddie Jones also, and I've filmed with him in the past. My first day on the set, I arrived here quite short notice from a film in Germany and I was put into a small enclosed space to do my first scene, there were four of us – an American, a Scandinavian, a German and myself, a truly international cast. The quality of the work and the atmosphere has been excellent.

KGG: What's your impression of Kyle, who's never worked on a film before?

PS: Is that true?

KGG: Yes, this is his first film.

PS: Then it's impressive, very impressive. I think that ... you know there was a considerable search to find the actor to play the part. I think they found someone with extraordinary talent, versatility and concentration. And what is more, he has an authority on the set, which with a role as complex as this is very important.

KGG: Did you know the book before ...

PS: I do now.

KGG: You hadn't read it before?

PS: No, no. I hadn't read it before. I started reading it on the plane from London. As I say, I came here at short notice. And it is an extraordinary piece of work. I think far richer than I had imagined. The pity of it is that, because the book is very big and a movie can only be so long, there's only portions of the book that we shall be able to include in the film. So much that will be left out, and those who know the book will miss it. But I feel, from what I've seen, that the work that goes on here, that something, a distilled quality of the book is present in the work. Perhaps we only have one scene where there might have been a sequence of four or five, or a sequence maybe only lasts five minutes which might have perhaps been forty pages in the book, but I think what David has done in the script and in his direction is to get a distillation, an essence of the qualities. And so the unique atmosphere of the book is going to be very present in the film, I suspect. But I've only read the first book and there are four, and I believe a fifth in preparation.

KGG: Do you like science fiction?

PS: I've only dipped in superficially to science fiction before. I like this kind of science fiction. It asks questions, it has a strong narrative and it concerns itself with important matters, with the questions of morality, honour, of faith, relationships of parents and children, and it invites the reader – as I think the film will invite the audience – to question their lives, to question the society in which they live. I think it can be very important. I think it's already been seen that science fiction can be much more than escapism. I think what is most impressive about the work is the way in which David Lynch is focusing everything. It's a vast project, and the story itself has so many different elements. This morning, going on the stage to watch a scene, a part of the story that doesn't concern me, it was difficult not to be impressed by the terrific focus of energy and concentration in the work. It's so easy to be general, to be vague, particularly when you're dealing with fantasy and science fiction, you can generalize about something. Instead, the work is as specific as if it had been Shakespeare. It's impressive.

Sting (Feyd Rautha) and Sean Young (Chani)

Sean Young as Chani, Paul's Fremen love interest. Photograph copyright Universal/De Laurentiis.

In Sting's trailer, Estudios Churubusco.

When Anatol got an opportunity to interview Sting (while I was off somewhere else, unfortunately), Sean Young was present and suggested that she should be the one to conduct it; he went along with the idea, although it possibly wasn't the best one.

Sting: Has the interview started yet?

Sean Young: I don't think so.

Anatol Pacanowski: It never started, will never end, it will just ...

SY: Well, tell us when the camera is rolling.

AP: It's going now.

S: Okay, let's start the, um ... my name is Sting and this is Sian Phillips ... [*laughs*]

AP: Sean Young!

SY: Oh yeah, right, he didn't know [*laughs*] ... Sean who?

S: Okay ...
SY: Okay. I want to, like, know what kind of car you drive?
S: I drive a Volkswagen.
SY: A Volkswagen? Is that the only kind of car you have?
S: No. I've got an MG.
SY: That's it? Just two?
S: That's it.
SY MG and Volkswagen?
S: I don't spend much time at home, so I don't have a car.
SY: Do you drive much?
S: No. I'm driven a lot.
SY: Okay, my question ...
S: If this is the level of questions you're asking ...
SY: I build slowly!
S: What do you think of David Lynch?
SY: Ah, now, that's a good question. Ooh, baby, David Lynch ... visually great [*laughs*] ... that's about it, no ...
S: Are you talking about his body, or his work?
SY: No, I'm talking about his work. Visually, he's very very good, and I think he is not used to dealing with actors.
S: Actresses.
SY: Actresses, yes.
S: I think he deals very well with actors.
SY: Oh, well, that's true. This is subjective ... actresses. "Actors" can mean actresses. You see, in America, actors means, encompasses both. Actress and actor.
S: Thank you for that information. It's your turn.
SY: Okay, it's a good question: why do people call you Sting?
S: Why do people call me Sting?
SY: Yes. [*laughs*] Because you were seventeen and you got bumble-bee'd.
S: Stung?
SY: Yes [*laughs*].
S: Look, are we going to do a serious interview?
SY: Yes, okay, it's the glasses. They kind of get me upset.
S: Look, let's be serious. The camera's rolling, it's costing money, there are people here ...

AP: Tape is cheap. Don't worry about it if you have fun, but obviously, you know, Sting's time is limited.

S: You must be serious. Look, you know, I'm here looking serious ...

SY: That's true, that's true. I have to take that into consideration. My mind's going completely blank. I don't know what kind of questions to ask you. Like, how do you feel about making *Dune*?

S: I think that *Dune* will be an event.

SY: That's [*laughs*] ... anything else?

S: Well, you've yet to see ...

AP: Now, Sean, seriously ...

SY: I know. I really should stop. It's this Harkonnen animal is on my body, I can't deal with it. Get this thing off me.

S: I think it's going to be an important movie. Not morally or philosophically. Visually I think it's going to be ...

SY: I feel better already.

S: ... extremely provocative, shocking, outrageous even, as a visual adventure.

SY: What's been the most difficult scene for you to do?

S: The most difficult scene was appearing nude.

SY: [*laughs*] Appearing nude ... which scene was that?

AP: In the shower.

S: The problem was I had my clothes on. It's difficult to be nude ... [*laughs*]

SY: [*laughs*] With your clothes!

S: That was the hardest acting I ever did.

SY: Oh, wow.

S: It's a physically hard picture to make, don't you think?

SY: Yes, I absolutely think so. Standing around eight hours a day in hot Stillsuits isn't exactly motivational.

S: Maybe you should explain to people what a Stillsuit is.

SY: Well, anyone who's read *Dune* would know that.

S: That's only forty million people.

SY: Right, that's why I didn't explain it. There's a thing called Stillsuits, which Fremen – that's what I am, a Fremen person – and you're not, you're a Harkonnen and we're mortal enemies ...

S: Bad!

SY: Very bad ... very good, very bad. And we have our life on the desert and it's very hot and if we don't wear these Stillsuits, we lose all our water, so by wearing these Stillsuits we get to keep all our moisture, except a thimbleful a day.

S: Does that include the normal sanitary ... um ...

SY: Yes, it includes like feces and everything, you know, just recycle the whole thing, yeah.

S: You recycle it ...

SY: In the Stillsuit, you know, and then we have it right here, a little thing that goes up ...

S: It's purified ...

SY: ... our nose like that.

S: It's purified, and then it goes back in. Doesn't that sort of collect toxic substances?

SY: I would think so, but the Fremen are very very clever people, so they manage to deal with all those things. I don't have to worry about it.

S: I prefer the Harkonnens, who are much more wholesome and don't have recycled feces running through their bodies. We're in fact normal healthy animals.

SY: What relationships with people on the film, the other actors, have you enjoyed cultivating?

S: I don't really want to talk about my relationships ...

SY: That's a good idea. I don't mean, like, you know ...

S: Sexual relationships.

SY: [*laughs*] No, I mean, like what actors have you enjoyed working with ...

S: Which actress!

SY: Ac-TORS!

S: Oh, actors. Well, I'm very very partisan, very partial to my own family, the people who ... I play ... my family, my uncle, he's played by Ken MacMillan. He's a brilliant actor, and he plays Baron Vladimir Harkonnen. And then there's my brother, he's played by Paul Smith, his name is Rabban. He's enormous, monstrous, a giant of a man. And then there's Brad Douriff, who plays Piter, who's a kind of servant. And then there's Jack Nance, who is the star of *Eraserhead*, and he's the kind of family retainer. We're a very amusing bunch. Much better than the Atreides, who this one is aligned to ...

SY: I'm not Atreides.

S: Well, you're kind of on their side, right.

SY: Yeah, well in the end, yeah.

S: In the end, yeah.

SY: Only because I fall in love, you know.

S: With the leading man.

SY: With the leading man!

S: And she could have had me all along.

SY: Well, yeah, that's true. I have to rethink that out.

S: The problem is, I mean, do we really want more good guys? I think the cinema needs bad guys. I think we're the life and blood and salt of the earth.

SY: Why?

S: Because you couldn't be good unless you had something relative to be good against, like us.

SY: That's true. No transformation can take place unless you go through Hell first, absolutely.

Sting as Feyd Rautha, challenging Paul to a knife fight. Photograph copyright Universal/De Laurentiis.

S: Who said that?

SY: You did!

S: Oh yeah.

SY: You write all my lines for me. Okay, let me think of another question ...

AP: I wish George were around because he very much – George Godwin, the guy that I work with – he thinks very much the same way, that Harkonnens are actually, you know, delightful ... better guys, more interesting ...

SY: George must think that.

AP: That the Atreides are all bland, you know, they're kind of ... well anyway, I've heard that you wrote a screenplay and I really wish he were around because he's a, you know, screenwriter and he knows, he's read the novel that you ...

S: *Gormenghast*, oh really.

AP: It's a trilogy, I understand.

S: Yes, three novels.

AP: And all I really know about it is that Francesca liked it a lot, she's read and she liked it a lot, so could we maybe talk a little bit about that?

SY: About *Gormenghast*?

AP: About his screenplay.

SY: You want to?

S: Yeah, why not?

SY: So it's based on three stories by Melvin Pierce? Pierce?

S: Mervyn Peake.

SY: Peake, Mervyn Peake. Melvin Pierce! [*laughs*]

S: It's a trilogy of novels written in England after the Second World War. It's a very arcane piece of literature, very dense, very difficult. Not terribly well read. Nonetheless, it's a book, or a series of books, which I've been ... I wish I could speak better ... a series of books which I've been obsessed with since I was at university. Since I became rich, I have enough money to buy things like the rights to books ...

SY: To books ...

S: So when I first started to make movies, you know, like every actor I was sitting by the telephone waiting for the jobs to miraculously materialize, jobs that I would like to do with people I want to work with. Of course, they rarely do. It's ... you know, you might as well wait to win the lottery.

SY: Is there a character in that screenplay you'd like to play?

S: Oh, yes! There's a character who's me, a character called Steerpike.

SY: It's Steerpike!

S: Of course ...

SY: Of course it's Steerpike, yes.

S: He's an evil genius.

SY: Yes.

S: He has a kind of grotesque charm.

SY: Well, he's very young in the beginning, right?

S: Very young, and then very old.

SY: And you play the both of those parts?

S: Perhaps.

SY: Or you'd have to get somebody, somebody who's a little more youthful?

S: Well, you know, I could stick a false head on for the younger parts.

SY: That's true. That's true ... Steerpike, of course. Steerpike's a character who manages to rise up from the low-lifes of the kitchen, all the way up to a very political, nice, powerful position ...

S: Like me.

SY: Yeah, like you. I'm trying to think of a question.

AP: Well, maybe about power, you know, how much power do you really have?

S: Yes, is power an end in itself?

SY: [*whispers*] Yes.

S: I don't know. I mean it's, it's not really a moral question. I think the story is a good one, it's a good adventure story first of all. It's about the rise of someone like me, an exaggeration of my own life. I came from a very lowly, humble background and …

AP: Working class hero.

S: Working class, and in England that means something because there's very little social mobility. And one of the routes for my escape was to be a pop star.

SY: But that was, was that when you were young? I mean, did you feel … was that something that was conscious with you when you were really young, or …

S: My roots … I always wanted to escape my environment. My first, the first root I took was to try education, to be academically successful, because I thought, you get a degree …

SY: You were smart.

S: … you can become middle class and you can have a garden round your house and you can have a car and a nice wife and wear a white shirt, and that was kind of what I thought. And then I realized that's a pretty shallow ambition. So then I decided to become a teenager. This was at the age of twenty-five. But …

SY: Backward! But better late than never …

S: It was a lot more fun than most people's adolescences, who have them when they're, like, twelve to eighteen, right. Mine was much better, much more fun.

SY: Why?

S: Because I could really enjoy it and I wasn't troubled by puberty.

SY: Yeah, right, that's it. That's it …

S: I'm still not troubled by puberty. I don't know when it's going to arrive.

SY: When you were in high school, you said you were really popular. I can't imagine how that would feel like.

S: To be really popular? Sean unfortunately is one of these gifted children who are loathed by parents, teachers …

SY: No, not parents! Not parents!

S: I know that your parents loathe you.

SY: No you don't.

S: This is a complete fabrication that they like you.

SY: No.

S: Teachers, classmates, they couldn't stand the girl. Too talented, you see, much too much personality. The only place left for her to go was to the cinema.

SY: No, the only other place left to go is Broadway at this stage, where I can dance, because that's much more interesting than cinema. Cinema's too difficult. It is. I don't mean that it's too difficult, but having to wait around all day and deal with the pace that's so slow is not nearly as gratifying as going up on stage and doing something. I mean, going on a concert tour must be like nothing else.

S: I agree, but it's like, it's the difference between having an instant thing where you just do it [*snaps fingers*] and it's spontaneous and wonderful and it lasts for that moment ... this film, although it's taking a lot of time and there's no spontaneity, will probably last forever. Or as long as there are cameras or ...

SY: People to watch films.

S: So there's that, you know.

SY: Well, don't you feel that the most important thing ... well, I like to look back on things that I have done too, but in terms of the philosophy of my life I can't look back. I have to let the steamroller of life just sort of happen, and try to be at the steering wheel all the time. And the moment that is right is the most important one, because there's no other goal besides that, you know, where I am right now, and if I can get the most out of that, it's more important.

S: But isn't it the skill on the studio floor to manufacture spontaneity for a tiny second?

SY: What do you mean?

S: Well, on stage you have, you know, you have an audience, you have the adrenalin going, the excitement, the danger of a live performance. Isn't the skill on the screen to do that as well without having all the things that help you, like an audience? You have to trust your director.

SY: Yes, and it's also doing it, it's much more doing it for other people for much less instant gratification back. You have to do it sort of like, put your money in the bank and wait for the interest to accumulate on it and hope that interest rates don't change by the time the movie comes out [*laughs*], so that you just have to trust how ... no film ... I stopped predicting what films were going to do, 'cause I've been in films that were going to be terrible and did great, and films that were going to do great and did terrible, and you can't ever tell when you're making it what's going to happen to it. Raffaella put it really well when she said this film could either be the greatest hit ever or it could be the biggest failure ever. It could be the biggest embarrassment ever, because of how many people have read *Dune* and how many people have their own conception of what it should look like.

S: You'll never satisfy the people who've read *Dune* and have their own ... you'll never ever get that.

SY: No, exactly, and that's why the movie, you know, it does a certain balance, a tricky balance which you have to be careful of.

S: I mean, this is David Lynch's *Dune*, you know, it's his conception of the novel, not ours.

SY: Not entirely.

S: I suppose we have to trust ...

SY: You have to ...

S: ... what percentage of directors have you trusted?

SY: One ... well, two. I trust David.

S: Can you name them?

SY: Ridley and David.

S: Ridley Scott and David, and the other directors you didn't trust.

SY: Well, they were ...

S: Can you give their names?

SY: [*laughs*] No, the only reason I didn't trust them, because we were dealing in comedy. We were dealing in comedy, and comedy for me was like, "Funny? What's funny?" What can I do that's funny, especially funny at the moment, you know, I ... *Stripes* was a great experience and I learned a lot on that and every time we made it, every time Bill Murray would do something, I'd watch behind the camera and go, "That's funny? That's not funny!" But when I saw the film, I laughed my head off. And then *Young Doctors In Love* was just, we thought it was so funny when we were making it, and when I saw it, it just didn't hit funny at all for me. So, comedy is what makes it more difficult, comedy people do different things than serious ... not serious, but more serious material. And that's why the directors, it was very difficult for me to trust them, because when you deal in comedy you have to re-write everything at the moment and if you don't have that capacity, well, what are you going to do? I mean, there's things that are omitted daily in *Dune* and stuff like that, but basically I have my lines to depend on. I can show up at work and know that I'm going to have my scene there in front of me to work, and say okay now this and this and this. I didn't have that in comedy because it was out the window before you knew it.

S: I suppose you ... in my case, when I perform I'm used to instant feedback from a very large audience and if you do well they respond in a very positive way, and yet on the studio floor, if I say my lines and I say them okay I don't get fifty thousand people "yeahhh!!!", I get the director going, "Okay, check the gate, let's get on with the next shot." Or he'll say, "Good." So you go from ...

SY: "Okay, try again," and you don't know what exactly you did wrong and you've got to do it again.

S: That's right. You go from fifty thousand people going "yeahhh!" to a director going ...

SY: I know when I'm doing it good, though, on film. I know when it's right and I know when it's ... I never know when it's wrong, 'cause I don't feel it's ever been an embarrassment to me, or it's never been, you know, I don't think wrong is possible, but there's always ... there's wrong in terms of meeting your standards and what you're capable of getting from yourself when the camera's on. You can't wait until the camera's off and your shot's over, and there's only one chance for your shot to be there because to make a movie you have to be relentless, you have to push on, you have to get your shots in and the budget and, oh the producer and all that stuff ...

S: The what?

SY: The producer and all the people who are hovering over you to get your film finished. You can't, you can't just say "well, we'll get that shot again tomorrow" if it didn't work. To get how you, to get that power going inside yourself, so that when the camera's there you're doing exactly what you want to do, it just takes so much balancing of your energy during the day, of how you feel about it and what's happening around you at that moment, and keeping, you know, present, being here for what's happening. Looking at Kyle's eyes this morning, I was saying "get there!", you know, "calm down, get there". Erase everything else, just look in his eyes and really don't let anything else affect you.

S: So there is a sense of danger in the studio.

SY: Yeah. It's personal, though, it's inward. It's like, it's a personal standard you have to meet up to or else, you know, you fail yourself. I mean, I would, I'd be terrified, I'd be terrified to stand in front of fifty thousand people. I'd be terrified. I don't know that I could ...

S: Tell you a secret, I'm terrified too. But I think terror is important, and like fear of just destroying yourself is a wonderful drive to be good.

SY: That's if you ... well, somewhere you must know you'll overcome it or else you wouldn't do it. I mean, that's why most people don't do it, because they don't feel they can overcome it. More people can overcome it than give themselves credit, but somewhere you couldn't do it if you didn't know that you were capable of overcoming that terror. And making ... do you, have you ever made a big mistake on stage?

S: Umm ... no.

SY: Really?

S: No, no. There are no mistakes on stage, because everything you do is visual. I deliberately, every night I will sing a very long high note, which makes me over-oxygenate, I think it is. And I get into a kind of trance and my head spins around and the whole auditorium goes backwards and forwards. It's a wonderful feeling, because you could actually fall over ... and you just pull yourself out of it, but it's a great feeling of danger. It's like dying on stage.

SY: Yeah, we talked about this. I'm afraid of danger. Well, I'm getting more accustomed to it. I mean, I'm getting so I can accept it better, but I really don't like danger all that much and I'm not comfortable with it, and I realize the necessity of it. The most dangerous thing I ever did was to quit my job and decide to become an actor, you know, decide to pursue what I really wanted.

Crew

Aldo Puccini, Construction Manager.

Construction workshop, Estudios Churubusco.
Dune was Aldo Puccini's final feature; he died the year the film was released.

Anatol Pacanowski: You can sit down if you'd be more comfortable, you know. As you like, Aldo.

Aldo Puccini: It's the same for me. I'm okay. It's better you get to the bridge to know me because ... [*referring to the bridge set built by his crew at the Aguilas Rojas location*]

Anatol: Aldo, you've been on television before, haven't you?

Aldo: Yes, I was on television some time. I was on television sometime because I ... I don't know how many films I shoot in my life. I make, I don't know, I never count because I ... long, long time in this job. And I love my job, believe me. Yes, suppose I born another time, I want to do the same work, because I love my work. This ... any man would think the same thing because you do things you love, you do right, you do good. Suppose you don't like, it's better you leave, do other things. No, this my job. You see my set, I like building all the set, it's okay for me.

Kenneth George Godwin: Is this the biggest film you've ever worked on?

Aldo: No, no, I built more big than this, yes much more big.

KGG: On what films?

Aldo: I can't say ... *The Bible, Barabbas, Waterloo, War and Peace.* I can't tell you, I don't know how many films I shoot in my life, I don't know. I never counted.

Anatol: When did you start making films, Aldo?

Aldo: I start in Rome, I was maybe ... before the war, I was seventeen years, eighteen years old, I start to work in Cinecitta in Rome. And I never leave, I do the same work.

KGG: You work all over the world?

Aldo: I work ... you know how many times I come in the States? Twelve times from Italy to the States, any part of America ... in Canada, America de Nord, America de Sud, any part of America, any part of the world, in Russia, in Africa, in Australia, in Polynesia, any part of the world. I like, I go round, I work. But my family, my heart, is in Rome, because my family is in Rome, all my family. I miss my wife now, now eight months, eight months, I got to stay here maybe for another five, six months. More than one year, too long, you know, too long. It's okay for the work I do …

[Brief interruption]

Aldo: It's very dangerous work. All my body got something broke … look here, look here, this mark from the *Orca*, you know the *Orca* picture? I was in Canada too for shooting the *Orca*, in Saint John. You know Saint John, you from Canada, no?

KGG: Yes.

Aldo: You know Saint John?

KGG: New Brunswick?

Aldo: Yes … no, no, in …

KGG: Newfoundland? St. John's?

Aldo: St. John's, Newfoundland.

KGG: Yeah, I lived near there.

Aldo: I was working there for the *Orca*. After I go to Malta Island, in Malta Island the special effect, I do the special effect of the house, it go down … I do that before the house, I broke my left … sometime I forget, you know, I forget to speak English. I speak Spanish, any language because every part of the world, new language … [*hammering in background*] Now, we make all in wood, no?

KGG: Yeah.

Aldo: After we do like that, you cannot recognize after we put in cement, put colour, put anything … see, like the stone you see here.

KGG: How long does it take to build it?

Aldo; Oh, this I start two weeks ago, two weeks ago, and another two weeks.

KGG: Another two weeks? Four weeks …

Aldo: Four weeks, four or five weeks, depends from the weather because sometimes raining and we've got to …

KGG: How long did it take to build the wall?

Aldo: The wall, I put … four weeks for the wall over there. It's a nice wall, huh?

KGG: Yeah, it's beautiful.

Aldo: Yes, you see, it connects everything from the stone, the wall … suppose somebody cut the stone, make the biggest …

KGG: It's very real.

Aldo: Yes, like real. It's no secret, we don't have any secret. You got to imagine it, you got to think what they did say, what they did want, what did they have in their mind, because we got to think what they have in mind, because we got to do everything they think, no? From the scripts, read the scripts, you think over here I need this, I need that. No secret. You got to think all the time, because every set a new building. You never do in this job, you never do what you do the day before. Everything's new, every day new. Because every day you do different job, different work, different things. I like that. I like it very much. You know the *La Strada*? *La Strada*? I make, I building the set for Fellini, *La Strada*, yes.

KGG: It's a beautiful film.

Aldo: Beautiful. *Cabiria. Le notti di Cabiria*, with Massina, Giulietta Massina, his wife. I building the set. I was work with Fellini for the *Casanova, Casanova*.

KGG: Big sets.

Aldo: Big sets, yes. Few picture, few films I work with him. I love him, I love him.

KGG: He's still making films, isn't he?

Aldo: Yes, I like make another film with him, yes.

Bob Bealmear, Apogee, Inc. supervisor.

On desert set in soundstage, Estudios Churubusco.
Bob Bealmear: ... well, it is when I work for John Dykstra.
Kenneth George Godwin: Is this the first time you've worked for him?
BB: No, no, I've done it ... are you interviewing me now, are we on the air?
KGG: It's sort of informal, we just want a few comments.
BB: I'm glad ... and I'm just happy to tell you, George ... what is that you want to know?
KGG: How did you get to be doing this business?
BB: You want to know what we're doing down here? Well, John Dykstra gave me a call and said that they were going to be doing *Dune* in Mexico City and wanted me to supervise the construction of two very large front-projection screens. So, I said yes, that I would do it, and it was a five-week job that turned into several months worth of work because, you know, special conditions and so on. But the front projection screen – I don't know if you see it behind me or not – but the front projection screen is not going to be used in a conventional manner and I think that that's the major difference, not only the size of it – it's thirty-five feet tall and this particular one's a hundred-and-four feet long, so we're talking maybe four stories and the side of a good sized building. The size of it of course, just logistically and from an engineering point of view, is an interesting project. What's particular about this, what's specific is that it's not being used as a front-projection screen, but rather it's being used as a bluescreen. Not a transmission bluescreen in this case, but we'll ... Apogee builds its own projectors, and Apogee's building a projector which has been nicknamed the "blue max" and that's going to throw an even blue light on this enormous screen and allow then for post-production, optical post-production special effects to be done. And that's pretty much it, unless you'd like a little more explanation of what that is.
KGG: Yeah, give us a little more detail.
BB: Well, when you have a bluescreen this size, it'll allow you then to take models of, say, worms that in the movie are going to be larger than a breadbox ... if people are this big and the worms are THIS big, obviously you've got a problem unless you want to deal with that optically. So you deal with model worms that may be any size, from here to THIS big, and then in post-production you put those in where the bluescreen is when you're shooting your live action. I don't know if that's any clearer or not. Except when you're shooting

your live action and you have this big blue screen behind you, and the people again are this big and the screen is this big, then that allows you a great deal of space that isn't going to be used in that original live action shooting, that in your post-production you can fit in whatever you like. So that allows you to put in gigantic worms getting ready to eat very small people, when in reality we know it's not like that. So that's what the bluescreen is about.

KGG: What do you normally do, when you're not building bluescreens?
BB: Well, I sleep a lot and study Spanish …

KGG: I mean before you came here to Mexico.
BB: Well, I'm a freelance writer, but … and I was working in television this past year for a CBS daytime program. But John Dykstra, who aside from the fact that he's a very good technician and very good at what he does, is just a very nice guy, a fellow I've known for a while, and he called and asked me if I would supervise this job … anything to get me away from my writing for a while, so I said "sure", came down and supervising this one … and I don't know if you've seen the other one on Stage 2, it's a little bit larger, and that's basically it. It's just, you know, hard work. No brains, just muscle. But the people that we have working for us, I think, are who we have to thank for the fact that it's going as well as it's going. They're very good with their hands, they're dextrous … god knows all kinds of things have disappeared since they've been [*chuckles*] … no, that's not true. They're just very good with their hands and they've taken a lot of care with this material. The material is a 3M 7610 high-contrast material, which is complicated and difficult to work with because you can't get it dirty, you can't touch it with your hands. You always have to wear gloves. You can't get it wet. Once you put it up, you have to cover it right away to keep the, just the ambient dust from getting on it because it'll destroy the integrity of it right away. It's a screen material that reflects light directly back to its source, a very particular kind of material. We have to handle it in small squares instead of large squares because it's pressure sensitive and has to be applied gently and correctly, without any creases or bubbles or mistakes. So you add all that up, and you don't pay your people well and allow them short hours, why you end up with no screen at all.

KGG: How much will it cost?
BB: I think that probably, George, if you really wanted a real nice Porsche, if you could just roll this material up, you could get a nice Porsche for what it costs. One of the bigger ones. What else do you want to know?

KGG: Say something funny.
BB: [*laughs*] When are you going to go to work? That's funny!

KGG: Thanks a lot.
BB: My pleasure.

John Dykstra, special effects director, Apogee, Inc.

Estudios Churubusco (a very noisy outdoor location).

John Dykstra became one of the major forces in special effects in the 1970s, largely through his groundbreaking technical developments during the making of the first *Star Wars* movie, innovations which formed the basis of Industrial Light & Magic. While working on the pilot of Universal's *Battlestar Galactica* in 1978, he formed his own company, Apogee, Inc., which for some years rivalled George Lucas' behemoth. Dykstra was initially hired to oversee *Dune*'s extensive, complex visual effects, but as the production's demands expanded, he ran into conflicts with the producers about the budget which was needed and eventually, realizing that it would not be possible to achieve what was wanted with the money that was available, he withdrew. Personnel from the Van Der Veer effects company took over optical work, with Brian Smithies supervising miniatures.

John Dykstra: Spaceships, no problem. Spaceships here in Mexico, we've got yellow ones, blue ones, almost any kind you'd like.

Anatol Pacanowski: You look good, looking good.

JD: Thanks.

AP: Good lighting, and we have good suntan.

JD: Hey.

Kenneth George Godwin: The most important question for our viewers is "Mr. Dykstra, why do they call it blue screen?"

JD: Why do they call it blue screen? Ah, okay. Well, turns out that in real life almost all things have red and green in them. Very few living things have blue in them. I mean, there's an old George Carlin line about there being no blue food. And as a result, when you do a blue screen process shot, which in fact, what you're trying to do is, you're trying to separate your foreground actors and whatever it is that you're using in the foreground from the background. So you use blue, because blue does not appear generally in the actors … unless of course you have blue eyes or if they're foolish enough to wear a blue tie or t-shirt or something like that. So, our approach to it is to use blue screen, which is a primary colour and is separable from the other two colours and that allows us to create a mask and that's kind of confusing because – the cameraman over here is waving his arms at me …

AP: We have a wind problem, and I can see your microphone, George.

KGG: Well how far back do you want me?

AP: It's a little windy. It was a bad idea …

KGG: What do you want to do?

AP: I can't stop the wind.

KGG Hey, what do you mean [*laughs*]. So it's windy, where do you want to go?

[We moved to a more sheltered spot]

AP: I'm ready, I'm rolling.

JD: I'm going to look at you when I'm doing this.

AP: Yes, that's ideal.

JD: I'm talking off camera ... so what's your first question?

KGG: When you first read the script, with all the effects sequences in it, what was your reaction?

JD: Well, I'd read the book, I read the book a long time ago and ... well, in technical terms, the excitement of all the things that had to be done for the story were inherent in the first go round. The script itself condensed all that material into six or seven really important sequences and every one of those sequences by itself is probably harder than any other movie I've done [*laughs*] in the past, so it's overwhelming, but it was very exciting because obviously this is a classic story, it's a story that everybody is going to want to go see, and of course the people who've read the book will have to go see it at least twice. So it's a great showcase for this kind of work. It's the toughest kind of work because in order to make these very very unbelievable things happen – huge worms, people floating around, you know, all of the impossibilities or improbabilities that are outlined in the story which is so much fun, they've got to look real. So the seams can't show, you can't realize it's an effects shot, otherwise it's a giveaway. And as it turns out, because this is a desert planet environment, most of the master shots, the big wide shots are going to have to be special effects shots. So we have to make something that looks as real as the vistas you saw in *Ryan's Daughter* or *Giant*, only we're going to have to put them together out of miniatures and trickery, so to speak.

KGG: Do you have to invent new techniques for a lot of this stuff?

JD: Oh sure, the techniques are really, the techniques that we're going to use in this film are going to be techniques that are born out of other techniques, will be new applications of those techniques, new combinations of those techniques. I mean, there's basically ... one of the things that you do initially is called a time frame change, meaning that you photograph a miniature subject of some kind at a very high camera rate to make it move more slowly, to give it scale or mass and make it look large. So that's moving, changing your time frame in photography from normal to high speed, and that's one way of converting a very small-looking thing into a very large-looking thing. Water, sand, explosions, etc. Then there's another time frame change that occurs when we photograph the miniatures for space travel and that sort of thing, where we go to one frame a second, which is one one-twenty-fourth the normal frame rate, and that when it's photographed moves very very slowly. Of course, when it's played back at twenty-four, it moves more rapidly and it gives you the sense of motion that you finally end up with on the screen. So that's one of the first techniques and that's inherent in almost every trick we're going to do for this movie. We're either going to run the camera too fast, run the camera too slow, or something like that to give it our basic time frame change. And that's mostly to provide scale to things, to allow us to hold everything in sharp focus, to allow us to expose for very dimly illuminated subjects and that kind of thing. Then the other thing we do is the construction of the miniatures themselves, of course. If you think about, as an example, a building someplace, it you look at that building from a distance the corners are absolutely square, right, they're razor-edged square, so when you build a miniature building that's only ten-inches tall or something like that, you have to work very very hard to make sure that's a precision corner, because it would, even if it was a funky corner on the real building, it still looks very square. So when you build your miniatures, that's one of the considerations. That's why it's a highly technical skill, building miniatures for this kind of work. And we tend to make our miniatures smaller than most people. Obviously the bigger the miniature, the closer it is to the real size, the more easily it is depicted as being real. So by making these very small miniatures, we press, again press the limits of capabilities in special effects. We're going to present a desert, in fact, in a sequence that is supposed to be two-hundred miles across, and we're going to do it with a miniature. And it doesn't make any difference how small the miniature is – I don't want to give away too many secrets here – how small the miniature is. It's not going to be two hundred miles across. In fact it's not going to be one one-hundredth of that. In fact, it probably isn't going to be one one-thousandth of that, and yet when we photograph it, it's going to have to appear to be this vast desert. So that's the kind of scale difference that we're working with in terms of the miniatures. Then there's a whole bunch of light effects, slit-scan laser effects and that kind of thing, that's really enhancement, it's an add-on to live action photography, to add on to the miniatures and that sort of thing, and that works in conjunction with all the live-action effects that are going on here on stage.

KGG: Since you've got on the project, there have been some changes. How much of that is due to impossible effects to make?

JD: It's mostly due to money. I mean, there is no impossible effects to make. You can make anything, I swear. You can take all the people – this is an old friend of mine's, his impossible scene and it was written into a script – it says I'd like a master shot, a wide shot to include the city of Detroit and all the people in the scene, I want them all to turn into Irish Setters before your very eyes in the master, right. Now that, that's an impossible special effects shot. However, it can be done. I guarantee you it can be done. It takes time and money, so [*high-pitched shriek in background*] … there's an effect, the killing of a chicken [*laughs*] … that was somebody being turned into an Irish Setter! The biggest problem with this picture is because of the scope of the material, and because there are so many opportunities, a wealth of opportunities in the book and a wealth of opportunities in the script to present this great imagery, the tendency is to make a movie that's half special effects, meaning half vistas, half scenes that include stuff that doesn't exist. So, many of the changes that have occurred, many of the deletions that have occurred have really been based on what's an effective way of describing this environment. I mean, you start out with three-hundred-and-fifty scenes, scenes showing dogs eating ants on stilts dressed as pigs, right, which are great, it's wonderful, but when you get down to shooting the picture, when you get down to thinking about how much of an epic this picture is and trying to get it into a reasonable screen time, it turns out that a lot of those scenes get dropped just by virtue of the fact that you have no time to put them in. So, it's picking the best of that stuff, and that always requires that it be integrated with the live action, which is critical, 'cause if it's not then it sticks out like a sore thumb. And that integration with the live action requires that as the live action requirements change, as they always do during shooting, the effects requirements change. So we've cut down on the number of shots, we've tried to pick out the best shots to describe this land, the planets, both the planets from which they came and the planet they arrive at, the big battle scenes and how the worms happen … so it's the classic problem of sort of an embarrassment of riches with regard to the story and an embarrassment of poverty with regard to the money to create the … and the time to show it.

KGG: Are there any difficulties in doing the film here in Mexico?

JD: There is almost no technology here, not on the level that we're used to working. I mean, the kind of things that we do require that you shoot two scenes at separate times, moving the camera through three axes of motion … it's got to be able to tilt down and pan and track, all at the same time and be able to do that within one ten-thousandth of an inch, let's say. Well, that's hard to do in a country like the U.S. where there's a high level of technology. Here, it's almost impossible unless you bring that equipment. But of all the people that I've met here, there's no question but what anybody who is a good worker, anyone here, any Mexican here who's a good worker, wants to learn the stuff. The technology doesn't exist here though, they don't make it here, it's not available here. But it won't be long before, I think, people will be making lots of films here and that technology invariably, via us, and via other companies, is going to be here, exist in Mexico for the use in making motion pictures. And other applications as well.

KGG: How is Mexico compared to a place like Greenland? [Dykstra had recently worked in Greenland on Clint Eastwood's *Firefox* (1982)]

JD: Mexico's warmer. [*laughs*] There's more girls here ... Technology's going to come to Mexico. It has to. I mean, there are people here willing to do the work and who are craftsmen. It's just a matter of giving them the tools to do it with. It's almost impossible to turn a machine part with a hammer and a nail, but when you get a lathe and when you have some training in the use of materials and just specifics, I mean, almost apprenticeship, to people with regard to special effects technology, video technology, all those kinds of things, then that stuff ... as a result, that stuff is learned and it's applied and then the technology has a base from which to work when it comes here, when it becomes available here. ... What was the other question you asked about the ...?

KGG: Just working ...

JD: Greenland! Greenland is cold, Mexico's hot. There's more girls here. I said that before.

KGG: It must be on your mind!

JD: No, ahm, Greenland is designed to kill people. Mexico is a much happier place. In fact, probably it's one of the happier places. But aside from that, there's sixteen million people or so in this city, and in Greenland we worked with twenty-five-hundred people, so significant differences. Actually, we worked as a kind of isolated unit up there, and here we're much more part of a whole production, which makes it much easier. There's more talent to call on, there's more equipment and personnel available, whereas we had to make do with what we had there. Here we can expand a shot, a specific shot a little bit more than what we brought with us if we have to, whereas there, boy, that was it, what you brought is what you used.

KGG: Is *Dune* more special than most films?

JD: Oh sure, *Dune* is very special. I mean, I think even within this business, the people who make special effects for sure, because it's tied into science fiction, but even people who make films in general know that this movie is a very special movie. It has that sense about it. The producer has that sense about her. The director has that sense about him. The people making this documentary have that sense about them. And it's pretty much an effort of love, I think. I mean, you know, there's a lot of anger and hate that goes on in those kinds of situations, and politics, but for the most part the feeling is one of everybody putting their best effort forth because they know it's a special movie.

KGG: Is there anything you'd like to add?

JD: Hi, Mom! [*laughs*] Ah, let's see. Well, I'll tell you this thing, I mean, this whole movie as an example, it's an interesting thing … there's people here from four or five different countries speaking four or five different languages, and that includes the people from Britain who speak English and I don't understand them either, but it's an interesting combination. I mean, it's not a thing that I've encountered before. There's sculptors and model-makers and plasterers, all who speak different languages, who have all become integrated into this one making of this one film, and it's great. I mean, it's pretty amazing. That alone is a difficult enough problem to overcome, just the language barrier, and then on top of that almost everybody except for the Mexicans working on the show are in a foreign country, I mean, away from their homes and most of them much further away from home than I am. So I'm pretty much overwhelmed by the lack of bitching, the lack of complaining, the lack of kind of putting problems off on somebody else. That's great. I mean, it's an accolade from me 'cause I've worked on lots of shows where people were more than willing to blame somebody else and it's just not that bad here, which is amazing.

KGG: Are you going to stick with special effects?

JD: No, I'm going to direct, produce, write and act! [*laughs*] No, sure, I'm going to continue to do special effects because that's how I make a living, and in fact if I expand into other areas it's going to be based on doing effects. The likelihood of somebody saying "here's a dramatic film, it's a love story and it's your first opportunity to direct" is unlikely. But at the same time, I think there are some opportunities right now that I'm working on, that'll give me a chance to do some direction in concert with doing special effects, which I think will result in a movie that absolutely will be technically better because of my relationship with the director as a special effects guy, but at the same time I think also I have … I'm interested in expressing myself in telling a story, and I think I can do that, so that's the next thing I want to do.

KGG: So you're working on something …

JD: Sure, I'm working on two or three scripts, but you know everybody is. It's the old story of you get on the bus and you say you just got turned down at Universal and a guy in the back says, yeah, I just got shut down at Columbia, and the bus driver … I mean, you know, that's the way the business is. Everybody's going to be a director. But there are some people I think right now who have stories, two or three stories in fact, that people I've been working with in an effects capacity, and also with the option or potential of doing some direction … it's a question, I'm untried as far as a dramatic director is concerned and that's a pretty stiff one for a lot of people to accept, because I'm so technical. But I mean it'd be good visuals [*laughs*] if nothing else.

I encountered John Dykstra again the following year, when I visited him in England on the set of Tobe Hooper's underrated *Lifeforce*. However, I didn't question him about what had happened on *Dune* to cause him to leave the project, other than to confirm that budgetary issues had made it impossible for him to do the kind of work which he felt the film demanded. I did get a chance to tour the *Lifeforce* sets, however, and was given a close-up look at the massive alien spacecraft model which was being rigged for motion control photography. I recall that Dykstra had some reservations about the project, particularly as it was still then called *Space Vampires*, after the Colin Wilson novel it was based on. As a fan of Wilson's work, I was able to assure him that the book was better and more serious than the title suggested.

Appendix
My adventure with Jack Nance on the fringes of Hollywood

I recently came across a small stash of old audio tapes. These were copies of several interviews I conducted while working on *Dune* back in 1983. I dubbed them from the original video tapes that Anatol Pacanowski and I shot while we were documenting the production for Universal Studios. I'm not sure now why I made the dubs – perhaps it was due to some premonition I had that the video tapes would be taken away from us, though I didn't imagine at the time that the studio would destroy them all a couple of years later. Whatever the reason, these rather poor-quality dubs are all that remain of the *Dune* making-of documentary. Although I don't think the interviews are very good (I didn't know what I was doing when they were recorded), if I can find the time and energy, I may transcribe them and post the text here on my site as an additional element of my record of that summer in Mexico City.

I have just over four hours of recordings of David Lynch, Max von Sydow, Jurgen Prochnow, Patrick Stewart, Sting and Sean Young, plus John Dykstra, Bob Bealmear, Giorgio Desideri and Aldo Puccini. Some of the interviews we did are missing, though whether that's because I didn't make a dub at the time or have since lost the tapes, I can't say. The most significant absences are cinematographer Freddie Francis and the film's star Kyle MacLachlan. The longest session was the one we did with Jack Nance one afternoon after lunch at Estudios Churubusco, when we were all a bit drunk. I can recall Anatol setting the camera up, with Jack perched on a chair and the rest of us lying on our office floor while we talked randomly about whatever popped into our heads.

My brief connection with Jack Nance in the '80s was one of the most important things to come out of my research on *Eraserhead* and my work on *Dune*. Jack was unlike anyone else I've ever known, one of the most charming and amusing people I've ever met; but that charm could be washed away when he was drinking. I saw him bright and intelligent, self-deprecating about his considerable talent; and I also saw him angry and even violent, looking for a fight as if he had some dark energy trapped inside which needed to explode out of him to relieve an intolerable pressure. Truth is, Jack was the first serious alcoholic I ever met and I found the pattern of mood swings confusing; he was like two completely different people, one I loved dearly, the other seriously scared me.

I first met him when I went to Los Angeles in December 1981 to conduct interviews for my article about the making of *Eraserhead*. The long lunchtime session at a Denny's on Sunset Strip was a highlight of my trip. As an added bonus, a day or two later he got me into Zoetrope Studios where I watched Wim Wenders at work for an afternoon on the Chinatown set of *Hammett*, a movie in which Jack had a small role. But after I returned to Winnipeg a few days later, I had no more contact with Jack until he arrived in Mexico City in late May 1983 to play Nefud in *Dune* (a role invented by David Lynch specifically to give Jack some work). He remembered me from the meeting a year and a half earlier and I gave him a photocopy of the typed manuscript of my article. He liked it so much that we became instant friends and I hung out with him a lot over the next three months. Which meant a lot of evenings out at bars, in one of which I first saw his dark side. But the next day he was his "normal" self again.

He told me about a project he wanted to get off the ground, a movie about a famous Texas gambler and gangster named Herbert Noble, nicknamed "the cat" because he survived so many attempts on his life. I actually still have a tape that Jack made for me on which he reads through his large collection of newspaper clippings about Noble. (Listening to his voice on that tape brings back vivid memories of the charming, impish Jack.) The idea of a movie about Noble never got beyond Jack's dream. Another project we discussed never got much beyond my own dream.

When principal photography concluded on *Dune* in early September 1983, and Universal took away all the tapes Anatol and I had shot, I returned to Winnipeg, pretty much kicking myself all the way for not having handled things better; Anatol and I never even had written contracts for the job we were hired to do and so were without rights and protections, despite verbal agreements with executives at the studio. The most amazing opportunity I'd ever been given ended ignominiously because of my own inexperience. But I kept in touch with Jack, by letter and occasionally by phone, and met up with him again in December 1983, when I took a brief detour to Los Angeles to see Jack Leustig, Kyle MacLachlan's agent, who had optioned the script I wrote during the summer in Mexico. That was when I got to see where Jack lived, a kind of scary apartment with a mound of trash spilling across the kitchen and a ragged old couch inside of which his pet rat lived.

When I was drifting around Europe in the summer of 1984, I wrote a long treatment for a script about a character based on Jack. It was a mix of sci-fi, noir and comedy, about a washed up, alcoholic detective who gets reluctantly drawn into a case when a young woman comes looking for help. Not an original premise, perhaps, but it goes off in unexpected directions involving cutting edge media and an invention which can open doorways in time and across dimensions. I turned the treatment into a script when I got back to England after fourteen weeks in Italy, Germany, Denmark, Holland and Belgium and sent a copy to Jack. I was a bit nervous that he'd take offence at what might be considered an unflattering portrait of him, but he actually acknowledged that I'd captured him quite accurately. He liked it, so we tried to figure out what to do with it – while he was a character actor with a cult following, I was nobody with essentially no experience. We didn't have a lot to build on!

Henry Spencer in Eraserhead, *as perplexed as Jack would eventually be during our surreal meeting in Las Vegas, Copyright David Lynch.*

I worked on polishing the script some more and Jack sent out some feelers, eventually getting a glimmer of interest far from Hollywood. Jack's brother Richard was a lawyer with business connections in the southwest and he had become involved with a consortium of Oklahoma ranchers who were getting a lot of money in royalties from oil wells on their land. And these ranchers were looking around for ways to invest that money which would help them avoid paying some taxes. Someone had suggested that the movies might be a good bet for generating some profitable tax write-offs and, one thing leading to another, my script was offered to them as a possible investment. Which is why I suddenly found myself in May of 1985 flying down to Los Angeles again.

I think it was a ten-day to two-week visit. I stayed a while again with Jack Leustig and his wife Elisabeth, and also crashed for about a week at Kyle MacLachlan's apartment. But the main point of the trip was a one day excursion to Las Vegas to meet with Richard and a representative of the Oklahoma oilmen. Jack and I were put up at some casino hotel (I can't remember which one), given some spending money and tickets to a show which, the representative told us, had some on-stage effects which would be ideal for the script's time/dimension-travelling sequences. I can't recall anything much about the show other than that it looked like numerous such shows I'd seen in movies: part magic, part cabaret, populated by long-legged dancers wearing glitzy yet skimpy outfits. I think there was a tiger involved too. The "effects" we'd been told to watch out for were just a scanning laser and stage smoke which produced a kind of swirling, liquid light … something already used in quite a few movies, so hardly ground-breaking.

But this was all mere preamble. The point of the visit was the meeting where we were going to discuss the project, what it entailed, ballpark some budget numbers and maybe toss around a few names of people we'd like to have involved. This took place in the representative's hotel room, with me, Jack, Richard and someone else present. I can't remember the representative's name, but he was a classic "good ol' boy", well over six feet tall, heavyset but giving an impression of being fit. He spoke with a big voice and even wore cowboy boots and had a hat. And it quickly became clear that he hadn't come with the same intention as Jack and me.

He immediately took out a copy of the script and opened it to page one. Then he proceeded to go through it line by line, objecting to individual words – and not just in the dialogue, but also in the scene descriptions. After his first comment about an inappropriate word, he paused and looked at me expectantly. Then he asked if I was going to write it down so I'd remember. I halfheartedly scribbled on a page of my notebook. A bit later, when he objected to a particular adjective in a scene description, I tried to explain that those parts would not actually be heard by an audience, but he still thought it should be removed because it was giving "the wrong impression".

Jack and I kept looking at each other; Richard started to look embarrassed. And I didn't have a clue how to handle the situation. Here was a guy who may have the power to make money available to us, so I didn't want to offend him by saying outright that we weren't there for detailed yet dumbass script notes, yet he was utterly impervious to any subtle nudges towards a more practical conversation. In short, this guy knew nothing about movies, nothing about either the business or creative side of filmmaking. But he was working overtime to impress us with his deep thinking about the script. It was excruciating and I was rapidly getting more and more depressed. This all started sometime shortly before midnight and went on for several hours. I think it finally stopped because he'd simply become bored. As I recall, though, he did make it to the end of the script.

I think it was well after three that the "meeting" broke up. Jack and I went downstairs to the casino, where we ordered drinks and stared at each other. There didn't seem to be much to say. Jack went over to the craps table and started shooting dice. I stuck around a little longer, then went up to my room and tried to sleep. I was pretty restless and eventually went down to the restaurant, where I met Jack for breakfast around 7:00. The oilmen's representative joined us, big and loud and seemingly unaffected by a lack of sleep, though both Jack and I were pretty exhausted.

He offered something like a priceless *pièce de resistance* at the breakfast table, taking a pen from his jacket pocket, flipping over his place-mat, and quickly sketching what looked like a football play diagram as he explained in all seriousness that you couldn't trust directors, so we had to work out a strategy to make the movie without allowing the director to make any decisions. He used little figures and arrows to show us how we had to "get around the director", because a director would only waste our money.

Jack and I caught a 9:30 A.M. flight back to Los Angeles.

I think we waited about three months to hear back from Richard. The good ol' boy had reported back to his ranchers and eventually they all decided to put their money into real estate.

Jack and I kept in touch on and off for a few more years. I turned the script into an (unpublished) novel, eventually doing a major rewrite of both script and novel in which I changed the gender of the protagonist.

Jack was in a cycle of drinking and sobriety and back to drinking again in those years. He moved around quite a bit and eventually I lost touch with him. I probably hadn't heard from him in about seven or eight years when I read a brief newspaper report of his death in 1996. The circumstances seemed peculiar, and yet remembering how he could be when he'd been drinking, aggressively getting in the face of people a lot bigger and stronger than himself, I could picture him in that donut shop parking lot getting into an argument with some guy who punched him in the face and knocked him down. Apparently the police never found evidence of a fight and we only have a second-hand account of what may or may not have happened from someone Jack told the story to later that day. The next morning he was dead.

From *Rough Cut*, the Cagey Films blog, August 12, 2015

www.ingramcontent.com/pod-product-compliance
Lightning Source LLC
Chambersburg PA
CBHW080634230426
43663CB00016B/2860